CARVING MASKS
Tribal, Ethnic & Folk Projects

ALAN & GILL BRIDGEWATER

Sterling Publishing Co., Inc.   New York

To Julian and Glyn for being there when we need them—they are good sons!
  Let's hope they can survive the course—mending our computers, looking after the car, mending the camera, working with us on new books, helping us move yet again...Our needs are endless—HA!
  And...don't forget our birthdays!

Library of Congress Cataloging-in-Publication Data
Bridgewater, Alan.
    Carving masks : tribal, ethnic & folk projects / Alan & Gill Bridgewater.
          p.   cm.
    Includes index.
    ISBN 0-8069-1336-3
    1. Wood-carving.   2. Masks.   I. Bridgewater, Gill.   II. Title.
TT199.7.B7285   1996
736'.4—dc20   96-13945
                                                               CIP

Edited and designed by Rodman Neumann

1   3   5   7   9   10   8   6   4   2
Published by Sterling Publishing Company, Inc.
387 Park Avenue South, New York, N.Y. 10016
© 1996 by Alan & Gill Bridgewater
Distributed in Canada by Sterling Publishing
% Canadian Manda Group, One Atlantic Avenue, Suite 105
Toronto, Ontario, Canada M6K 3E7
Distributed in Great Britain and Europe by Cassell PLC
Wellington House, 125 Strand, London WC2R 0BB, England
Distributed in Australia by Capricorn Link (Australia) Pty. Ltd.
P.O. Box 6651, Baulkham Hills, Business Centre, NSW 2153, Australia
Manufactured in the United States of America
All rights reserved

Sterling ISBN 0-8069-1336-3

Contents

5 PREFACE

7 WOODCARVED MASKS—RITUALS & TRADITIONS
    Origin of Masking   8
    Tribal, Ethnic & Folk Masks   9

13 TOOLS, TECHNIQUES & MATERIALS—A–Z GUIDES
    Tools & Techniques   13
    Good Wood for Carving   23
    Timber Faults   24

27 PROJECTS
    1   Green Man Mask—Britain   27
    2   Flour Spout Mask—Alsace, Europe   37
    3   Fool Mask—Europe   47
    4   Ugandan Mask—Africa   57
    5   Baule Mask—Ivory Coast, Africa   67
    6   Fang Mask—Africa   77
    7   Bapende Mask—Congo, Africa   87
    8   Kwakiutl Mask—Northwest Coast of North America   97
    9   Haida Mask—Northwest Coast of North America   111
    10   Tsimshian Mask—Northwest Coast of North America   121
    11   Barong Mask—Bali, Indonesia   135
    12   Lombok Mask—Timor, Indonesia   149

158 METRIC CONVERSION

159 INDEX

Color section follows page 96.

Acknowledgments

We would like to thank all of the manufacturers who have supplied us with the best of the best:
- Tim Effrem—President, Wood Carvers Supply (woodcarving tools)
- Jim Brewer—Research and Marketing Manager, Freud (Forstner drill bits)
- John P. Jodkin—Vice President, Delta International Machinery Corp. (band saw)
- Nick Davidson—Managing Director, Craft Supplies Ltd UK (wood)
- Dawn Fretz—Marketing Assistant, De-Sta-Co (clamps)
- Paragon Communications—Evo-Stick (PVA adhesive)
- Frank Cootz—Public Relations, Ryobi America Corp. (thickness planer)

A big thank-you to Mike Lewis—The Mews Studio—for his beautiful color photography in the color section that follows page 96.

Preface

Our ambitions for this book have to do with our wanting to share with you some of the enthusiasm for what is a wonderfully powerful and dynamic area of woodcarving.

Carving Masks has been painstakingly researched, written and illustrated, and shaped into a series of 12 step-by-step projects. On the premise that the best way to learn about woodcarving is by doing, each of the projects has been designed to include inspirational drawings, photographs of the finished masks, scaled working drawings that show the various views, hands-on-tool illustrations, and a series of photographs that show close-ups of the procedures and stages of progress. All of these elements accompany a numbered easy-to-read text that instantly puts you in touch with the various hands-on-tool procedures. A concluding section on problem solving helps you sort out potential difficulties. A short introduction at the start of each project sets that particular mask in the context of a special time and place.

Whatever your woodcarving needs, we believe that this book will go a long way toward answering them. As to the choice of projects, it must be noted that a good number of them are, as far as we know, described here for the very first time. Of course the number of masks is limited by the size of the book. Choices had to be made; we just couldn't do justice to some important traditions such as those of East Asia. You may rightly ask, where are Japanese masks and Chinese masks? Another book, perhaps!

We feel that by working through the projects in this book you will be engaged in the discovery of something about yourself while being granted a respite from the mundanity and passivity of much of everyday life. No matter what your roots—African, Mediterranean, Northern European, South American Indian, Native North American, or whatever—this book will help you find something out about your humanity: where you came from, where you are going, and what you are about.

What could be more stimulating and satisfying than to decorate your home with one or more masks that you have carved and painted? A visually exciting and thought-provoking trip to a world where masks, mystery, and magic are one, an insight into customs and traditions both long gone and still practiced, a woodcarving adventure, an inspirational companion—*Carving Masks* is all of these and then some.

Alan & Gillian Bridgewater

Woodcarved Masks

Rituals & Traditions

Masks are uniquely fascinating and enigmatic in that they physically and psychologically transform the wearer. A masked person is able to take on the identity of the mask, to become one with the mask, or, you might say, to become "two-faced." For us, the very word *mask* conjures up a whole mishmash of thoughts and pictures that have to do with disguise, veils, concealment, Native American shamans, European masquerades, tribal Africa, the supernatural, trick-or-treat spooks, and, above all, magic! We would say that, without a doubt, the key word is *magic*.

(Top left) An Ugly Perchten mask—a monstrous creature—Bischofshofen, Austria. The masker dresses up with animal horns and skins; the mask is painted black with red lips and eye rims. (Top right) Roitschaggata mask—from Wiler in Lötschental, Switzerland. (Center left) Modern Devil mask—Teloloapán, State of Guerrero, Mexico. (Center) Devil mask—Mexico. (Center right) Grotesque mask—Tyrol, Switzerland. (Bottom) Kekch mask—early twentieth century, Belize. The snake additions are made from leather and cloth.

Carved and painted dance mask—Zaire, Africa.

Helmet mask—Sierra Leone, Africa.

ORIGIN OF MASKING

Masking is alive and kicking, a worldwide phenomenon that goes way back to the very beginnings of human activities. If we were able to time-travel back to the deepest darkest Neolithic cave in Palestine, France, or Spain—perhaps 9000 years ago—we would see masks being made and worn. This is borne out by cave paintings that show men in animal masks. Of course, we can't possibly know why such masks were made and worn, but many people suspect that it had something to do with beliefs that masks are a sort of spiritual conduit, a means of opening up lines of communication with the other world—with spirits, with ancestors, and with the dead.

In some traditional African and South Pacific tribal societies, just about everything that had to do with masks was considered to be taboo—the carver was thought to be gifted, the wood to be special, and, of course, the wearer to be more a spirit demon or god than a man.

In tribal Africa, the masked dancer occupied a special category. A 1930s written account describes how the mask was so powerful that in some villages the women couldn't look at masks without risking death. The account goes on to describe how the masks had to do with sympathetic magic—meaning that if, for example, the mask portrayed an antelope, then the wearer was thought to acquire some of the powers attributed to that animal. And then again, a mask that was made from a number of "fused" characteristics—the nose of a pig, the jaw of a crocodile, the beak of a bird, or whatever—was considered to have all the combined powers of those animals. Masks have had a function in nearly all African societies—on ritual occasions, at burial feasts, fertility and harvest festivals, as well as in initiation ceremonies. When they wanted variously to thank, appeal to, or propitiate a deity, then a special tribe member wore a mask and performed a dance.

Perhaps it is enough to say that, generally speaking, the motivation for masking has to do with the conviction that the mask protects the wearer from unfriendly spirits and/or makes him in some way or other sympathetic to the spirits.

TRIBAL, ETHNIC & FOLK MASKS

When we first saw examples of woodcarved masks in museums, we were at that time on the lookout for Pacific Northwest coast American carvings, Bali carvings, and European Green Man images. We were struck, more than anything else, by the wonderful confident power of the carvings. And, as carvers schooled in the rather restrained traditions of English decorative unpainted carving—Grinling Gibbons, church pews, and the like—we were more than a bit stunned by the sheer brilliant boldness of the carved masks: the size, the symmetry, the uninhibited forms, and above all, the color! Having been inspired by the Northwest Coast masks, we were presently searching out masks from Africa, India, East Asia, Europe, and other regions.

Carved and painted Northwest Coast Native American mask—late nineteenth century, Tlingit tribe.

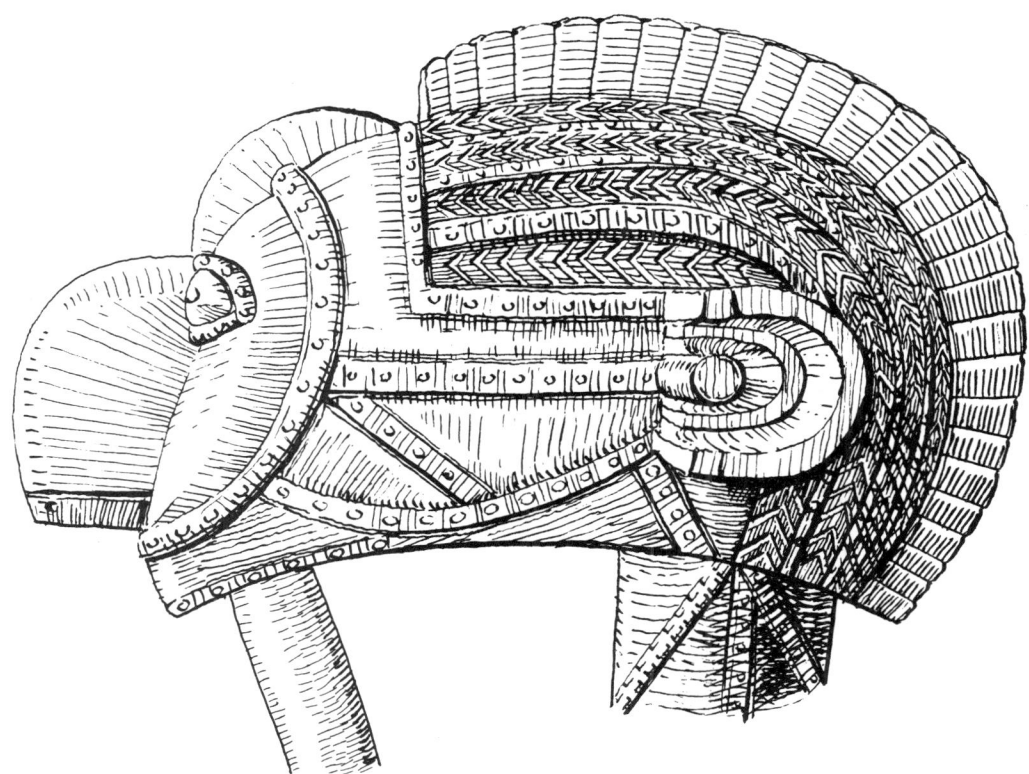

Nimba fertility mask, detail of the head—late nineteenth century, Baga tribe, Guinea, Africa. Masks of this type are worn high up—like a child being carried—on the shoulders so that the berobed wearer looks to be about 9ft (2.7cm) tall.

Barong Ket mask: carved, painted, and gilded wood with leather, hair, and mirror glass additions—Bali. The Barong Ket represents the Lord of the Jungle, a symbol of positive male energy, who protects villages. The mask and costume are very costly and elaborate, and are kept in the temple when not in use.

Green Man mask, carved on a misericord in St. Mary Magdalene Church, Newark, England—sixteenth century. The pre-Christian Green Man or Jack-in-the-Green character has to do with nature worship. It is thought that he has his roots in the earlier Roman Floralia masks.

It soon became more and more apparent, whenever we came across tribal, ethnic, and folk masks in museums and galleries, that masks are uniquely special on at least two counts: wood-carved masks were/are made the world over, and generally the form of the mask bears little or no relation to European notions of decoration and beauty.

African mask—front, side, and back views—carved all-of-a-piece with characteristic bird–horn motifs, plumb-slit eyes and zigzag corona. The dished back, with the eye slots and the thong holes, suggests that this is a dance mask. Thought to have been carved by the Baule tribe.

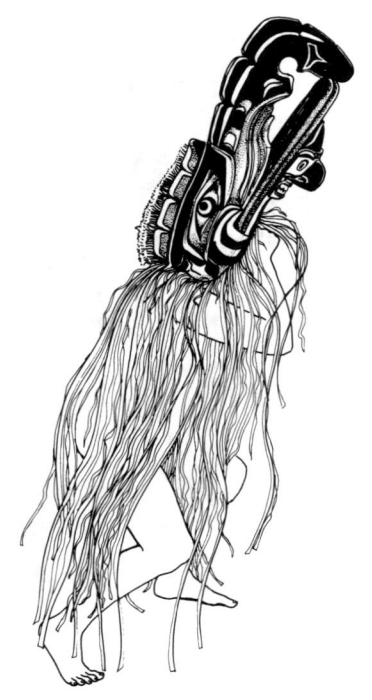

Dancer wearing the Crooked-Beak-of-Heaven mask—Kwakiutl tribe, Northwest Coast of North America. According to myth, the monstrous bird lived in a house in the sky and preyed on men. The mask was worn by women during the Hamatsa dances.

Having said that masking is a worldwide phenomenon, and although we have mentioned Africa, the South Pacific, and the like, you must not make the common mistake of thinking that masking is somehow or other only limited to third world tribal societies—not a bit of it! Masking was common throughout the ancient Egyptian, Greek, and Roman worlds, and, of course, we in the West—in Europe and America—still have our masked theatre performances, masked mummer plays, masked carnivals, and all manner of other celebrations, festivals, and special times when masks are worn. Certainly, in most instances, we don't know *why* we wear masks, but nevertheless the tradition is still strong.

If you have any doubts at all as to the real power of the mask, then I suggest that you put a mask on a child or adult. You will see straightaway that the wearer does in reality begin to lose his or her inhibitions and take on a new identity. And why is it that many of our comic book cartoon heroes and anti-heroes—Batman, Catwoman, Spiderman, the Lone Ranger, Zoro, to name but a few—are masked? Could it be that just under the surface we still have thoughts that the mask gives us—nice workaday people—special powers?

Tools, Techniques & Materials

A–Z Guides

TOOLS & TECHNIQUES

Band Saw If you enjoy *Carving Masks*, and have ambitions to do more of the same, then a small benchtop band saw is a tried and tested, relatively low-cost machine that will save you a great deal of sweat and time. In essence, a band saw is a power-operated tool consisting of an endless metal loop blade running over and driven by a number of wheels. It is the perfect tool for cutting tight curves and shapes in small-section wood.

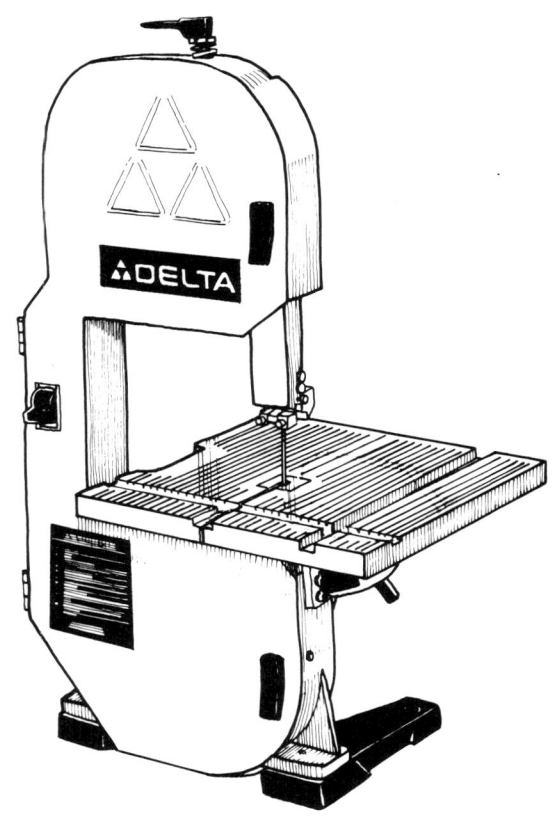

The Delta band saw is a good machine for light to medium work.

Bench In the context of mask carving, all that is required is a stable wooden surface that is strong enough to take a vise and a variety of clamps and holdfasts.

The workbench needs to be strong, stable, and the correct height.

Blank A prepared block or slab of wood—a piece of wood that is ready to be carved. We usually get our wood from a specialty supplier for the plain and simple reason that they are prepared to sell small mask-size pieces and off-cuts, whereas large mills are either unwilling or unable to deal with small orders. That said, woodturning suppliers usually have a good stock of mask-size wood.

In the context of *Carving Masks*, we tend to favor easy-to-carve woods like jelutong (or, if that's hard to find, any straight-grained hardwood like maple), linden/lime, and bass, with the blanks being built up from small sections.

Bow Saw If you can't get to use a band saw, then you might use a traditional hand bow saw. Such a tool has a thin blade set in a wooden H-frame. In use, the blade/handles can be rotated as much as 360 degrees to enable the carver to clear the workpiece when cutting curves. This is a good saw for cutting the profile edges of masks.

Brushes We favor using long-haired brushes such as those used by watercolor artists. Always wash the brushes immediately after use and store them bristle-up.

Calipers A two-legged compass-like instrument used primarily for measuring widths, spans, and thicknesses—usually consisting of two "C"-shaped legs that are pivoted at the crotch, or two "S"-shaped legs that are pivoted at the intersection to make a figure eight.

Clamps Screw devices for securing wood while it is being worked are called variously clamps, cramps, C-clamps, holdfasts, hold-downs, and any number of trade names. In the context of gluing up a mask-sized laminated slab, we usually smear all mating faces with a generous amount of glue, set the whole works in the vise, and then use extra clamps around the edges. It's always wise to have a trial dry run at clamping before you smear everything with glue!

Clasp Knife, Penknife & Hand Knife Just about any folding or straight knife used when carving. Mask carvers need a good selection of knives. It's a good idea to start a collection so that you have a knife to fit the task in hand. We currently use:

- an American Northwest Coast Indian crooked knife—for workings dips and hollows,
- a Swedish sloyd knife—it holds a wonderfully sharp edge—one of our favorite tools,
- a large English jackknife—for roughing out,
- and a selection of small penknives—for fiddly details and modeling.

Compass or a Pair of Compasses Two-legged instruments used for drawing circles and arcs, and sometimes for stepping off measurements —best is a long-legged screw-operated type.

Coping Saw A small "G"-shaped handsaw used for cutting thin small-section wood. The frame allows the thin blade to be swiftly fitted and removed. This is a good saw for cutting curved profiles—meaning around the edge of the mask.

If you plan to build most of your masks up from very thin sections, and if you can't afford to get an electric band saw, then get yourself three relatively inexpensive hand tools—a coping saw, a fret saw, and a bow saw.

Cushion or Bag A leather or canvas bag loosely filled with sand or sawdust. In use, the mask is nestled by the cushion. It is especially useful when you come to hollowing out the back of a partially carved mask that you couldn't easily secure in a vise. (See *Hollowing*.)

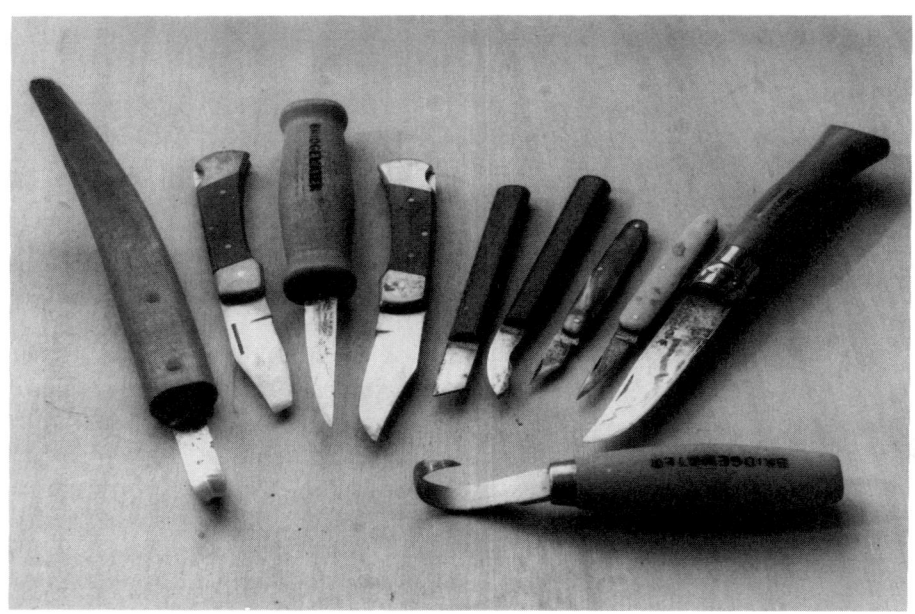

Knives are good for carving. Each knife gets to be used for a slightly different task, and you can easily shape the blades to suit your own needs.

The drawknife removes waste relatively fast. The workpiece must be held secure in a clamp or holdfast.

Deep-Carved In the context of *Carving Masks,* a surface that is deeply carved with hollows and undercuts, such as, for example, the hollow at the back of a mask or the modeled details at the front of a mask—around the nose, horns, or deeply set eyes.

Designing Working out the structure, pattern, or form of the carving by making sketches, drawings, outlines, and maquettes. If we see an exciting mask—in a museum, pictured in an old book, in an ethnic gallery, or wherever—we usually take on-the-spot photographs, make sketches, and construct a Plasticine maquette, all before we start carving.

Dividers A two-legged compass-like instrument used for stepping off measurements.

Forstner drill bits are the best tool for swiftly clearing waste.

Drawknife A two-handed knife used for swift shaping and roughing out. The two-handed usage makes for a totally safe tool—it's almost impossible to cut yourself.

Dust-Free Before you start painting, make sure that the workpiece is completely clean. Sweep up the debris, vacuum the surfaces, wipe the mask with a damp cloth, and then move to a dust-free area in preparation for painting. If at all possible, try to keep the carving area and the painting area completely separate. Our carving workshop is at one end of the garden, and our painting room is in the house.

Finish The type and quality of a finish depends upon the project at hand. For example, in the context of a mask being tribal, ethnic, or folk, it might traditionally have been carved, used, and then discarded. It might have been carved in a dark oily wood, or it might have been rough carved and then burned, and so on. Masks were given any number of different surface treatments. That said, as our masks are intended primarily to be hung on a wall in a house or gallery, they are usually sanded to a smooth finish, given one or more washes of watercolor paint, and then waxed and burnished.

Forstner Drill Bit Forstner drill bits are large-diameter bits used for boring out flat-bottomed, clean-sided holes—they are just perfect for drilling the various pilot holes at the back of the mask. (See *Hollowing*.)

Glues & Adhesives Although there are all manner of glues and adhesives—everything from animal glues that need to be heated, to instant glues and resins—we favor using PVA, meaning polyvinyl acetate. Such glue comes ready to use in a squeeze bottle, has a long shelf life, can be washed off when wet, and has no unpleasant smell.

Gouges & Chisels In the context of *Carving Masks*, the woodcarver needs a good selection of relatively small-size gouges and chisels. Although we use a broad range of tools, we tend to favor small-size flat chisels for setting-in and chopping holes, small-size U-section straight gouges for roughing out, straight V-section tools for setting-in and detailing, and various, straight, spoon, and bent gouges for modeling.

We usually define and describe gouges by the shape of the cutting edge, rather than by any number or code. For example, a gouge might be described as a "shallow curved/sweep straight gouge," or a "large U-section scoop gouge," and so on. The "large" refers to the width of the cutting edge, the "shallow curved/sweep" describes the shape in cross section of the blade, and "straight" (or "bent") refers to the shape of the shaft.

In use, chisels and gouges can be held in one hand and pushed with the other, or held in one hand and struck with a mallet. Much depends on your individual size and strength. For example, as Gillian is petite and not so strong, she tends to use a small mallet to strike the tools, whereas I can usually manage simply by putting my shoulders behind the tool and pushing. We both get there in the end—one "tap-tap-tapping" and the other "push-push-pushing"!

A collection of tools bought secondhand: (from left to right) a veiner, two spoon tools, three gouges, an old Henry Taylor V-section tool, a large gouge with an unpleasant-to-hold handle, and, finally, an old Henry Taylor dogleg tool.

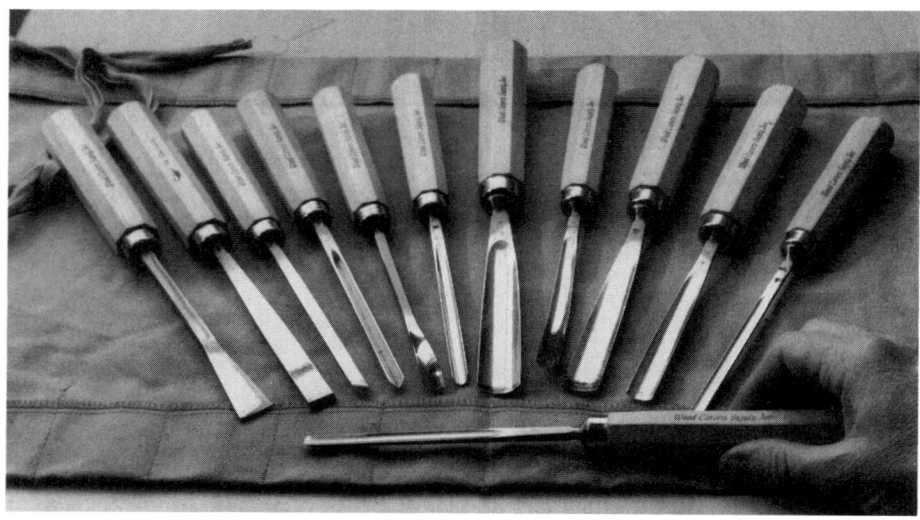

A quality set of chisels and gouges that come ready to use.

Gridded Working Drawing A scaled, square grid placed over a working drawing. In use the mask illustrated can be reduced or enlarged simply by changing the scale of the grid. For example, if the grid is described as "one square to one inch," and you want to double the scale, then all you do is read off each square as being equal to two inches. When you come to transferring the drawing to the wood, you just draw out a grid at the suggested size and transfer the contents of each square. At four grid squares to one inch, you draw out a ¼-inch grid—where one square is ¼ inch. (You might also consider making use of an office-type photocopying machine that can reduce or enlarge the original—and then simply transfer the new-sized drawing directly or use it to step off measurements to the workpiece.)

Grinding The act of using a grindstone to bring the bevel of a gouge or chisel to the correct angle and finish. (See **Sharpening.**)

Grounding or Wasting Cutting away the wood in and around the design, with the effect that the ground is lowered and other parts of the design—the nose, lips, and cheeks—are left in relief.

Inspirational Designs Meaning our sources—all the traditional masks that we get to see in museums, collections, gift shops, old books, on our travels, and such. It's a good idea to keep a sketchbook and to make notes and sketches whenever you see a particularly interesting mask. We draw most of our inspiration from pre-twentieth century, African, Native American, European, and East Asian masks. We usually study the forms and profiles, try to get a close-up look at the back of the mask, make notes about size and finish, and then modify the mask to our own design. In many ways the design of your mask—its wood type, weight, size, and finish—depends on its intended usage. Ask yourself whether you are going to hang it on the wall and so on. Is it going to be worn on stage or in a carnival? Is it going to be used in a lecture hall? Is it going to be a faithful copy of the original?

Hold-down A bench hold-down, or holdfast, is the perfect piece of equipment for clamping down masks while they are being carved. In use, the shaft is fitted into one of a number of holes in the bench, the workpiece is set between the

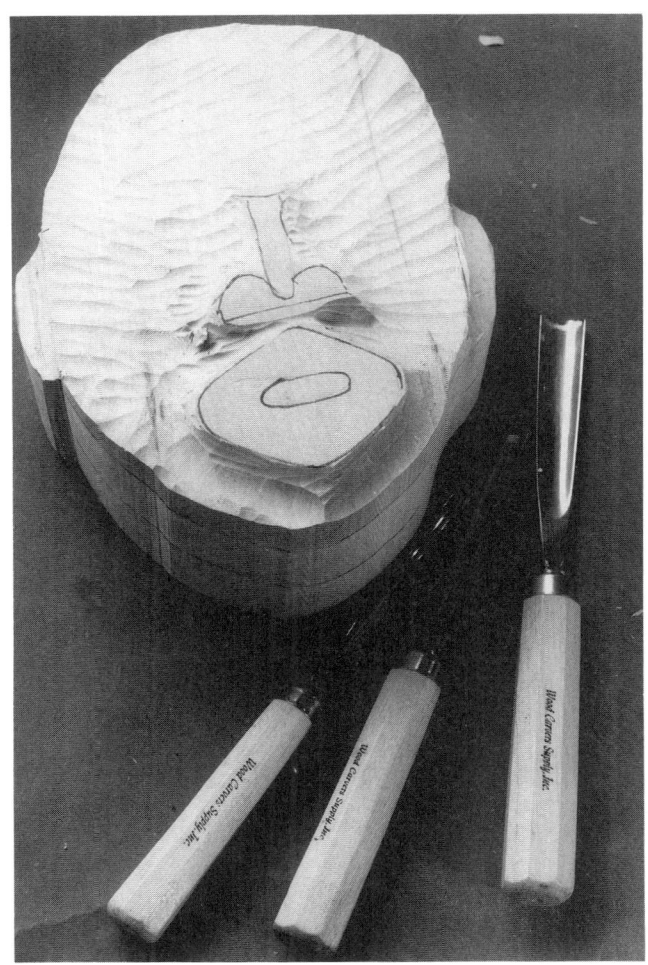

Grounding or wasting.

This Record holdfast is perfect for flat work. Note the little pad of plywood stuck to the face of the working end to protect the workpiece.

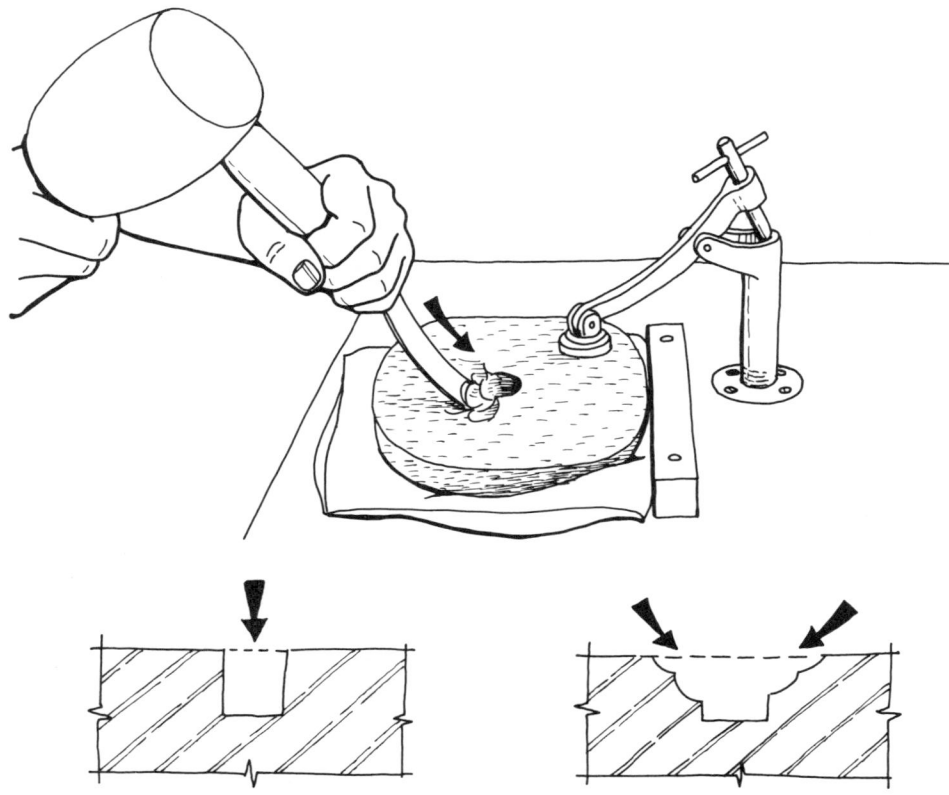

Hollowing—working with the carving protected on a sandbag and held securely, drill out a pilot hole/holes. Then, working from the center, use a gouge (straight or bent) to remove the waste.

swivel pad and the bench, and the screw thread is tightened up. Holdfasts are good on many counts; they are relatively inexpensive, most benches and tables can be easily modified for their use, and in use they can be instantly released and relocated.

Hollowing In the context of *Carving Masks*, hollowing is the procedure of clearing and dishing the waste from the back of the mask. Our working procedure usually goes something like:
- Carve the front face of the mask first—the features and the eye and mouth holes.

Hollowing. Using a gouge and a Forstner bit to remove waste.

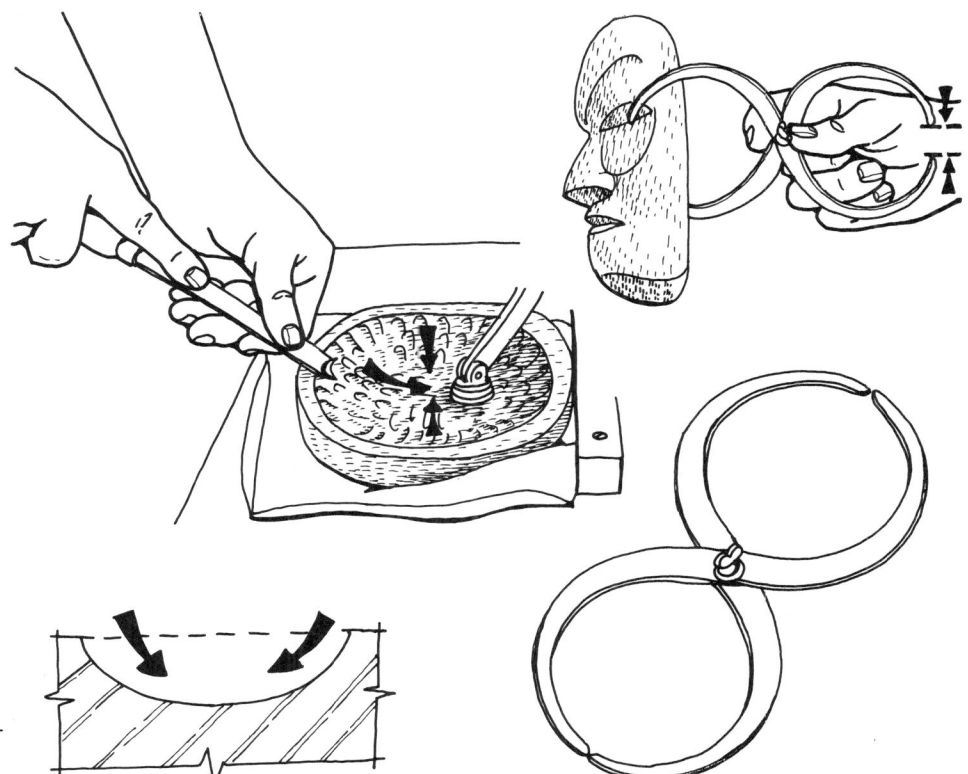

Hollowing—remove the waste carefully and use the double-ended calipers to check the thickness of the remaining wood.

- Bore out a pilot hole area at the back of the mask—to the greatest possible depth and width—nestling the mask in a cushion.
- Use straight and bent gouges to clear the waste from around the hole.
- Every now and then along the way, check the thickness of the mask wall with the calipers.
- Use spoon gouges and the Northwest Coast crooked knife to tidy up the dished shape.

Incised Cut A shallow, knife- or gouge-worked V-section trench or scoop cut.

Laminated or Built Up A carving that is constructed or built up from a number of blocks or layers. A good many of our masks are built up from a number of thin prepared sections. We favor lamination on at least three counts: we can use inexpensive offcuts, we can prepare the sections on our small benchtop band saw, and, once carved, laminated masks are more resistant to warping and splitting than those carved straight from the tree.

Mallet A wooden-, plastic-, or rubber-headed hammer that is used primarily with a chisel or

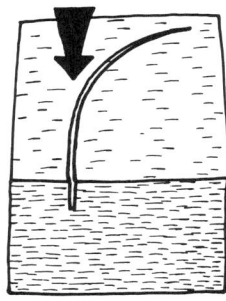 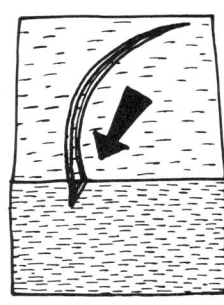 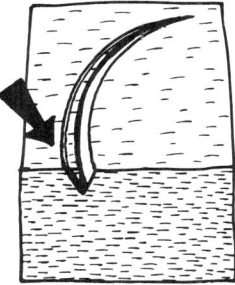 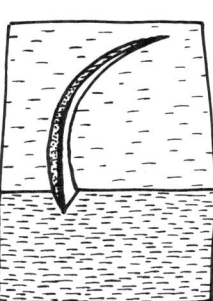

Making an incised cut. Once you have drawn in the shape and position of the trench, take a sharp knife and cut-sink a deep, straight-down stop-cut along the spine of the trench. It is best if this is achieved with a single stroke. Then make the two follow-up angled cuts.

gouge. Many carvers like to make their own mallet. For example, one carver we know uses a cut-down baseball bat covered with a leather sleeve, and another favors a club turned from a piece of stump wood.

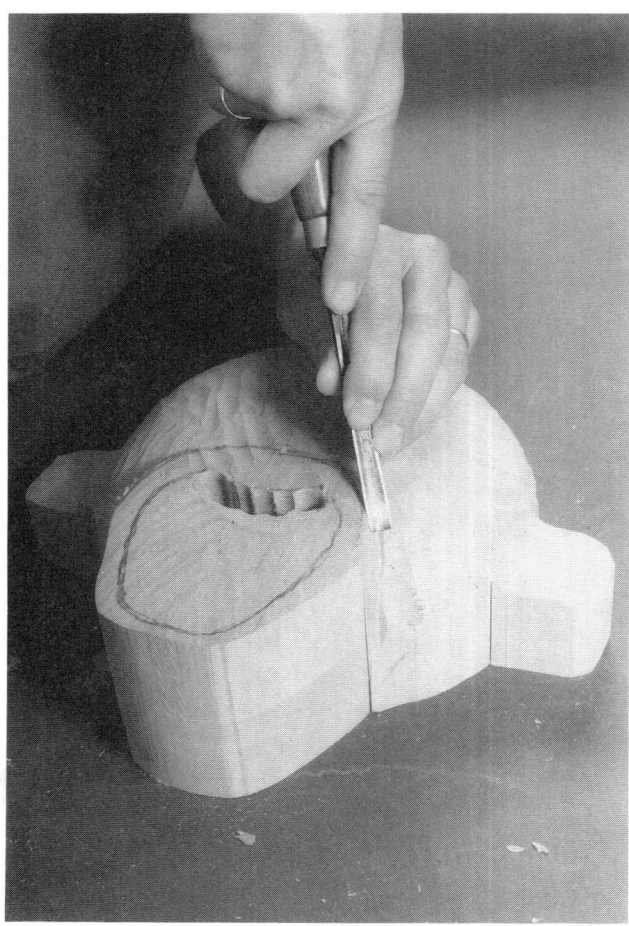

Cutting a plateau with a gouge.

Measure A measure might be anything from a wooden or metal ruler to a flexible tape or even a piece of string.

Modifying Changing and redesigning a mask so that it is bigger, smaller, worked from thicker or thinner sections, made from a more exotic wood than the original, and so on. For example, we decided to modify the Northwest Coast Bird Monster mask to make it half size. And then again, we made one of the African masks from an inexpensive, easy-to-carve wood that we stained black rather than use an expensive, difficult-to-carve ebony type wood.

Paints & Painting Before painting, always clear away bench clutter, wipe up dust, and carefully set out your tools and materials so that they are conveniently at hand. It is best, if possible, to do the painting well away from the carving area. In the context of masks, we prefer to use watercolors protected and enhanced with burnished beeswax.

Pencil-Press Transferring The act of tracing a master design, and then pencil-pressing the traced lines through to the wood.

Plateau Wood In the context of making masks, when a design has been roughed out—meaning the eye sockets and side cheeks have been cut away and lowered—the remaining high-relief features such as the lips, forehead, and nose are termed plateaus.

Roughing Out The act of using the saw, band saw, gouge, or whatever tool seems to be appropriate to swiftly clear away the bulk of the waste—the carving stage prior to modeling.

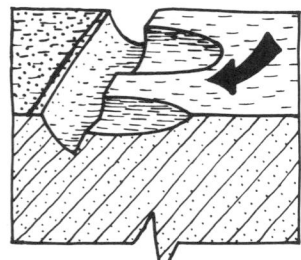 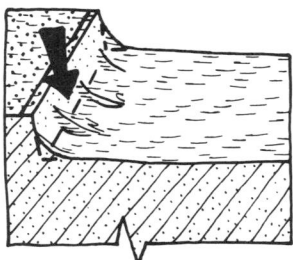 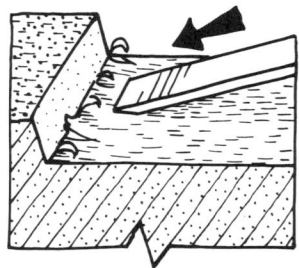

Setting-in and grounding: (left to right) Having cut a V-section trench to the waste side of the drawn line, swiftly clear the bulk of the waste. The ground still needs to be skimmed slightly lower and the small strip of waste between the drawn line and the ground needs to be set-in with a stop-cut. With the drawn line crisply set-in with the stop-cut, skim the ground to a smooth, tooled finish.

Rubbing Down or Sanding Rubbing the wood down with a series of graded sandpapers so as to achieve a smooth ready-to-paint finish. In the context of carving masks, the wood usually needs to be smooth, but not so overworked that you blur the marks left by the cutting tools. That said, some masks are traditionally rubbed down so that they are absolutely smooth.

Note that because wood dust is—to a greater or lesser degree—toxic, we usually wear a cotton hat to protect the forehead, and a full-face forced-air filter/respirator. When the sanding is complete, we vacuum up the dust—from ourselves and the masks—and then move to a special dust-free area that we have set aside for painting. If you find that a particular wood dust makes you wheezy, your eyes red, or whatever, then switch to another wood.

Setting-in The act of cutting along the drawn lines of the design prior to lowering the waste. A design might be set-in either before or after cutting the V-section trench—it depends upon the size, type, and character of the mask. We might cut a V-section trench to the waste side of the drawn line, clear away the waste with a gouge, and then tidy up the drawn line with a knife or chisel. Or then again, we might set the drawn line in with a stop-cut, and then slide the gouge toward the stop-cut, and skim off the waste.

Setting-out The act of transferring the design lines to the wood and generally preparing the wood, the tools, and the working area prior to carving.

Sharpening It's most important that woodcarving chisels, knives, and gouges are kept razor sharp. To this end, we have a sheet of fine-grade emery cloth mounted on a 9in (23cm) disk of ½in (13mm) thick plywood, at the cen-

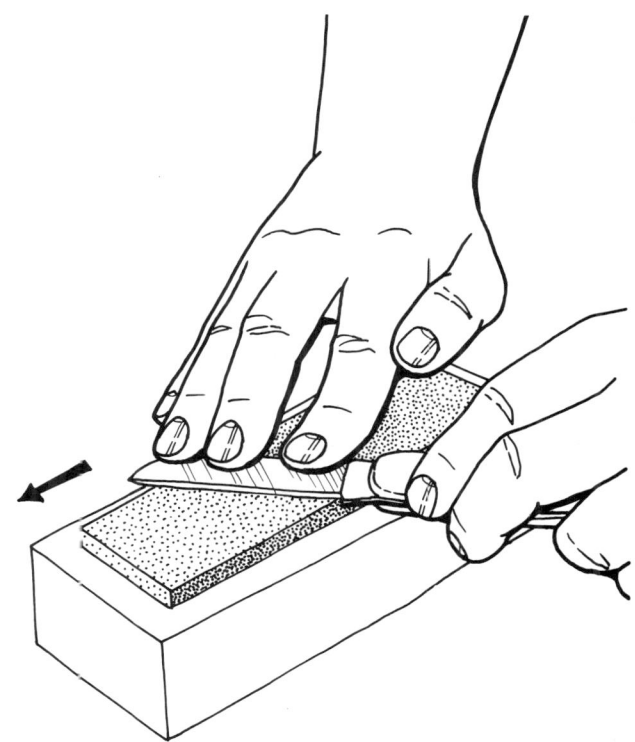

Once the edge is ground to a bevel, then the blade must be honed. Honing is what is commonly meant by "sharpening." The locked and braced action of the knife and the two hands ensures that the angle of the bevel to the stone is constant.

ter of which there is a 6in (15cm) diameter disk of leather, flesh side out, and an even smaller 4in (10cm) disk of leather with smooth side out. It looks a bit like a target. The whole works is screwed and mounted on a faceplate on the outboard end of our lathe, but it could just as well be mounted on a bench motor or grinder. In use, we first stroke the blade on the emery cloth, and then strop, or you might say burnish, the bevel edge to a finish on the two inner leather

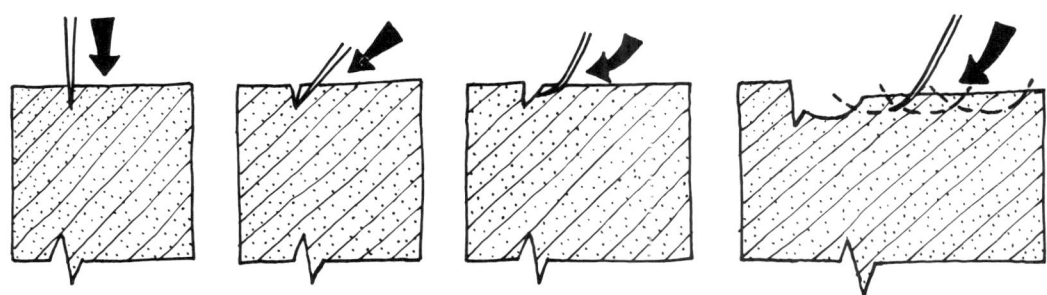

Setting-in with a stop-cut: (left to right) A shallower cut is then set-in to the waste side of the stop-cut and waste is scooped out with a bent tool.

You need a collection of honing stones as well as smaller slips, both flat and cone shaped. The large stone in the center front is medium on one side and coarse on the other. The lidded box contains a medium-fine stone and the misshapen stone in the wood base is super-fine.

disks. The whole operation is completed in a few seconds.

Chisels are held flat-down on the grit or leather, whereas gouges are gently rocked from side to side so that the whole bevel comes into contact. The inside curve of the gouge is stroked with a small tapered slip to remove the edge-of-blade burr.

When you come to sharpen the V-tool, you follow the same procedure as for sharpening a chisel—rub one side of the V and then the other—the only difference being that you have to adjust the bevel angle slightly so that you don't break through the point of the V. Mostly we sharpen knives on a stone.

Slips Small shaped stones used when sharpening gouges. The stones are designed to fit the various convex and concave sweep shapes and sizes of the gouges.

Stop-cut An initial straight-down or V-section cut, into which subsequent skimming cuts are made (see also **Setting-in**). A stop-cut acts as a brake—it literally stops and controls the cut. For example, where a straight-down stop-cut might split the wood—say, around the eye or nose—we first run a V-section incised stop-cut to the waste side of the drawn line, and then make the stop-cut so that the remaining rind of waste crumbles away into the trench.

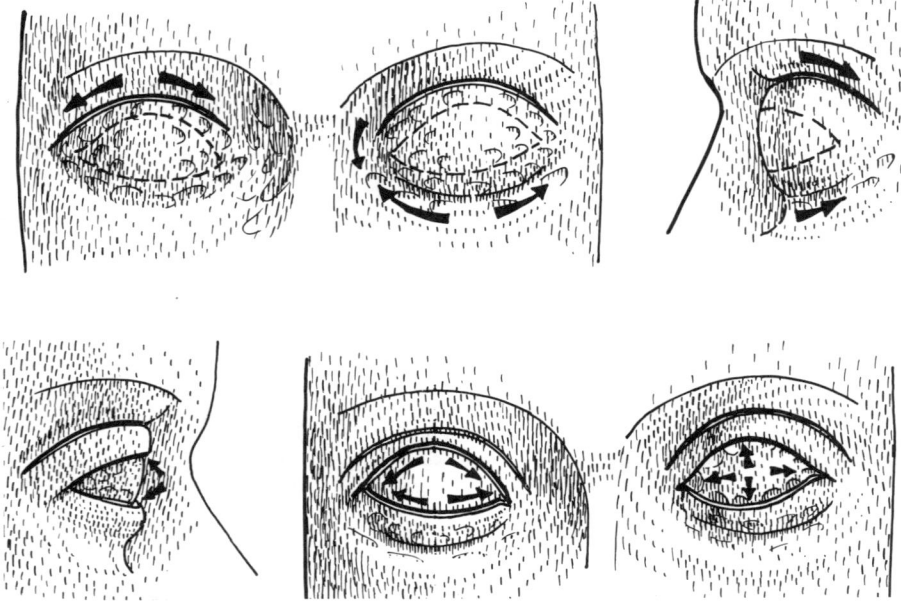

A stop-cut defines the length of subsequent cuts and acts as a brake; it literally stops the cut.

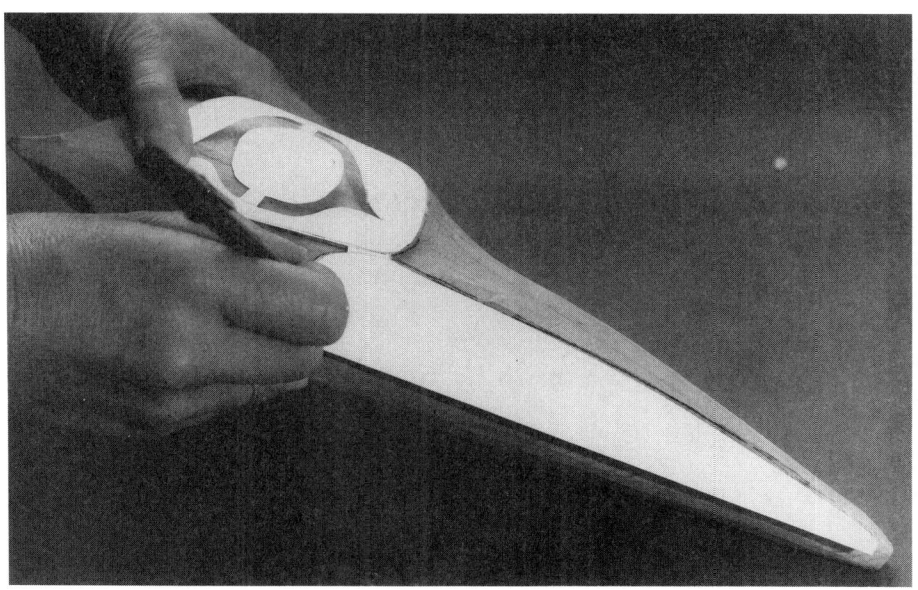

Using a template to mark out a design.

Template A cut-out shape or profile—usually cut from thin cardboard—that we use to transfer design features from the tracing to the mask. Almost invariably, a template made from a tracing will need to be adjusted to fit the contoured surface of the mask.

Tracing Paper A strong, translucent paper used for tracing. We usually work up a good design, take a tracing with a soft 2B pencil, line-in the reverse side of the tracing, and then rework the lines with a hard pencil to press-transfer the lines to the wood. If we are pretty sure that such and such a line on the mask is going to be cut away with the waste, we might well draw it in with a ballpoint pen.

Undercutting The procedure of lowering the waste to reveal a vertical face at the edge of a plateau, and then scooping out the face to create a cave-like cavity or overhang. An undercut—such as under a lip or the nostrils—might be likened to a cave under an overhanging cliff edge.

V-cuts A V-section trench, such as might be made with a knife or V-tool.

Vise A bench-mounted clamp. In the context of *Carving Masks,* we favor a simple vise with sacrificial wooden faceplates, or jaws.

Workout Paper Inexpensive paper as might be used for initial roughs and workout drawings—it is best to use slightly matt white paper.

Workshop In the context of *Carving Masks,* a workshop can be quite a small space, anything from a shed or lean-to shelter out in the garden to a corner of the basement or a small spare room within the house. All you need is a sheltered space with light and electrical power. The good thing about working with traditional hand tools—a mallet, a knife, and various gouges and chisels—is the minimal dust and noise. We tend to do the mallet and gouge carving in a garden shed workshop; the cutting, sawing, drilling, and sanding in the end of the same building; and the final painting in the house or under a covered porch.

GOOD WOOD FOR CARVING

Apple A hard, dense close-grained wood that comes in small sizes, carves well. A good wood for small masks.

Basswood Almost identical to English linden or lime, and also sometimes confused with canary—American whitewood—basswood is wonderfully easy to carve. A good wood for masks that are going to be painted.

Canary (American whitewood) A yellowish soft wood—but classed as a hardwood—even-grained and knot-free. Very much like linden/lime/basswood. A good wood for carvings that are going to be painted.

Cedar There are many varieties—western cedar, pencil cedar, Australian red cedar, and so on. Our best advice is to try a bit and see how it carves. Most Native American Northwest Coast masks were traditionally carved in close-grained red cedar.

Jelutong A pale cream, easy-to-carve, inexpensive wood that can be carved and worked almost without regard to the run of the grain. If you want your carvings to be painted and varnished, then we recommend using jelutong. Nevertheless, in North America jelutong may be difficult to come by; any straight-grained hardwood such as linden/lime or maple is a good alternative.

Linden/lime A close-grained, knot-free, easy-to-carve wood. The perfect wood for beginners. A bit like canary—American whitewood. Linden is a family of trees—*Tiliaceae*—of which the genus *Tilia* is generally termed linden, but also known as lime and sometimes mistakenly called "basswood" or "whitewood," especially in North America. It was/is famous for being the wood used by Grinling Gibbons (1648–1721), the legendary English woodcarver who in 1714 was appointed master carver in wood to George I and is well known for a lifetime's work including carvings in great cathedrals and great houses.

Pine There are so many varieties of "pine" that our best advice is to try carving an easy-to-find type, then take it from there. Search around for a straight-grained, knot-free white variety.

Sycamore A beautiful milk-white wood with a close grain and a smooth, silky surface. Although sycamore was traditionally used for dairy/food bowls and other domestic wares, it also was used sometimes in Europe for carnival masks.

TIMBER FAULTS

There is no such thing as a perfect wood—from piece to piece it might vary from being wonderful to being unworkable. You can never be sure that your piece of wood is sound throughout. If you look at one or two of the mask projects, you will see that we sometimes started carving, only to find that the wood had a cavity or split knot.

The best you can do is go for a recommended wood, look out for possible problems, and then work around any flaws. There are many faults and flaws to be on the lookout for—everything from foreign bodies within the wood, hidden cavities, stains, and molds, to cup shakes, dead knots, unexpected grain twists, insect holes, and wet sappy areas. Before you put tool to wood, start by checking the wood over for obvious problems, and, if you have any doubts, set it aside and go for another piece.

If by chance you are well into a project and a knot, split, hollow, or another problem shows up, then either modify the project to work around the problem, or cut your losses and start over with another piece.

Blemishes This refers to just about anything that is uncharacteristic. One person's beautiful knots or run of grain might well be your blemish.

Checks A check is a split or crack in the length of the plank/board/section—a split runs down the length of the grain. Since the check is an indicator of possible larger problems, it is best to look for another piece of wood.

Decay If the wood is soft, spongy, or crumbly, or it looks to be affected with worm holes, fun-

Decay and insect holes are timber faults that can make a piece of wood unsuitable for carving.

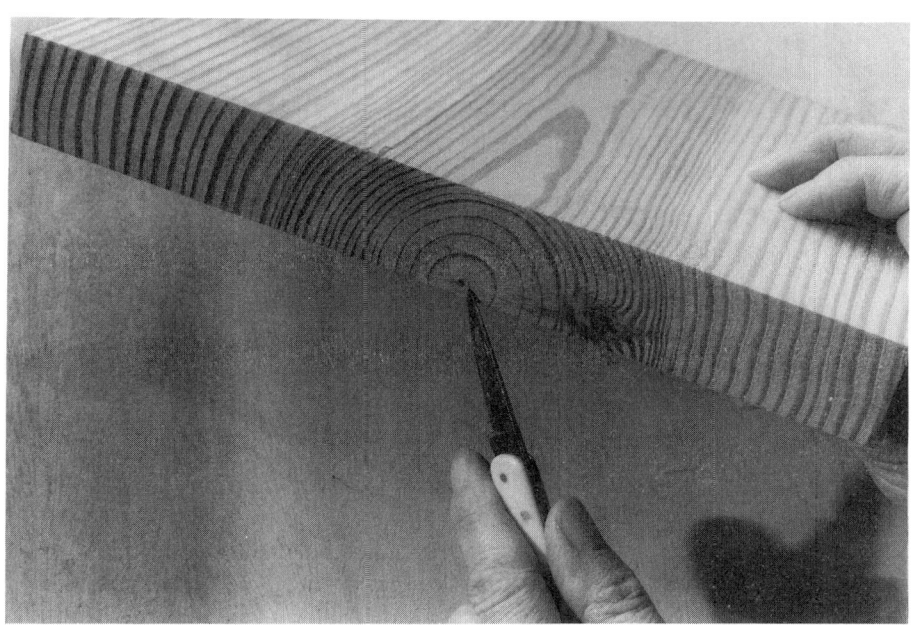

End grain is difficult to carve, and so needs to be approached with care.

gus, or white stains, then the chances are that the wood is starting to decay. If this is the case, then put it to one side and look for another piece.

End Grain Cross-section grain at the end of a piece of timber—the section seen when you make a clean cut through a tree. In the context of *Carving Masks*, end grain usually occurs at the crown, the chin, and the bottom edge of the nose and lips. End grain is always difficult to carve, and so needs to be approached with care. If you drive a tool directly into end grain, then there is a good chance that you will split the wood.

Grain Meaning the annual rings that run through the wood—all the lines, colors, and textures that characterize a piece of wood. Woodcarvers spend most of their time trying to angle the thrust and direction of their tools in order to cut the grain to best advantage. Ideally the woodcarver cuts either across or at a slight angle to the run of the grain.

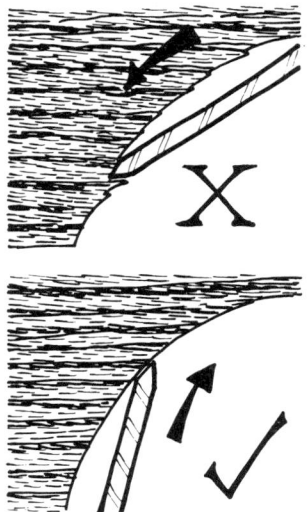

Ideally the woodcarver cuts either across or at a slight angle to the run of the grain. There is a right way and a wrong way.

Complicated grain patterns can add beauty to a carving but also create great difficulties in execution.

25

Green Wood Wood that still contains sap—unseasoned wood. Green wood is wonderfully easy to carve; the only problem is that once it has been worked, it continues to dry out, usually to the extent that the mask warps and splits.

Hardwood & Softwood Botanically speaking, hardwoods come from broad-leafed deciduous trees, whereas softwoods come from evergreens, such as pines. Hardwoods aren't necessarily harder to work or even harder in strength than softwoods. The terms are no more than very general descriptions for the reproductive characteristics of the various trees.

Knots Knots are termed dead, hollow, loose, spiked, encased, and many other local names besides. They are difficult, sometimes impossible, to carve.

Shakes & Splits Separations that occur throughout the length of a log are termed "shakes" and "splits." If, when you look at a log or plank end-on, you see a heart-shaped crack in the middle of the wood, or star-shaped cracks around the edge of the wood, then there might be hollows, cracks, and splits within the wood. Always, but *always*, spend time looking the wood over for possible problems.

·1·
Green Man Mask

Britain

It's an uncomfortable, spine-tingling experience, when visiting a quiet English country church, to catch sight of carved Green Man masks peering out from the gloom—grotesque and malevolent, foliage-crowned man-tree faces, with snaky tendrils crawling in and out of the eyes and mouth.

It's all the more disturbing when you stop and consider that the Green Man—sometimes also called Jack-in-the-Green or the Man of the Trees—is an ancient pagan god or spirit that has to do with tree worship, sacred groves, Druids, human sacrifice, and the like. But then again, per-

1-1 Inspirational drawings. (Left) Detail of a Green Man—from a Renaissance mirror frame—thought to be sixteenth century Italian. (Center) Detail from a misericord—Holy Trinity Church, Coventry, England, fifteenth century. (Right) A grotesque fairground mask, carved by Alexander Devos—early twentieth century. (Bottom) Fairground detail—a panel from a merry-go-round carved by C. J. Spooner—England, early twentieth century.

haps the Church/Green-Man connection is not so strange given that Christianity was grafted directly onto the old religion, with churches being sited on or near sacred groves and sometimes even built of "spirit" oaks.

Primitive humans somehow or other saw their lives as being controlled, or at least mirrored, by nature—by the growth, death, and renewal of trees. These tree spirits were given three-dimensional form as foliate figures and masks that are characterized by being an unsettling mix of man and plant.

Although not much is really known about the ancient origins of the Green Man, there are all manner of eighteenth and nineteenth century accounts that describe ritualized tree-worship and masking celebrations, with villagers dressing up and parading as the Green Man, Jack-in-the-Green, Hairy Men, and Lord-of-the-Trees. And, of course, even today in Britain there are throwback masking traditions and ceremonies, where men and boys dress up in masks and foliage.

If you enjoy this project, and are interested in the British Green Man tradition, there are all manner of Green Man and Jack-in-the-Green pubs, Green Man place names, hundreds of carvings in, on, and around churches, cathedrals, and old buildings, carvings on medieval furniture; and there are one or two village dances and carnivals that still feature Green Men.

THOUGHTS ON SHAPE, FORM & TECHNIQUE

Have a look at the working drawing (see **1-3**) and see how, at a grid scale of three grid squares to one inch, the mask measures about 12in (30.5cm) high, 11 to 12in (28 to 31cm) wide, and 1½in (3.8cm) deep.

Note how the mask is in the form of a flat carved image or motif, as might be found on a chest panel or maybe a church pew. That said, this particular Green Man mask draws its inspiration directly from an English merry-go-round panel carved in the late nineteenth century by C. J. Spooner. (This particular panel is on display in the Charlotte Dinger collection, New Jersey, USA.)

Have a look at the project photograph (see **1-2**), and note how, within the limitations of the 1½in (3.8cm) thickness of the wood, the imagery is carved to give the illusion of depth, with the areas around the nose and mouth being dished. Note how the near-symmetrical image is enlivened and made all the more dynamic by having the design of the foliage ever so slightly off balance.

CHOOSING YOUR WOOD

Although traditionally most of the church masks were worked in oak and chestnut, whereas the fairground carvings were carved in just about everything from pine and elm to lime and fir, we think that a flat panel of this character is best worked in a smooth-grained, easy-to-carve wood like linden/lime, basswood, or pencil cedar.

Have a look at the working drawing for overall size (see **1-3**).

Special Tip

The mistake most woodcarving beginners make is that they try to cut costs by using the first inexpensive wood that comes to hand. What invariably happens, of course, is that they have so many problems with the wood—it splits, warps, is so sticky that it ruins the tools, and generally brings tears of frustration—that they lose heart and give up. So choose your wood with care.

1-2 *Project picture—the finished mask.*

Suggested Tools

- workbench with a vise and holdfast
- medium-weight mallet of a size and shape to suit your needs—meaning your height and strength
- good selection of medium-sized carving gouges and chisels
- a good sharp, long-bladed knife—we use a Swedish sloyd knife with a laminated steel blade
- use of a scroll saw
- pencil, ruler, and pair of dividers
- one sheet each of workout and tracing paper
- small quantity of clear beeswax furniture polish
- typical workshop tools and materials such as sandpaper, oilstone, oil, sharpening slips, Plasticine, dust mask, and PVA (polyvinyl acetate) adhesive

1-3   Working drawing—the two sides that make up the total front view. Grid scale equals three squares to one inch Have a look at the two halves, and see how the mask is indeed asymmetrical.

PROJECT MAKING STAGES

Drawing Out the Design

1. When you have carefully studied the inspirational drawings (refer to **1-1**) and the working drawing (refer to **1-3**), and when you have carefully chosen your slab of wood, take a pencil, ruler, and the workout paper, and set to work drawing the mask out to size.

2. With the tracing set out with a centerline and with height and width parameters, use a soft pencil to draw out each half image.

3. Use the two halves of the working drawing (refer to **1-3**) to create an image that is slightly asymmetrical (see **1-4**). Spend time making sure that the profile line is clearly established.

Making the Blank

4. Once you are happy with the drawn imagery, make a master copy, and then use the tracing to press-transfer the total design onto the best face of the wood.

5. Having reworked the profile line so that it's clearly defined, cut the image out on the scroll saw. The best procedure with a profile of this character is to first work around the wood making straight cuts into the "valleys," and then to follow up by fretting out each of the leaves or lobes (see **1-5**).

6. With the image cleanly fretted out, spend time reworking the drawn lines until you have what you consider is a good image (see **1-6**). Shade in the areas that are to be deeply carved.

1-4   Use the two halves of the working drawings—both tracings—to draw out the design.

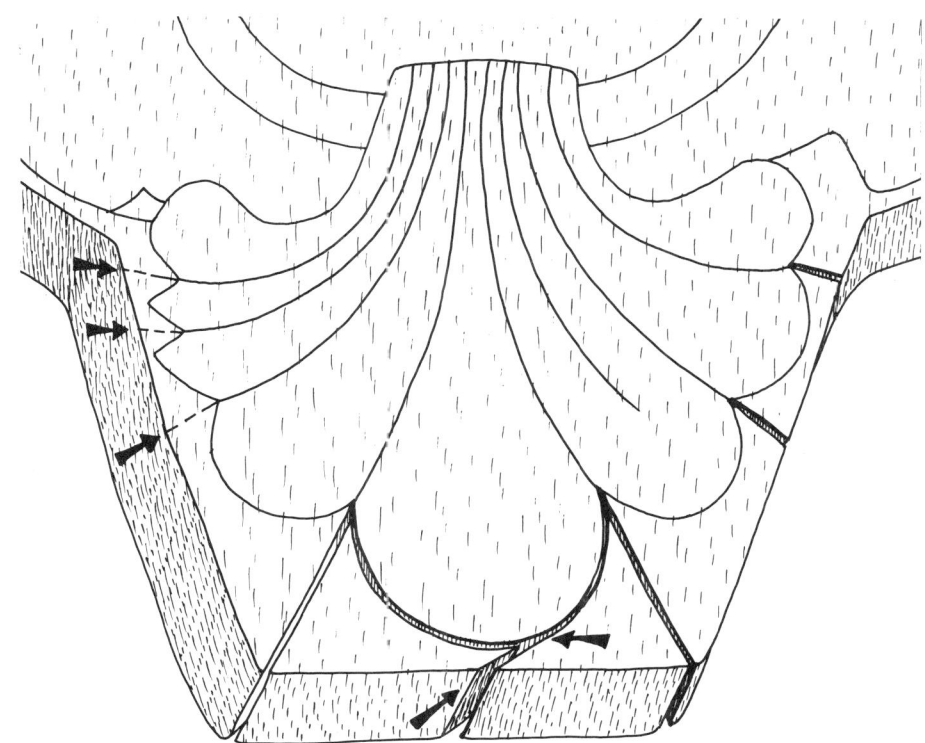

1-5 First run straight scroll saw cuts into the point of the "valleys," and then follow up by fretting out each individual leaf or lobe. Make sure that the line of cut is slightly to the waste side of the drawn line.

1-6 Rework the drawn guidelines, and shade in the areas that need to be deeply carved.

Roughing Out

7. Clamp the wood firm down on the bench, and use one or another of the small-size V-tools to cut in the main lines of the design—the between-leaf valleys, the lines around the nose, eyes and mouth, and so on (see **1-7**). If you are worried about overrunning the tool, to the extent that it digs into the grain and lifts up splinters of wood, then use the knife.

8. With the design crisply set in with V-section stop-cuts, next take a shallow-sweep straight gouge—we use a fishtail—and set to work rounding over the edge of the profile and dishing the areas around the nose and eyes (see **1-8**). Continue until the nose stands out in relief.

9. Continue working the profile—meaning the leaf lobes—until each leaf is rounded at the sides and at a slightly different curve from its neighbor. If you are doing it right, the leaves should run uphill from the dishing around the nose, and then run in a smooth curve downhill toward the outer edge profile.

Modeling

10. When you come to lowering the mouth—meaning the small areas between the lips and the sides of the tongue—first deepen the initial V-cuts with a knife, and then use a small-width gouge to lower the waste. Repeat this procedure to lower the waste as a series of layers (see **1-9**).

1-7 Use a V-section tool to set-in the stop-cuts around the main areas of the design.

1-8 Use the shallow-sweep straight gouge to dish the areas around the nose and eyes. Note the bench holdfast or hold-down—it's a great low-cost piece of equipment for holding the work secure.

1-9 Modeling the mouth. (Top, left and right) A detail and cross section showing the depth and angle of the various cuts. (Bottom, left to right) Deepen the initial stop-cuts on the inside of the mouth by cutting V-section trenches. Remove the waste between the trenches, and then repeat the whole procedure. Use the small-width gouge to clear away the remaining waste.

11. The waste at either side of the nose needs careful handling, inasmuch as the vertical sides of the nose need to run down in a smooth curve so that cheeks meet the nose in a curve rather than an angle. The best procedure is to first clearly define the area that you want to work (see **1-10** and **1-11**), and then to scoop out the waste with a shallow-sweep bent gouge.

1-10 Shade in the areas that are to be deeply graded.

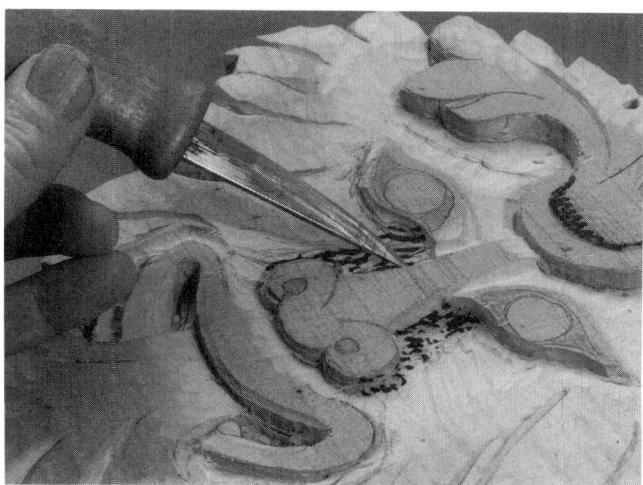

1-11 The sides of the nose need to run down in a smooth concave curve to meet the cheeks.

33

1-12 Deepen the areas around the eyes by first running stop-cuts along the "hairline," and then scooping away the waste from between the brows and the stop-cuts.

1-13 When you come to define the nostril creases, work with a tight, controlled two-handed action—to prevent the tool slipping and doing damage to the cheeks.

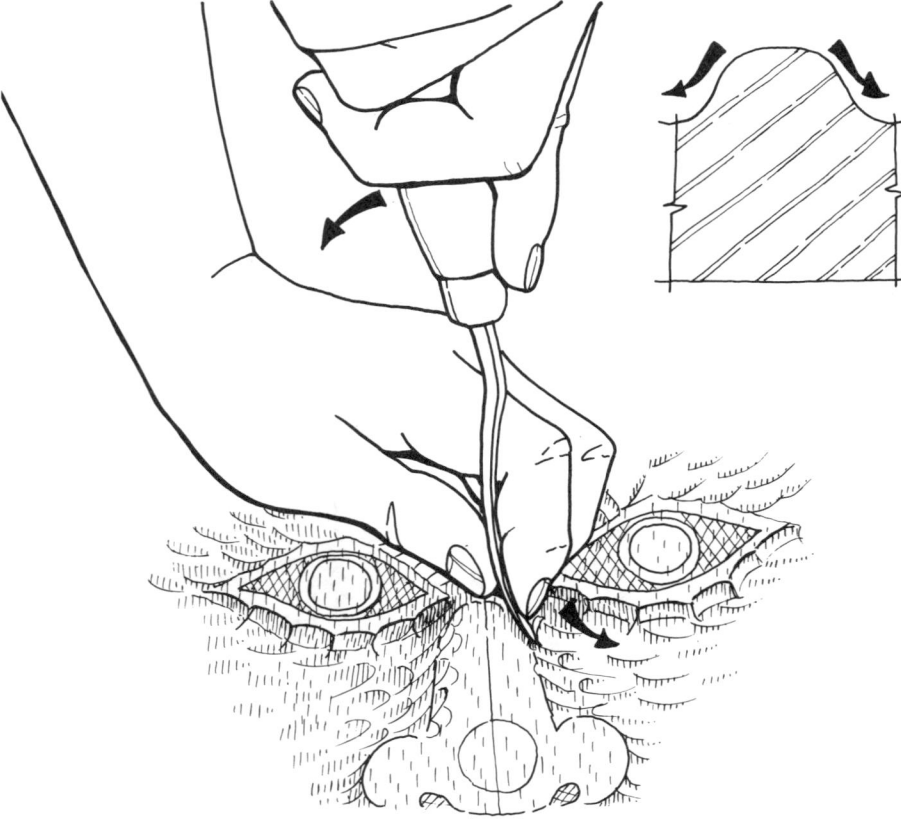

1-14 Having drawn a centerline, use the shallow-sweep, bent gouge to carefully model the curves and contours that make up the bridge of the nose. Be sure not to remove any wood from the tip of the nose—meaning the area marked by the circle.

12. When you come to deepen the areas above the eyes, first use a mallet and gouge to set in the "hair line"—meaning the underside line of the foliage—with a stop-cut. Then slide a small gouge down from the eyebrows and into the stop-cut to remove a level of waste. Repeat this procedure until the forehead runs in a smooth curve from the eyebrows to the underside of the foliage (see **1-12**).

13. You will find that there is no easy way to model the area between the sides of the nose and the underside of the eyes other than to first define the nostril creases with a knife or V-tool (see **1-13**), and then to scoop away the waste from the sides of the nose with a shallow-sweep bent or spoon gouge (see **1-14**). The working procedure is to set the back of the tool hard up against the sides of the nose, positioning and holding the shaft of the tool with one hand, and then to lever back with the other hand. If you are doing it correctly, the waste will come out as smooth curls—like scooping out a hard-boiled egg.

14. To model the eyes: after first lowering the waste around the eyes so that they are standing in relief like plateaus—take a small U-section gouge and carve out a channel around the total almond shape (see **1-15**) so that the sides of the eyes run in a smooth curve into the surrounding features. This done, use the point of the knife to lower the inside-eye areas that occur around the iris and the pointed ends. Finally, use a small scoop gouge to dish the center of each eyeball (see **1-16**).

1-15 Use a small U-section gouge to carve a channel around the eyelid. For maximum control, have one hand pushing and the other guiding and being ready to brake.

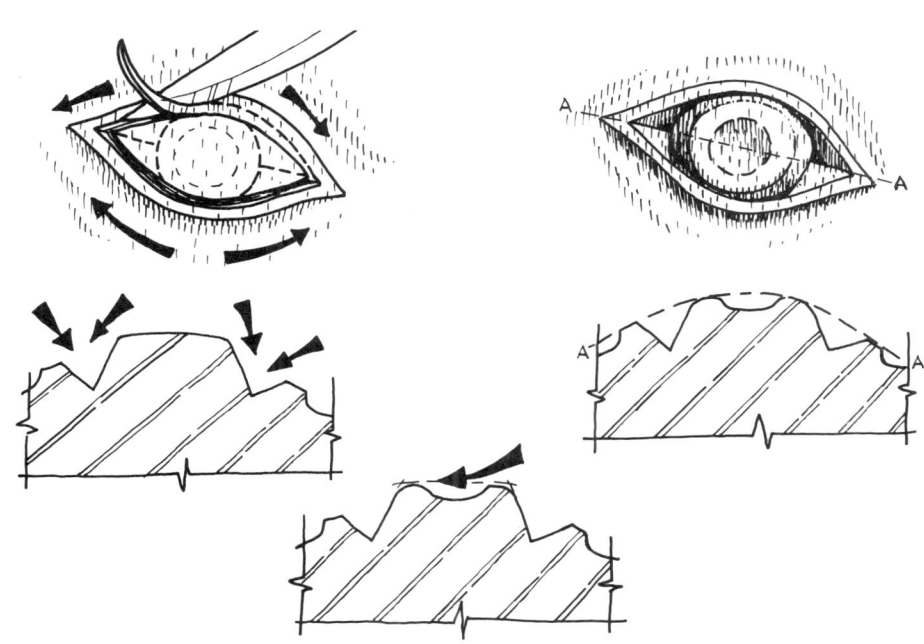

1-16 Modeling the eyes. (Top left) Use the point of the knife to cut a V-section trench around the inside edge of the eyelid. (Middle left) Lower the wood around the side of the eyeball. (Bottom center) Model and dish the pupil. (Right, top and middle) The finished eye, and the cross section showing the raised pupil and the overall arched contour.

FINISHING

15. When you have taken the carving as far as you want it to go—or maybe as far as you dare go—then comes the task of tidying up and generally pulling the whole carving together. It is best to start by clearing the work surface of as much clutter—meaning debris and all the tools that you have finished with—as possible.

16. After clearing out the crevices with the point of the knife, take a scrap of fine-grade sandpaper and go over the whole carving, rubbing down all the sharp edges and corners. Make a real fuss of the nose, the lips, and the foliage lobes that come out of the mouth.

17. Having sanded the whole carving—all the creases, cracks, cavities, and crannies—vacuum up the dust, give the entire carving a generous coat of pure beeswax furniture polish, burnish to a high-shine finish, and the job is done.

Special Tip

Be warned—there are lots of horrible smelly, toxic, expensive, polishes out there that pretend to be beeswax. One such polish we have has pictures of bees and flowers all over the lid; the wordage suggests that it is natural and "green," and yet the contents are so yucky that they require a whole list of health warnings. Only use **beeswax**!

PROBLEM-SOLVING

- If you want to change the scale and go for a larger carving, that's not a problem—but if you want to go for a much smaller carving, then you do need to carefully consider your choice of wood. A small carving requires a wood that is hard and tight-grained—for example, some species of linden/lime or maybe sycamore.
- If you decide to carve a Green Man in the English church tradition, and to use a slab of English oak, then be sure to go for a piece of half-seasoned oak—a piece that is still moist at its center. Such a project will need to be dried very slowly—once the carving is complete—or the surface will crack along the grain.
- Look through the other projects, and you will see that we tend to favor polished German and Swiss gouges rather than the unpolished type. The reasons for this are plain and simple—the polished tools are sold honed and ready to use, whereas the unpolished tools need to be honed.

·2·
Flour Spout Mask

Alsace, Europe

Although it is commonly perceived that masking is somehow or other a tradition that only has to do with exotic tribal cultures—African, Indian, South American, and such—it also needs to be remembered that there are European masking traditions that date far back to pre-Christian times, besides the later British traditions exemplified by Project One.

This particular type of mask and masks of a similar character—usually described as being "flour spout" or "bran" masks—must have been relatively ordinary everyday objects in rural pre-twentieth century Alsace. From its structure—flat back, gaping spout mouth, and large ears or lugs complete with spike holes—it seems likely that it was intended to be fixed to a large, flat-sided box

2-1 Inspirational drawings. (Top right) Alsace spout mask with devil imagery. (Top left) Alsace spout mask with fertility or god of plenty imagery. Note the characteristic corn "crown" motif. (Bottom left) Black Forest bran spout mask, Germany. (Bottom right) Spout mask from Alsace. The soldier imagery, complete with epaulettes, nicely dates this mask as being early nineteenth century.

or container in such a way that the contents could be poured forth.

Although almost nothing is known about Alsace flour spout masks, we suspect that they are rooted in the ancient belief that certain gods were responsible for fertility, harvest, and bountiful supplies of food. However, there are also ancient Celtic customs having to do with a cult of the head and with the practice of taking decapitated heads and nailing them above doorways—as an offering to the gods to ensure a good harvest or a good hunt. Nevertheless, the origin and use of these spout masks is so obscure that we don't really know whether they were in general use or used only by millers, for instance.

It's interesting to note that lots of food containers have parts and names that relate to the human body. For example, large old farmhouse jugs have a pouring "lip," one or more "lug" or "ear" handles, a "neck," a "billy," a "foot," and sometimes even modeled mask decoration.

We find the whole topic of flour spout masks intriguing. Is there anyone who can tell us more about their origin and use?

THOUGHTS ON SHAPE, FORM, & TECHNIQUE

Have a look at the working drawings (see **2-3**) and see how, at a grid scale of four grid squares to one inch, the mask measures about 9in (23cm) high, 10in (25.5cm) wide across the span of the ears, and 3½in (9cm) deep.

Note especially how the blank is laminated from six 12in (30.5cm) lengths of prepared 1¾in (4.4cm) by 4in (10.2cm) section wood—three side-by-side lengths for the back layer with the grain running across the span of the ears, and three side-by-side lengths for the front layer with the grain running down from the top of the crown to the bottom of the pouring lip.

This lamination is designed to give the mask maximum strength across possible weak-grain areas. The ears need to be strong with the grain running from side to side, and the pouring lip needs to be strong with the grain running from top to bottom. The cross-lamination technique seemed to be the easiest option.

As to whether or not this mask needs to be hollowed out, the design is such that there really seems very little choice other than to go for the hollowing option. We say this because by the time you have carved the spout, pierced through to the back of the mask, and generally carved the chin and lips, the task of hollowing is three parts finished.

CHOOSING YOUR WOOD

Although we could have solved the grain and strength problem by using a single slab of dense-grained hardwood, like say maple or plum, for

2-2 Project picture—the finished mask.

reasons of speed and stability we decided to use laminated pieces of linden/lime. A carefully chosen slab of well-seasoned maple would be strong and stable enough for the task, but, then again, it would have taken twice as long to carve. That said, if you do intend actually using this mask in the kitchen with food—on the front of a food box for pouring rice, grain or whatever—then it's best to use a traditional, tried-and-tested, nontoxic, kitchenware wood such as sycamore.

Have a look at the working drawings for overall size (see **2-3**).

Suggested Tools

- workbench with a vise and holdfast
- medium-weight mallet of a size and shape to suit your needs—meaning your height and strength
- good selection of carving gouges and chisels, including a wide spoon or bent gouge for hollowing out the mouth
- a good sharp, long-bladed knife—we use a Swedish sloyd knife with a laminated steel blade
- drawknife
- use of a band saw
- small handsaw
- bench drill press with a wide selection of Forstner drill bits
- pencil, ruler, and pair of dividers
- one sheet of workout and tracing paper
- quantity of plant oil—such as walnut or sunflower oil
- typical workshop tools and materials such as sandpaper, oilstone, oil, sharpening slips, Plasticine, dust mask, and PVA (polyvinyl acetate) adhesive

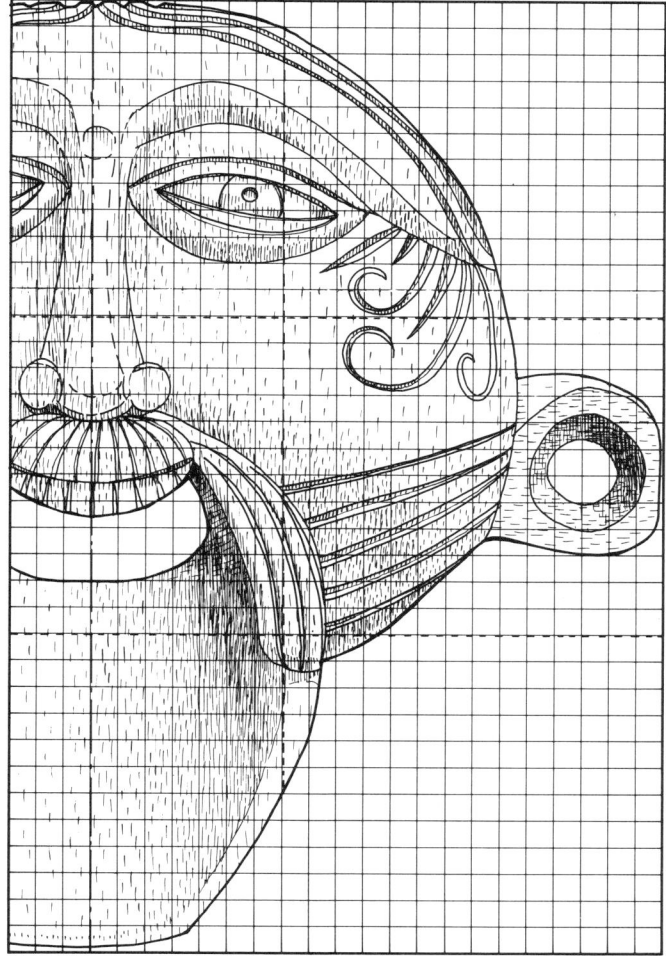
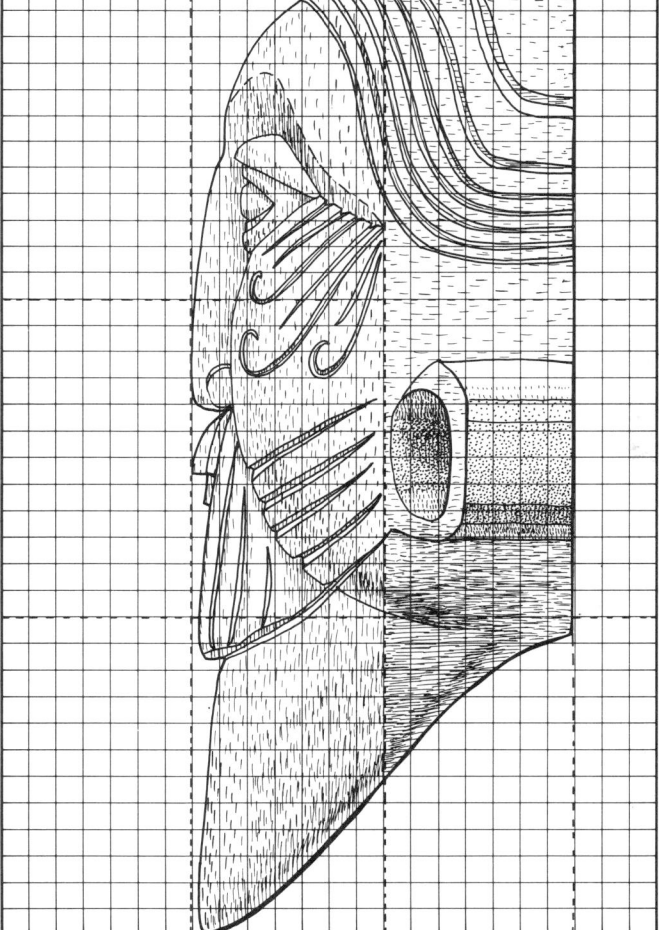

2-3 Working drawings—front and side views. Grid scale equals four squares to one inch. On the front view note the centerline. Also note in both views the lamination lines, and the ear holes that double up as fixing points—for the mask spout to be attached to a box, drawer, or whatever. We cross-laminated the grain to ensure that the ears were as strong as possible—with the grain running from side to side.

PROJECT MAKING STAGES

Drawing Out the Design

1. When you have carefully studied the inspirational drawings (refer to **2-1**), and the working drawings (refer to **2-3**), and when you have made decisions as to the best type of wood, take a pencil, ruler, and the workout paper, and draw the mask out to size.

2. With the front view complete, use the imagery and the various guidelines to draw out the side view. If you have problems visualizing how the two views relate to each other, then build a maquette from Plasticine.

3. Having achieved two good, well-related views, make clear tracings, and then pin your original working drawings on the wall so that they are within reach, but out of harm's way.

Special Tip

We always make tracings for the plain and simple reason that the tracings tend to get folded, dropped on the floor, splashed with glue and coffee, and generally messed up. By the time the carving is finished, the tracings are usually a write-off. Doing it this way, we always have a clean, crisp set of master designs, our original working drawings, which we keep for reference and for use a second time around.

Making the Blank

4. Take your prepared 1¾in (4.4cm) by 4in (10.2cm) length of wood, and cut it into six pieces—three for the back layer and three for the front layer—as shown in the working drawings (refer to **2-3**).

5. Arrange the lengths side by side, mark them so that you know clearly what goes where and how, and, then, one layer at a time, smear glue on mating faces and clamp them together (see **2-4**). When the glue is dry, take the two layers, smear glue on the mating faces and clamp those together. If you have done it right, the back layer should have the grain running horizontally from ear to ear, whereas the front layer should have the grain running vertically from the crown to the lip.

Special Tip

Although we nearly always use water-resistant white PVA (polyvinyl acetate) glue—because it's

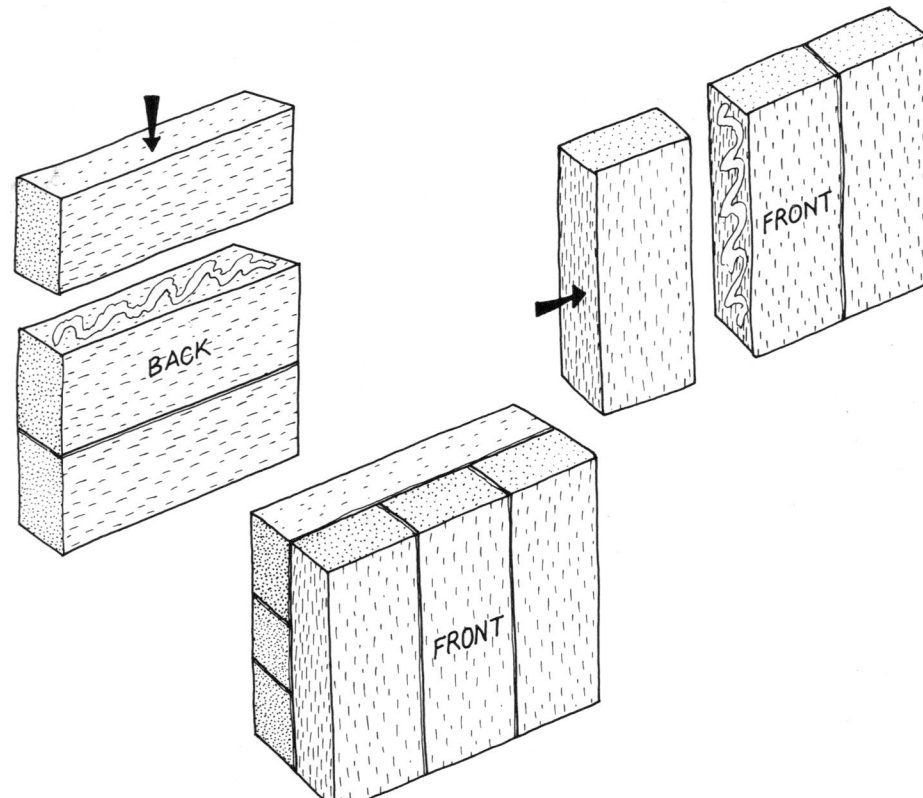

2-4 (Top left) Glue three lengths horizontally, label them "back," and clamp and leave them to dry. Make sure that the middle "ear" length is completely free of splits and knots. (Top right) Repeat the procedure with the other three lengths, and label them "front." (Bottom) When the glue is dry, clean up the mating faces, and glue the two layers together. Be sure to use newspaper or other padding between the workpiece and the clamps.

so easy to handle and store—you might well prefer to use a natural product like animal-derived hot-melt glue. If you do go for such a glue, be mindful that it breaks down when it gets wet.

6. Pencil-press-transfer the imagery to the front face, draw in the various center- and guidelines, and cut the profile out on the band saw.

Roughing Out

7. Having crisply fretted out the profile, and having made doubly sure that the grain is running from top to bottom on the "front" face, draw in the line of the ear. Then take the handsaw, and cut down to the waste side of the drawn line until you reach the glue or lamination level. This done, take the mallet and chisel, and slice off the waste. If you have done it right, the resultant ears will be half the thickness of the blank (see **2-5**).

8. Mark in the centerline and the line of the top edge of the mustache. Use the gouge of your choice to round over the front of the face. Carve the sides and cheeks so that they run in a smooth-curved sweep down to the level of the ear and then to the line of the whiskers.

9. Having drawn in the shape of the mouth hole—meaning, at this stage, the small hole that occurs below the level of the teeth—use the drill press and the ¾in (1.9cm) diameter Forstner bit to sink the mouth hole in to a depth of no more than 2in (5cm) (see **2-6**).

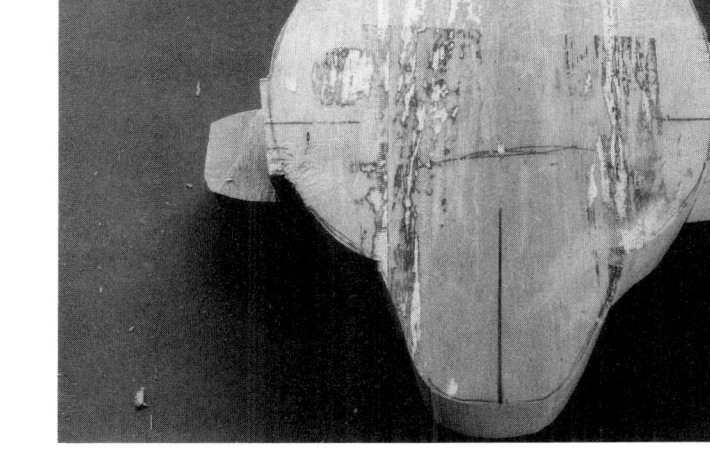

2-5 Having cut out the overall profile on the band saw, saw through the top lamination level, at the point where the ears meet the sides of the head, and then use the mallet and chisel to chop away the waste. Note the mess left by the newspaper.

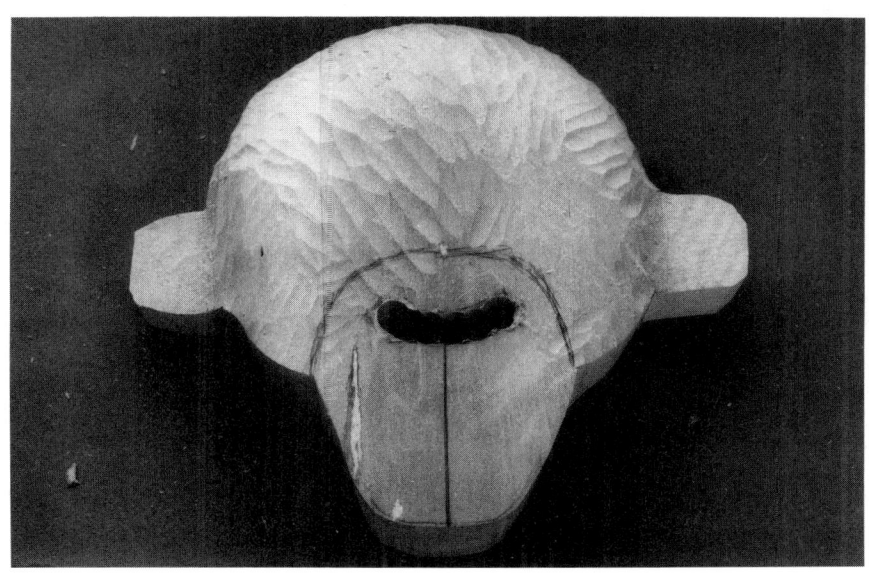

2-6 Drill out the mouth/throat—that is, the small area below the top teeth—to a depth of about 2in (4cm).

10. Turn the mask over so that the back side is uppermost, and run a large-diameter pilot hole down into the center of the mask—to a depth of about 1½in (4cm). We used a two-inch-diameter Forstner bit.

11. With the pilot hole in place, secure the workpiece with the bench holdfast, and use a ¾in (1.9cm) wide shallow-sweep, straight gouge to systematically lower the waste so that it slopes down to the bottom of the drilled pilot hole. Continue by working round and round, and deeper and deeper, until you break through to the mouth hole that you initially drilled in the front (see **2-7**).

12. Once you have achieved what is probably the trickiest part of this project—meaning running the hole through the thickness of the blank—turn the mask over and round over the cheeks so that the top of the whiskers are left standing proud (see **2-8**).

2-7 Working from the back—and having first drilled a centrally placed hole about 1½in (3.8cm) deep—use the shallow-sweep, straight gouge to systematically lower or dish out the waste. If you are doing it right, there will be a breakthrough between the front and back holes.

2-8 Lower and round over the whole face, leaving the mouth and beard area flat and standing in relief. Use the V-section tool to achieve a crisp angle at the line where the cheeks meet the sides of the beard.

Special Tip

If you try to organize the order of your work so that difficult procedures are tackled at the earliest possible stage, you can quickly recognize when you make a mess-up, stop, and start over.

13. With the front roughed out, run the mouth hole through to the back, partially hollow out the back, and generally bring the blank to a consistent state of completion. Then comes the good-fun bit of modeling.

Modeling

14. Start by using the handsaw to swiftly cut away the angle of waste from behind the mouth spout.

Special Tip

Once the mask has been roughed out, it's always a good idea to tidy up the working area—clear up the shavings, put away some of the tools, and spend time honing up the gouges.

15. With the mask held secure with the holdfast so that it is front face uppermost, with the chin towards you, draw in the line of the teeth, the whiskers, and the inner lip. This done, take the large-spoon gouge, and set to work shaping up the mouth and the spout hole (see **2-9**).

16. Work with a cautious, little-by-little approach, all the while being ready to modify the angle of cut to suit the changing direction of the grain. Keep in mind that, halfway through the thickness of the wood, the grain changes direction from vertical to horizontal.

17. Continue by carving from the front, then turning the mask over, and carving from the back. Use the knife to skim the wood to a good finish, and assess the thickness of the spout, and so on, until the surface of the mouth and spout run in a smooth-flowing curve into the hollow at the back of the mask.

2-9 The spoon gouge is held at a high angle, one hand guiding and pivoting and the other hand doing the work. The working action is one of digging and scooping.

18. Once you are happy with the overall shape of the spout, secure the mask in the bench vise so that it is upside down, with the spout looking towards your body. Then use the drawknife and sloyd knife to shape up the back of the spout (see 2-10). This is a pretty straightforward procedure, as long as you hold the drawknife so that the bevel is on the underside, work with a short, tight stroke, and are ready to modify your approach to suit the ever-changing direction of the grain.

2-10 With the workpiece well secured, hold the drawknife so that the bevel is facing the work, and then shape the back of the beard. Work with a series of short, tightly controlled strokes. The ''bevel down'' action ensures that the blade doesn't dig too deeply into the grain.

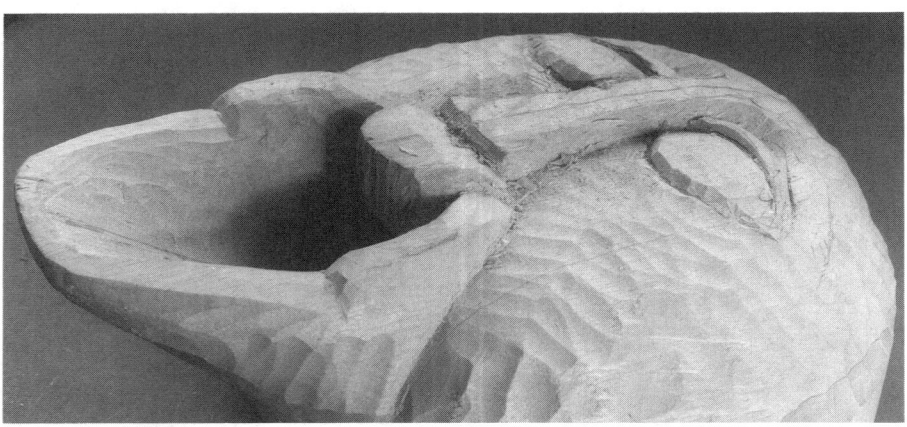

2-11 Use the knife and gouge to remove the waste from around the nose, mouth, eyes, and whiskers.

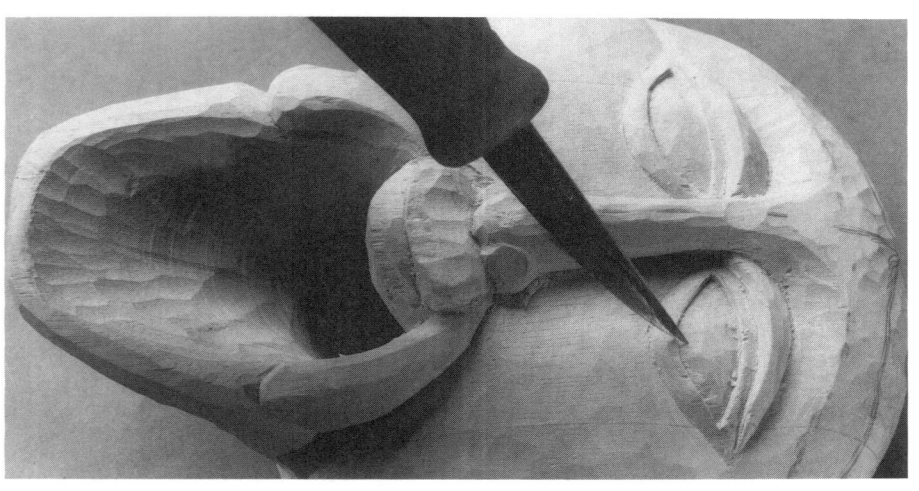

2-12 As the short-grained eyelids are very fragile, it is most important that the knife doesn't run out of control. Work towards your body, with small, two-handed paring cuts, all the while being ready to stop the stroke if the cut looks to be going in the wrong direction.

2-13 (Left) A top view and a cross section through the eye—showing the various steps and contours. (Right) Use the point of the knife to remove the small core of waste wood from the center of the eye. Work with a twisting action.

19. Having drawn in the shape and position of the various features, and double-checked that they are correctly placed, use the gouge and knife to lower the waste so that the nose, mustache, eyes, and eyelids stand out in relief (see **2-11**).

20. To model the eyes: set the almond shape of the eye in with a stop-cut, and then carefully lower the inner eye so that the lids step down by about 1/8 in (3mm) (see **2-12**). *Be warned:* there is a great risk at this stage of overshooting with the tool, and doing damage to the lids—so go at it nice and easy. Once you are happy with the profile and depth of the almond shape, draw the shape of the iris, set-in the two curves with incised cuts, and then lower the whole of the iris area. To carve the pupil, simply spin the knife on the spot, until the point cuts its own hole (see **2-13**).

FINISHING

21. When you have finished the modeling, give the whole surface of the carving a swift rubdown with the fine-grade sandpaper, and then wipe away the dust.

22. The details are pretty straightforward inasmuch as they can all be achieved by making incised lines. For example, the pattern of the hair, the side whiskers on the cheeks, the mustache, the teeth, and the curls are all made up from knife-worked incised cuts. All you do is make a single stop-cut to define the shape and depth of such and such a line, and then make slanting cuts at either side of the initial cut to create the V-section trench. Even though it's uncomplicated, you do have to keep changing the direction of the stroke when you come to cutting the curls (see **2-14**).

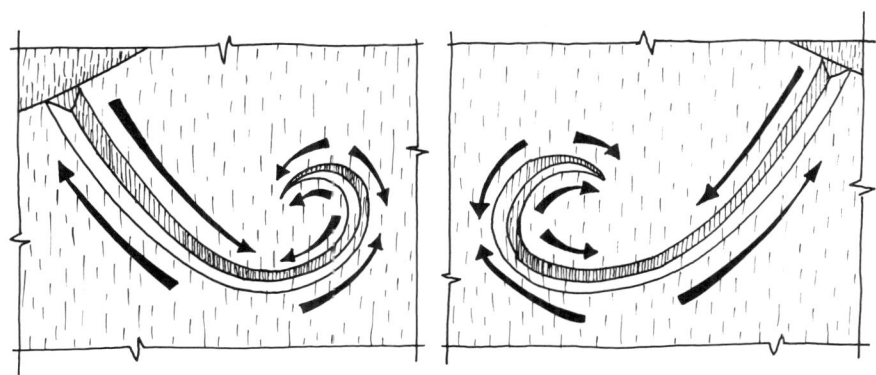

2-14 When you come to cutting the decorative curls, you will have to be constantly changing the direction and angle of the cut to suit the run of the grain. We use a knife, but you could just as well use a small V-section tool.

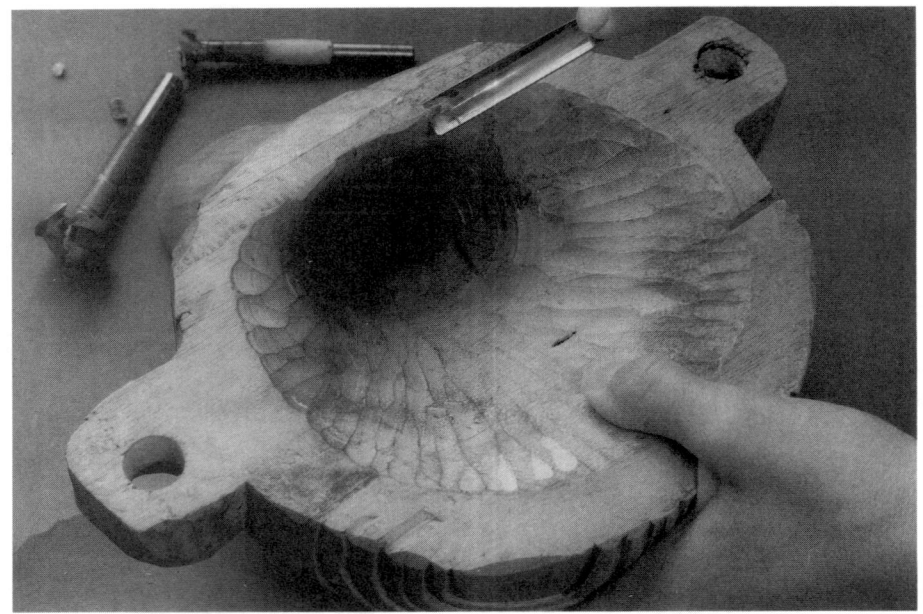

2-15   If you intend using the mask as a pourer, then be sure to tidy up the small ledge at the back of the mouth so that the pouring action is free-running.

23. If you intend mounting the mask on a container and using it to pour grain or something similar, then you need to skim away the small ledge on the inside bottom edge of the hollow—meaning at the back of the mask—to encourage easy flow (see **2-15**).

24. Finally, when the carving is finished, and you have bored out the ear holes with two drill bits—1in (2.5cm) and ⅝in (1.6cm)—give it another swift rubdown with the finest-grade sandpaper, wipe it over with vegetable oil, and burnish it to a sheen finish. As needed, give it several coats of oil.

PROBLEM-SOLVING

- If you like the idea of laminating the blank and want to go for the perfect arrangement, then stay with the front layer as described, but change the back layer so that the area below the horizontal ear line is made up from vertical grain. This arrangement would make carving the spout that much easier.
- Regarding using a drawknife for carving the outside of the chin or spout (refer to **2-10**), it would be better done with a tool half the size of the one shown.
- If you'll have a look once more at the project photograph (refer to **2-2**), you will note that the modeling is naive, or, you might say, even a bit swift and immediate; this is how it needs to be.
- If you do decide to carve this mask from a single slab of wood, then you could reduce the risk of the ears splitting off by having greater depth of wood and much smaller fixing holes.

·3·
Fool Mask

Europe

The European masking tradition of playing the "fool" is both ancient and widespread. Not so long ago—at least until the end of the nineteenth century—just about every other village had a carnival tradition that had something to do with a masked fool being hounded through the streets.

Some fools played out masked dramas that turned the tables on the onlookers, with the fool being given all the privileges of a king or church official—just for a day. Do you remember, in the classic film *The Hunchback of Notre Dame*, when Quasimodo was carried through the streets? Well,

3-1 Inspirational drawings. (Top, left and right) Ugly face masks—Bavaria, late nineteenth century. (Bottom left) "Old Winter" mask—Alpine, early twentieth century. The mask was worn during the midwinter festival to celebrate "Young Spring's" victory over winter. (Bottom right) Alpine mask—end of the nineteenth century. The mouth hole enabled the wearer to blow a pipe or horn.

as we recall, he was dressed up as the pope, and his face looked very much like the mask featured in this project.

The dark side of the fool masking tradition almost certainly has to do with making people with physical and mental disabilities scapegoats for all the ills of the community, these unfortunates actually being dressed up and hounded around the village. This line of thinking is borne out by the surviving fool masks and outfits which are characterized by having such features as lolling tongues, twisted and deformed faces, and crooked backs.

Our particular European mask comes from an Italian tradition that not only always portrays the fool as having a protruding tongue, but, even more interesting, also makes use of crooked-grained knotty wood in such a way that flaws and open knots become abscesses and hideous boils. On first seeing such a mask, we felt it must surely have something to do with the horrors of the Black Death and criminals being hanged or garroted!

THOUGHTS ON SHAPE, FORM, AND TECHNIQUE

Have a look at the working drawings (see **3-3**) and see how, at a grid scale of four squares to one inch, the mask measures about 8in (20cm) high, 6in (15cm) wide, and 3½in (9cm) deep.

Note how the mask is laminated from three layers of wood, with the layers being arranged in such a way that a large open flaw—a knot with a crack running through it—occurs on the left cheek. Take into consideration that one of the primary characteristics of this particular mask is the thick, heavy tongue that hangs and lolls out of one side of the mouth.

All that said, this is one of those projects where you could stay within the tradition, and yet still choose to go your own way. For example, if you have in mind to go for a caricatured self-portrait, or you would simply like to carve a face with a huge nose and fat cheeks or just an ugly face—meaning a mask that still has the lolling tongue and abscess—then this is the project for you.

3-2 Project picture—the finished mask.

CHOOSING YOUR WOOD

If you have been following our advice with the other projects—only choosing wood that is free from flaws—then the chances are that you will have a good size stockpile of wood that is generally twisted and knotty. If that is the case, then now is the time to put a piece of that wood to good use. Find a piece—it might be a single slab, or several thin layers—that is straight grained for the most part, but has a good-sized knot to one side. However, the knot must not be loose or dead, and it must not contain a split or cavity that will threaten the integrity of the rest of the carving.

We chose to build up the mask from three pieces of linden/lime, the wood being organized so that the knot ran through the middle layer.

Suggested Tools

- workbench with a vise and holdfast
- medium-weight mallet of a size and shape to suit your needs—meaning your height and strength
- good selection of medium-size carving gouges and chisels
- a good sharp, long-bladed knife—we use a Swedish sloyd knife with a laminated steel blade
- bench drill press with a ¾in (2cm) diameter Forstner bit
- use of a band saw
- pencil, ruler, and pair of dividers
- one sheet each of workout and tracing paper
- selection of watercolors—white, red, green, and black
- long-haired watercolor brushes—a large and a fine-point
- small quantity of clear beeswax furniture polish
- typical workshop tools and materials such as sandpaper, oilstone, oil, sharpening slips, Plasticine, dust mask, and PVA (polyvinyl acetate) adhesive

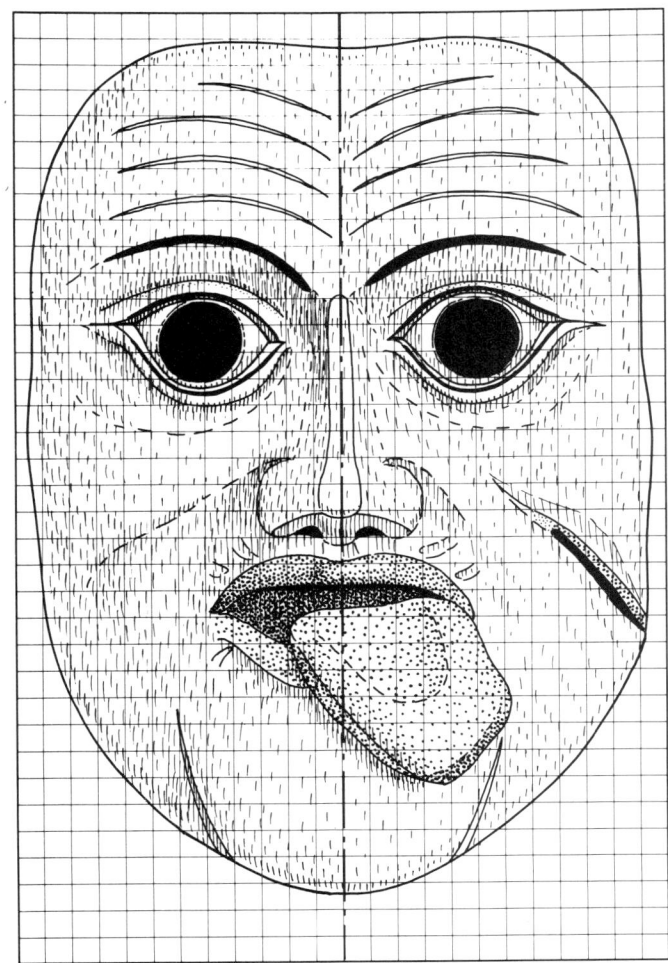
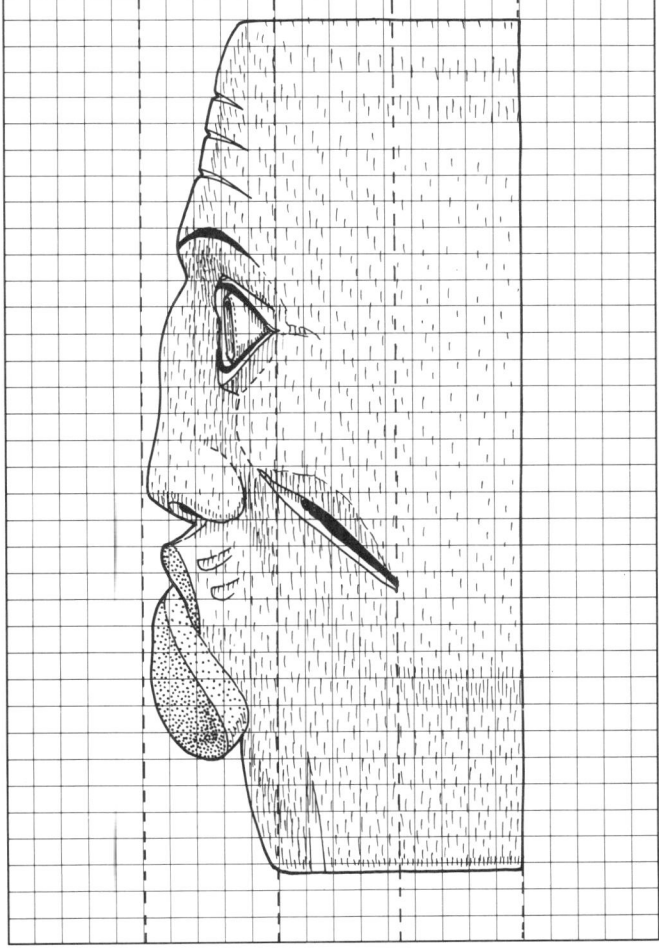

3-3 Working drawings—front and side views. Grid scale equals four squares to one inch. Note the centerline on the front view and the lamination lines on the side view.

PROJECT MAKING STAGES

Drawing Out the Design

1. After you have studied, if possible, European masks in museums and had a good long look at our inspirational material (refer to **3-1**), sit back and give some thought to just how you want your mask to be.

2. Keep in mind that the design needs to relate to your particular chosen piece of wood, take the Plasticine, and either make a maquette of the mask, or at least make a model of the lips and the tongue details (see **3-4**).

Special Tip

Whenever you are presented with a difficult-to-visualize detail—such as the lips and the lolling tongue—it's always a good idea to build a maquette or model so that you can see the problem in the round. With this mask, you could sit in front of a mirror and make faces to get an idea of the possibilities.

Note: It might well be a good idea to tell your friends, family, and neighbors why you are sitting in front of the mirror and making faces—just in case they get the wrong idea!

3. Draw the design at full size—front and side views (refer to **3-3**). Then make clear tracings.

Making the Blank

4. Once you have made tracings and chosen your wood—either a single slab or a laminated stack—take the front view tracing and try out various placings. Fiddle and fuss around so that the grain runs from crown to chin and so that the knotty flaw occurs on the left side of the face, midpoint between the eye and the mouth.

5. Bearing in mind that half the fun of this project is the unpredictability of the knot, set the wood out with a good clear centerline, and press-transfer the traced imagery. Make sure that you preserve the centerline; redraw the centerline as the carving progresses and see to it that the area marked by the circle—on the end of the nose—remains untouched until the final modeling stage.

6. With the imagery in place, run the wood through the band saw, and cut out the front view outline. Run the line of cut as close as possible to the waste side of the drawn line (see **3-5**).

Roughing Out

7. Before you start work, spend time arranging the workpiece so that it stays put. Look over the various photographs, and you will see that we opted for a couple of pieces of wood nailed to the bench—to stop the wood from sliding around—and a holdfast to hold the wood down.

8. Secure the workpiece flat-down on the bench, take a medium-width, straight gouge and a mallet, and start by cutting away the waste from around the nose, mouth, and tongue (see **3-6**). Clear the waste from around the sides of the face so that the surface slopes down from the sides of the nose.

9. Taking care not to let the gouge overrun into end grain, carefully lower and grade the center of the forehead, the dips of the eye sockets, the channel between the bottom of the nose and the upper lip, and the chin area around the tongue.

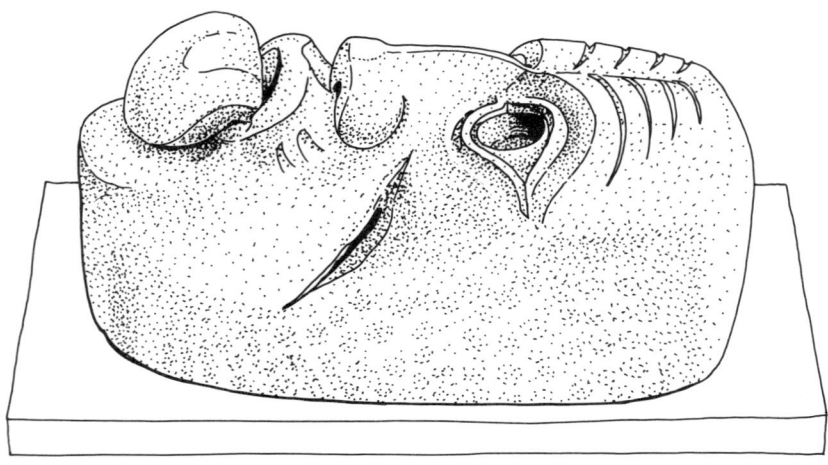

3-4 Once you have drawn out the various views, then make a Plasticine maquette so that you have a clear idea just how the mask looks in the round. If you can make the maquette full size, then so much the better.

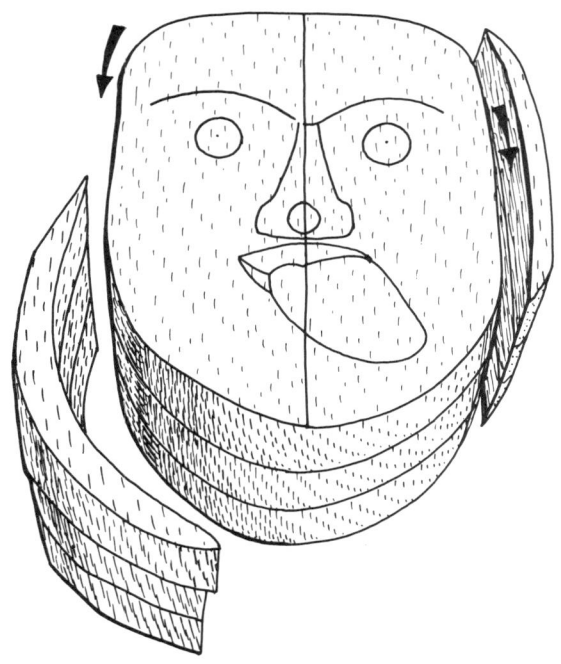

3-5 Use the band saw to slice away the waste from around the front-view outline.

10. Once you have removed the bulk of the waste wood, trace the eye details onto some scraps of tracing paper. Then use the tracings to establish the position of the eyes on the lowered sockets.

11. Mark the center of the eye holes with a spike, and then use a V-section tool to set-in the outermost shape of the eye—that is to say, the almond shape (see **3-7**).

3-6 Use the medium-width straight gouge and the mallet to quickly chop away the waste. Aim to create a sloping plane that runs down from the nose, mouth, and tongue.

3-7 With the center of each eye clearly marked, use the V-section tool to set-in the shape of the whole eye and the top lids.

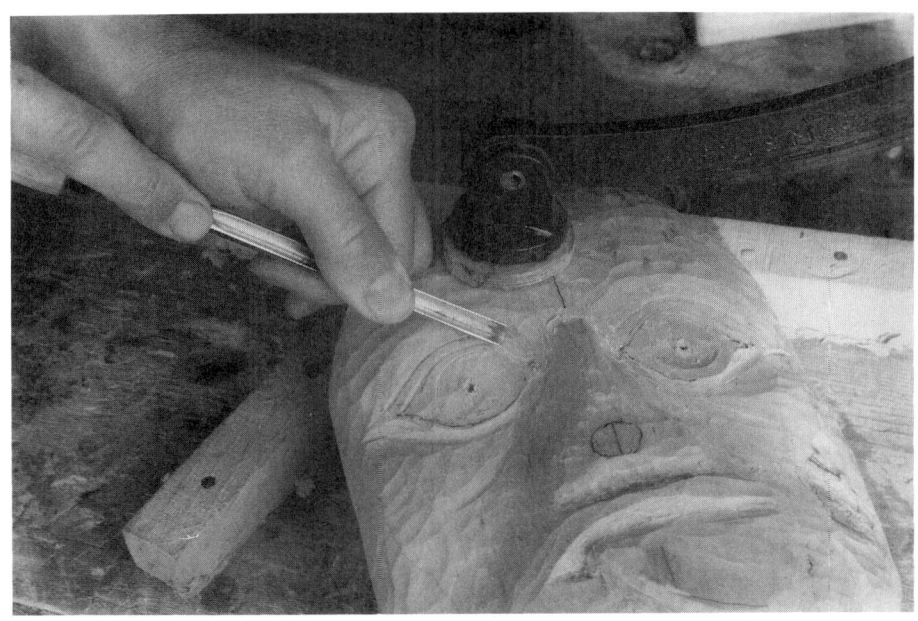

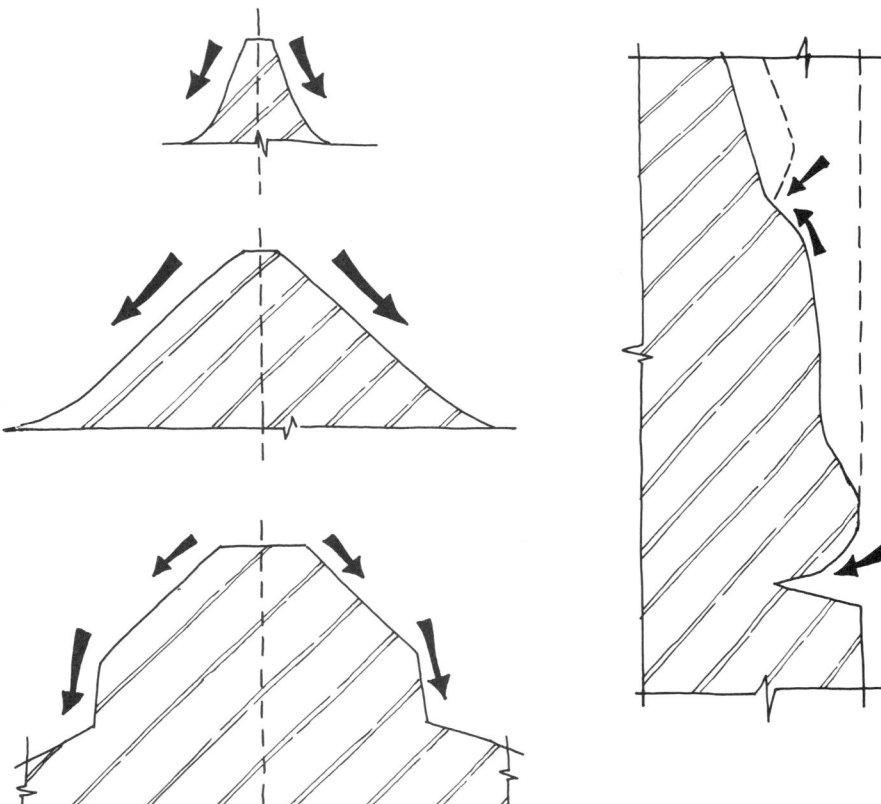

3-8 (Left, top to bottom) Three cross sections through the width of the nose—the top, the middle, and the nostrils. (Right) A cross section through the centerline of the nose to show the shape of the nose in side-view profile.

Modeling

12. To model the nose: remember to keep redrawing the centerline and the circle at the end of the nose, and, starting with the triangular shape, use the tools of your choice to create a hooked nose. Lower the top of the nose where it meets the brow. The area between the end of the nose and the puckered lips is particularly tricky; it is best managed with bent and spoon tools. You need to

3-9 Use a U-section gouge to deepen the channel, or moat, around the eye to form the eye socket. Then use the knife to sink stop-cuts around the eyelids.

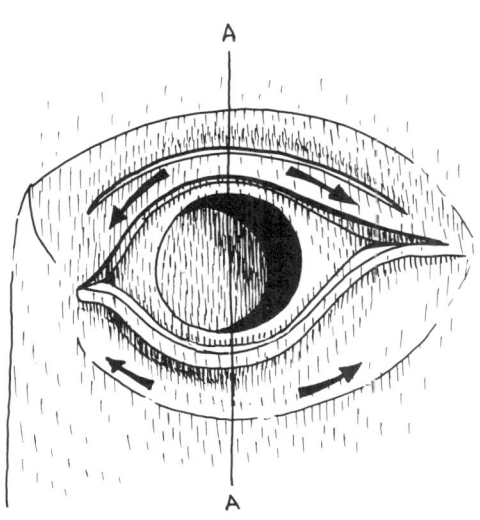 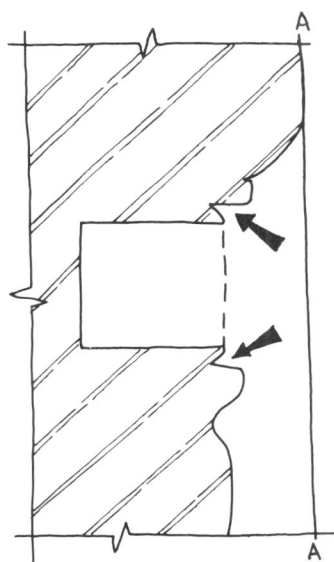

3-10 (Left) Detail showing the fully modeled eye. (Right) A cross section through the eye, showing the drilled hole and the V-section channel between the eyeball and eyelid.

lower the cheeks so that the nostrils wrap around the face (see **3-8**).

13. To model the eyes: first reestablish the center of the eyes with spiked holes, and then set-in the outline with a shallow incised line. Move to the drill press, and run a ¾in (2cm) diameter hole down into each eye to a depth of about 1¼in (3cm).

14. With the ¾in (2cm) diameter holes in place, first use a U-section gouge to deepen the channel around the eye—that is, the outer eye socket—and then use the knife to set-in the shape of the eyelids with a stop-cut (see **3-9**).

15. Slide the knife at a low angle around the inside of the stop-cut to lower the surface of the eyeballs. Repeat this procedure several times—setting-in with a stop-cut, and then lowering and undercutting—until the surface of the eyeballs looks as if it runs under the edge of the eyelids (see **3-10**).

16. To model the tongue: first lower the area around the tongue, study the maquette details, and generally familiarize yourself with how the tongue needs to roll over the bottom lip. Then use the V-tool, the straight U-gouge, and the knife to shape the lips and to undercut the tongue (see **3-11**).

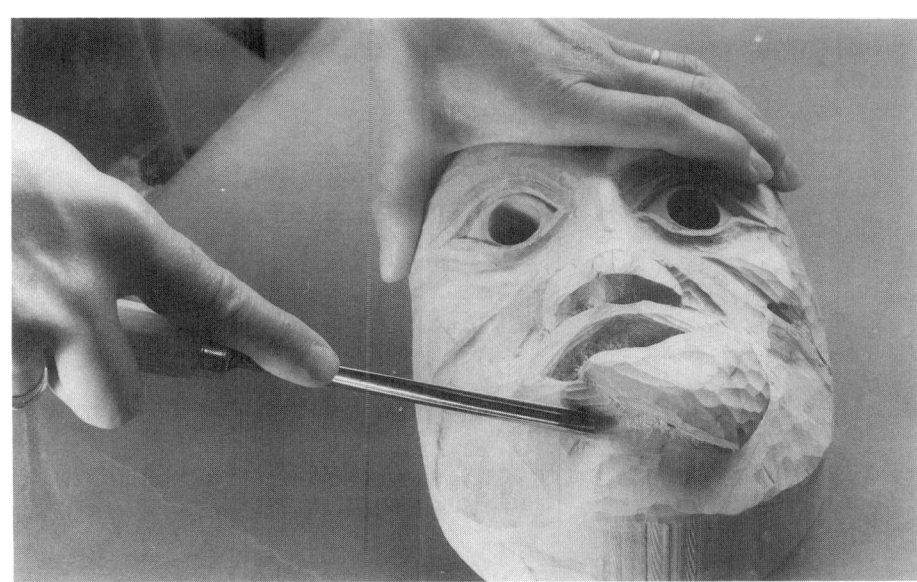

3-11 Use the U-section gouge to undercut the tongue, and to create the roll-over effect of the bottom lip.

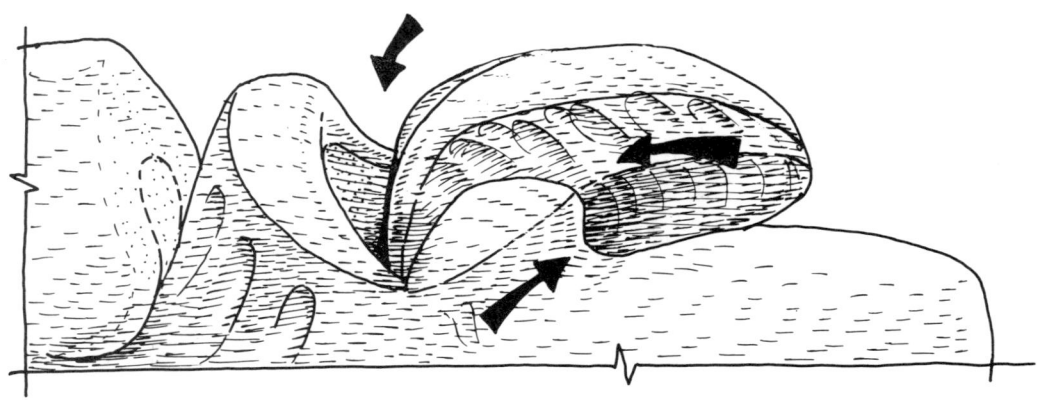

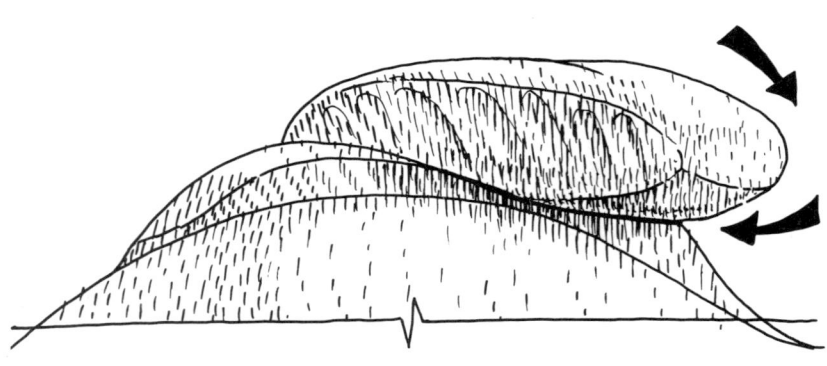

3-12 (Top) View of the tongue, seen from the left side of the chin. (Bottom) Side view of the mouth showing the underside of the tongue.

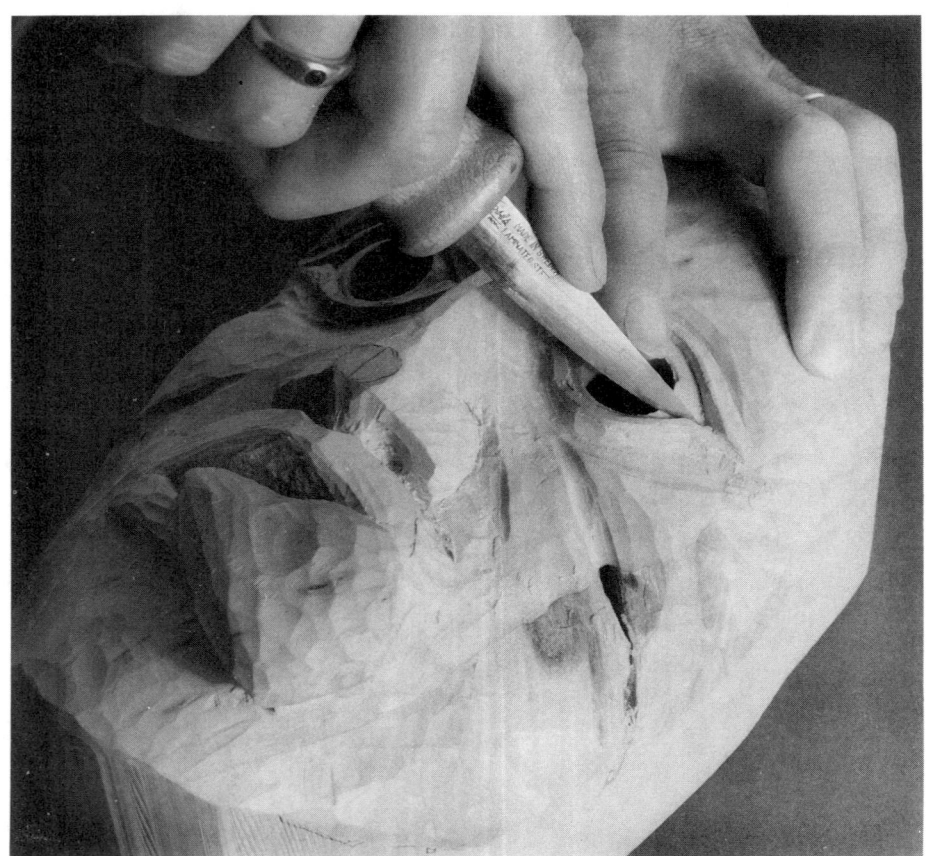

3-13 Use the point of the knife to slice away and lower the wood at the corners of the eyeballs. Lower the wood to a depth of about 1/4in (6mm) to create the bulging-eye effect.

17. Use a shallow-sweep straight gouge to carve a slight concavity down the center of the tongue, and then use a smaller gouge to scoop out the waste from within the mouth (see **3-12**).

18. Continue by shaping and hollowing the nostrils, finalizing the shape of the nose as seen in the side-view profile, deepening the hollow that runs up through the center of the forehead, deepening the channel between the top lip and the underside of the nose, and so on. (Refer to *Hollowing* in the "Tools, Techniques & Materials—A–Z Guides" for the back of the mask.)

FINISHING

19. When you have taken the broad modeling as far as you want it to go, pause to refresh the image in your mind of what you want your mask to be. Have another look at the working drawings, our photographs, and any other research clips that you have gathered along the way, and then hone your tools in readiness for finishing.

20. Use the knife to tidy up the eyes (see **3-13**), and to cut the worry creases across the forehead (refer to **3-2**).

21. Use the full range of tools to variously skim, trim, and tidy up the details so that you have an exciting and convincing profile (see **3-14**). Then take a piece of fine-grade sandpaper, and rub the tongue, lips, chin, and nose to a smooth finish. Leave all the tool marks on the cheeks, around the eyes, and at the sides of the forehead.

22. With the mask well carved and rubbed down, clean up the dust and debris, and move to the area set aside for painting. Lay a thin wash of off-white over the whole mask to give it an unhealthy pallor. Then paint the lips and tongue a thin red-pink wash, the eyebrows black, the lines around the eyes green, and the eyeballs white. Last, dab the wound/abscess on the side of the cheek with a nice juicy bloom of puss-green and puss-pink.

23. Finally, when the paint is completely dry, give the whole mask a quick rubdown with the fine-grade sandpaper to remove nibs and whiskers of raised grain. Then use the beeswax to burnish the mask to a sheeny finish.

3-14 The carving is ready to be finished. Note that the lips and tongue need to be well finished so that they contrast with the surrounding areas of tool-textured wrinkles and creases.

PROBLEM-SOLVING

- If you like the idea of this project, and want to know more about European "ugly" masks, then visit a museum and look primarily for Italian, Bavarian, Swiss, French, and Yugoslavian masking traditions.
- As with many of the other masks, if you can't quite visualize a detail—an eye, the way a lip curls, how a nostril swells, or whatever—then the best thing is to sit in front of a mirror and study your own face.
- If, when you are well into this project, you find that the knot is going to run into the mouth, or up into the eye, then be ready to accentuate the details accordingly. For example, if the dark color and the twisted grain of the knot does run into the eye, you could model the eyelid so that it pulls down like a scar.

·4·
Ugandan Mask

Africa

Although making and wearing masks is a near-universal activity, Africa is commonly thought of as being the center of the masking tradition. It's important to note, however, that this is a popular perception that has more to do with the phenomenon of early twentieth century European Cubist artists such as Braque, Picasso, and Epstein, who drew their inspiration and energy from so-called "primitive" African art, than with any real basis in knowledge or understanding.

Nevertheless, for most people the terms mask, African, and tribal tend to be closely linked, with African culture being symbolized by masks (see 4-1).

4-1 Inspirational drawings. (Top left) Igbo "Maiden Spirit" mask—8¾in (22cm) high. (Top right) Maonde mask—Mozambique—8in (20cm) high. The wax outlines on the eyes, nose, and upper lip are thought to depict traditional tribal scarification marks. (Middle) Songye, female mask of the Kifwebe Society—Zaire—about 15in (38cm) high. It is believed that the white lines were inspired by the marks on certain antelope. (Bottom left) Lulua mask—Zaire—about 14in (35.5cm) high. (Bottom right) Bembe "two face" mask—Zaire—about 19in (48cm) high. A two-faced mask gives the wearer superhuman powers of vision.

When we purchased this mask—the original that inspired the project (see **4-2**)—we were motivated not only because it is a beautiful and dynamic carved wooden object in its own right, but also by the label that read "an old Ugandan mask." It's an exciting notion to think that it might actually be genuine and old.

The original mask, with its cord netting at the back and unpierced eyes, was probably worn high up on top of the head—more like a helmet. On close-up inspection, we see that the wood is light in weight and color, the surface being covered with a dark stain or patina. Inside the hollow-carved back there is a crusty deposit that looks to be made up of a mix of ash, fat, and vegetable matter—perhaps it was used in some sort of libation ceremony or rite? We can see also that there are three tribal marks on the forehead and crescent marks on the cheeks. Is it really old or only made to look old? We would love to know if there is someone who can identify the tribal origins and ceremonial function of this particular mask.

THOUGHTS ON SHAPE, FORM & TECHNIQUE

Have a look at the working drawings (see **4-3**) and see how, at a grid scale of three squares to one inch, the mask measures about 10in (25.5cm) high, 7in (18cm) wide, and 4in (10cm) from back to front.

Note how, with the grain running from top to bottom, the mask is blocked up—or you might say laminated—from two 4in (10cm) by 4in (10cm) sections. Why we decided to do it this way is delightfully simple: our workshop is spilling over with 4 × 4 wood and we wanted to speed up the procedure by using the band saw. If you want to carve the project from a single slab, that's fine as long as your chosen wood is reasonably soft and easy to carve.

Study the side view, and you will see that the form steps down in sequence from the forehead to the brow, eyes, cheeks, lips, and chin, with the nose standing up as a smooth-sided peak. This "stepping"—with all of the levels being clearly defined—means that the necessary technique is relatively straightforward and uncomplicated. In fact, apart from the thin, short-grained ridges that make up the brows and the lips, this is a beautifully simple project—really good for beginners. Whether you want to hollow out the back of the mask depends on how you personally see the carving. You may decide you want to go for an authentic mask with the back hollowed out—a mask complete with holes around the rim and a supporting net of cord—or you may be happy to have a solid decorative piece to hang on the wall. If you choose to hollow out the mask, then see *Hollowing* in the "Tools, Techniques & Materials—A–Z Guides."

CHOOSING YOUR WOOD

Although it is commonly thought that African masks were traditionally cut from dark, heavy woods such as Iroko, mahogany, ebony, and the like, we see from various old accounts that since the end of the nineteenth century, at least, African woodcarvers have traditionally used lightweight, easy-to-carve, pale-colored woods such as cottonwood, obeche, and sapele.

We opted to use jelutong, but you could just as well go for linden/lime, basswood, or just about any wood that takes your fancy, as long as it is well seasoned, straight-grained, free from knots, nontoxic, nonresinous, and generally recommended as being easy to carve.

4-2 *Project picture—the finished mask.*

Special Tip

If you have any doubts about a particular wood—for example, you might have a piece of African wood—then check it out just to make sure that it's not allergenic. We say this because certain easy-to-carve African woods can give off unpleasant vapors and/or the dust can irritate the eyes and nose. If you have any misgivings, then it's best to seek the advice of a specialist supplier.

Suggested Tools

- workbench with a vise and holdfast
- medium-weight mallet of a size and shape to suit your needs
- good selection of carving gouges and chisels—including a small-size straight gouge, a straight chisel, a spade or fishtail gouge, and a small V-section tool
- a good sharp long-bladed knife—we use a Swedish sloyd knife with a laminated steel blade
- small gent's or tenon-type saw
- use of a small band saw
- pencil. ruler, and pair of dividers
- small open-toothed rasp
- one sheet each of workout and tracing paper
- black boot polish
- beeswax polish
- typical workshop tools and materials such as sandpaper, oilstone, white spirits, oil, sharpening slips, Plasticine, dust mask, and PVA (polyvinyl acetate) adhesive

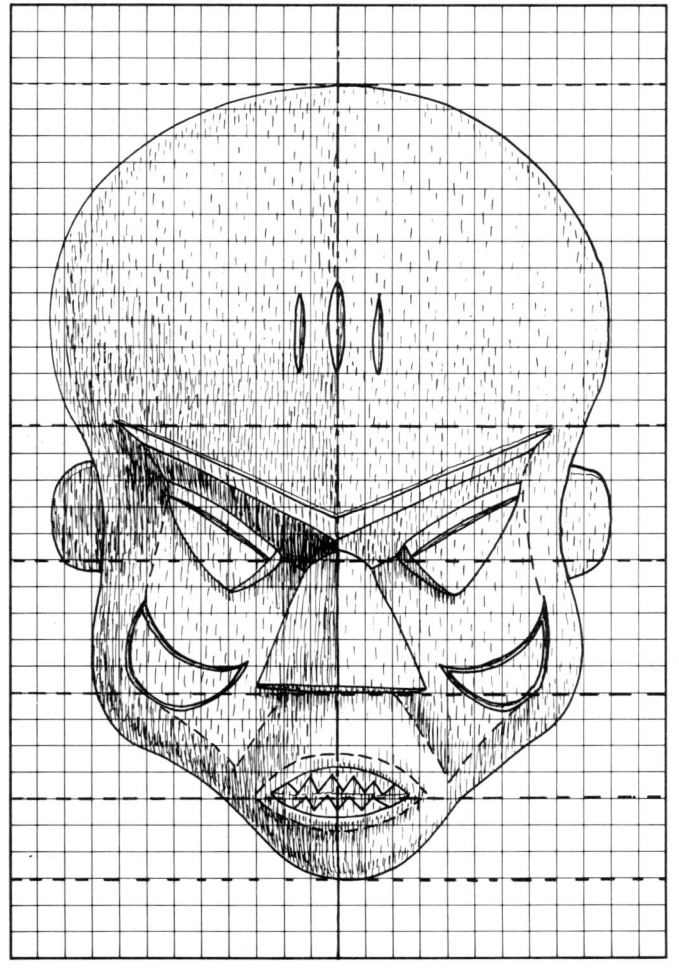
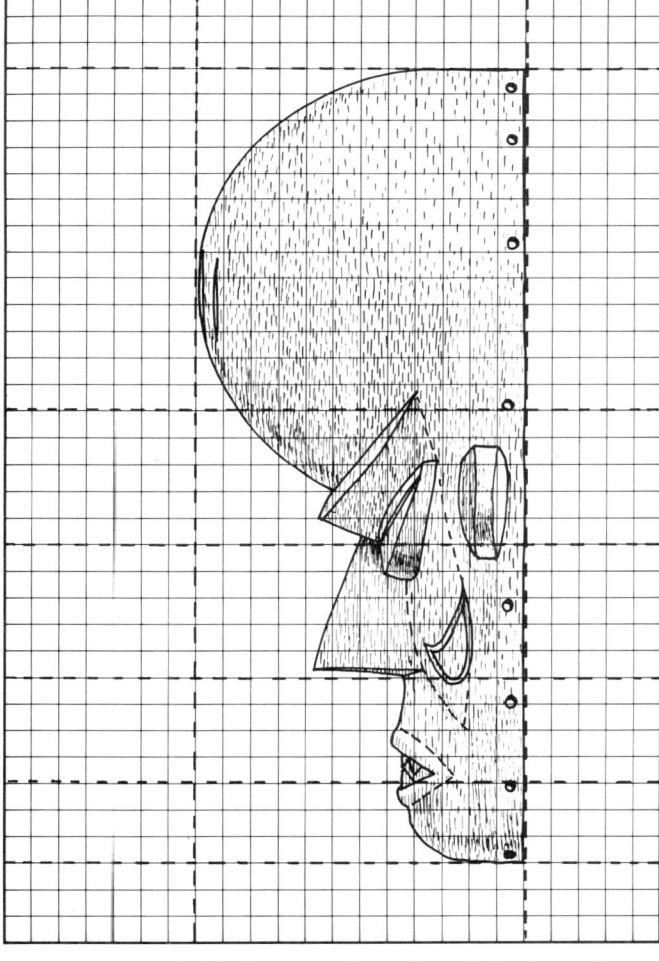

4-3 Working drawings—front and side views. Grid scale equals three grid squares to one inch. Note the optional drilled holes—used on the original mask to attach a string net or head support.

PROJECT MAKING STAGES

Drawing Out the Design

1. After you have gathered your tools and selected your wood, take a sheet of workout paper and draw the front view of the mask at full size. Have a centerline run from top to bottom—through the center of the nose and mouth. Mark in the precise position of the features, and generally make sure that the mask is symmetrical (refer to **4-3**).

2. Once you are happy with the front view, then run lines out from the primary features of the front view—marking the position of the brow, eyes, tip of the nose, and mouth—and carefully draw in the side-view profile (refer to **4-3**). Make sure that the depth of the mask fits into the 4in (10cm) thickness of the wood. If you have trouble visualizing the features, then make a full-size Plasticine maquette.

Special Tip

If Plasticine isn't in your budget, then settle for using hard block soap. You could carve a selection of feature details—one with each block.

3. With the drawn design measuring no more than 8in (20cm) wide, 4in (10cm) deep, and 10in (25.5cm) high, make a clear tracing. Draw a box—corresponding to your workpiece—around the edge of the views to allow a good amount of all-round cutting waste.

Making the Blank

4. Once you have drawn the designs to size and generally thought through how best to tackle the project with respect to your workshop and tools available, set the wood out with guidelines, align the tracing, and pencil-press-transfer the drawn lines to the wood. Shade in the waste areas so that there is no doubt what wood needs to be cut away.

4-4 *Front view showing the two half-blanks after they have been roughed out on the band saw.*

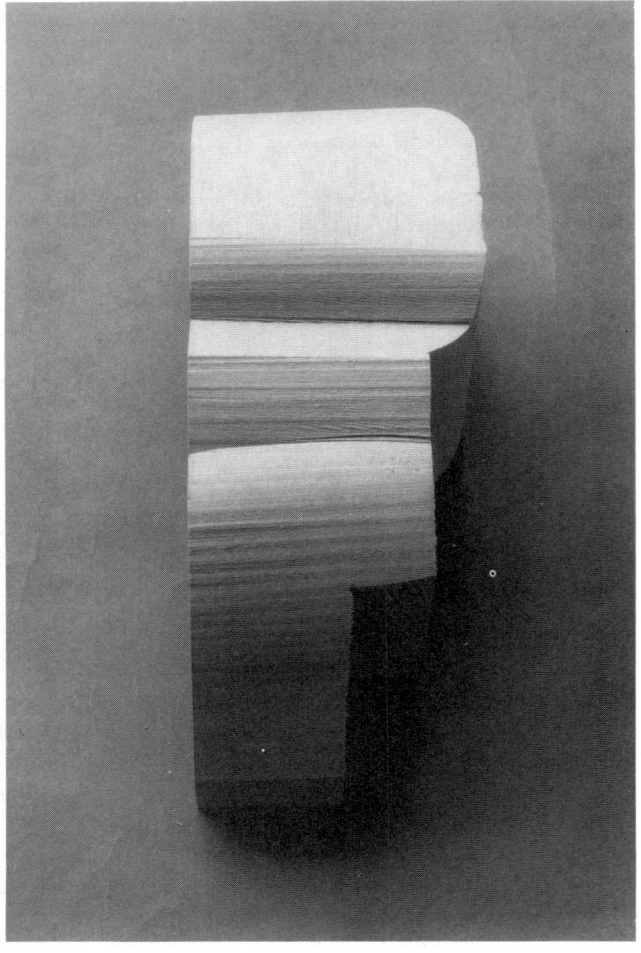

4-5 *Side view of the blank as it leaves the band saw.*

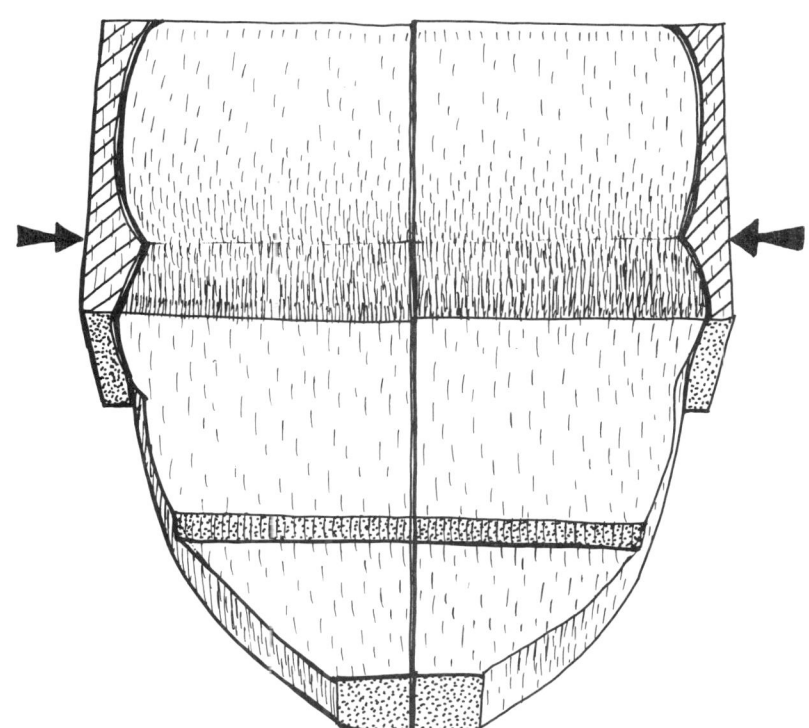

4-6 Gluing up. Use the pieces of waste wood—those cut away on the band saw—to provide a flat bed or seating for the clamp.

Note: We set both 4 × 4 wood sections out with front and side views; but of course, if you are carving a single slab, then you will need to modify the approach and draw the front view out on the face, and a side profile on the edges.

5. Being sure to allow a generous amount of cutting waste, run the wood through the band saw and cut out the drawn profiles. Do this with both views on both 4 × 4 sections (see **4-4** and **4-5**).

6. When you are satisfied that all is correct, smear glue on the mating faces, set the two cutouts together so that the glue line becomes the centerline of the mask, and then clamp up (see **4-6**).

Roughing Out

7. Having first pinned up your drawings and tracings so that they are in clear view, and brought your tools to good order, take the straight gouge and the mallet, and swiftly cut away the sharp edges of the blank. Aim, at first, to do no more than establish the bulging skull-like shape of the head, the slant of the brows, and the different levels of the nose and mouth. Be sure to cut across the direction of the grain—meaning out at an angle from the centerline and down from high to low wood (see **4-7**).

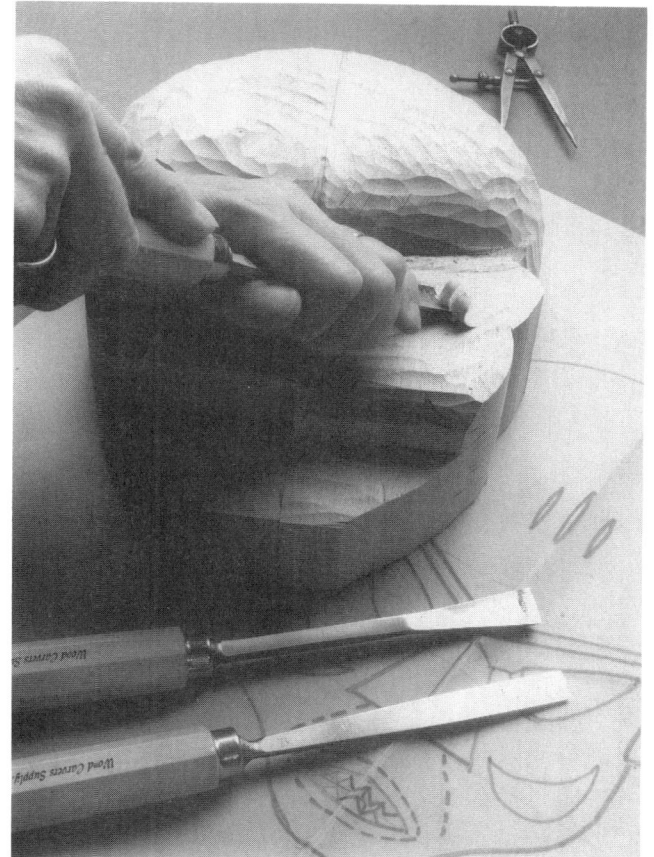

4-7 Having established the characteristic shape of the skull, round over the edges to rough out the other primary forms.

8. Use the ruler and dividers to establish the position and width of the nose, and then use the saw to cut through the wood to within ¼in (6mm) of the full depth of the nose—meaning deeper than the depth of the eyes, but not so deep as the nose (see **4-8**).

9. Keeping in mind that you *can't back off* once you have cut wood away, take the tool of your choice—we used a shallow-sweep, straight gouge—and *very carefully* clear the waste at either side of the nose. Cut down to the depth of the surface of the eyes (see **4-9**).

Modeling

10. After you have lowered the wood down to the level of the eyes, and drawn in the eyes at the new level, then, at one and the same time, slice down at either side of the centerline to achieve the triangular block that goes to make up the nose. Continue lowering the surface around the eyes until you get down to the level of the cheeks (see **4-10**).

11. Although we did say at the start of the project that this mask is a pretty straightforward piece of

4-8 Establish the overall shape of the nose by using the saw to make two straight-down stop-cuts. Be very careful not to cut too deep.

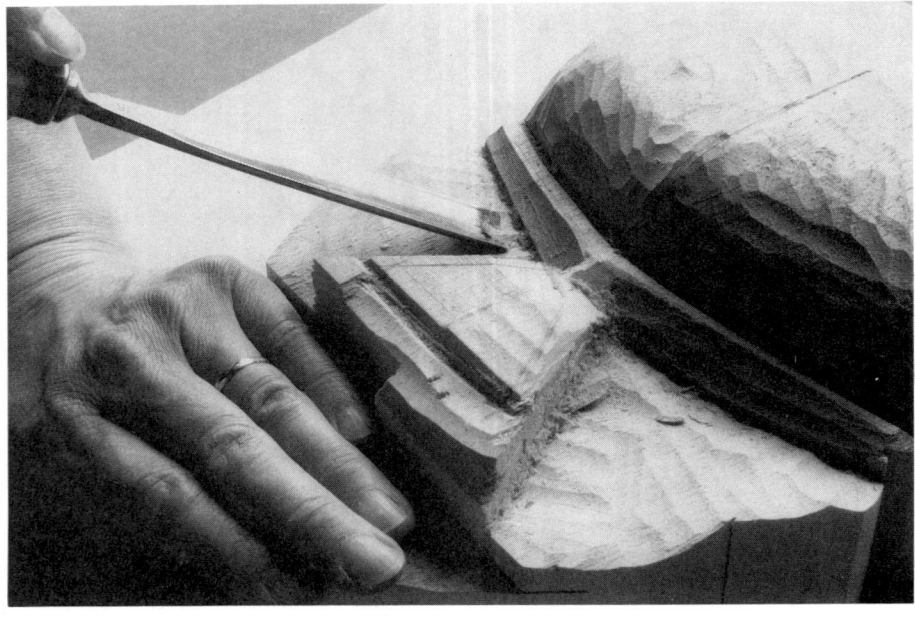

4-9 After first making the two saw cuts and roughing out the shape of the brow, then clear the waste between the nose and the brow. Lower the wood to the level of the eyelid. Be on your guard that the tool doesn't over-run into the short-grain brow.

carving, we should have added the proviso: but only if you take it slowly and spend time checking measurements. We say this because although the forms are indeed easy enough to model, the crisp character of the carving requires that the features be well placed, cleanly cut, and, above all, symmetrical.

To this end you need to repeatedly check and double-check measurements with the ruler and dividers (see **4-11**). The best procedure is to select critical reference points such as the tip of the nose, the width of the nose, the distance from the tip of the nose through to the corners of the mouth, and then to make sure that these measurements stay constant one to another.

12. When you come to carve the cheeks and chin to shape, first rough out the overall form with one or other of the gouges, and then skim off with the knife. It's all easy, as long as you avoid running the knife into end grain. For example, having rounded the cheeks, you will come to a point where you are presented with end grain around the underside curve of the eyes and end grain where the cheeks run into the chin. At this stage, you will have to modify the direction of your cuts so that they always run from high to low wood—downhill.

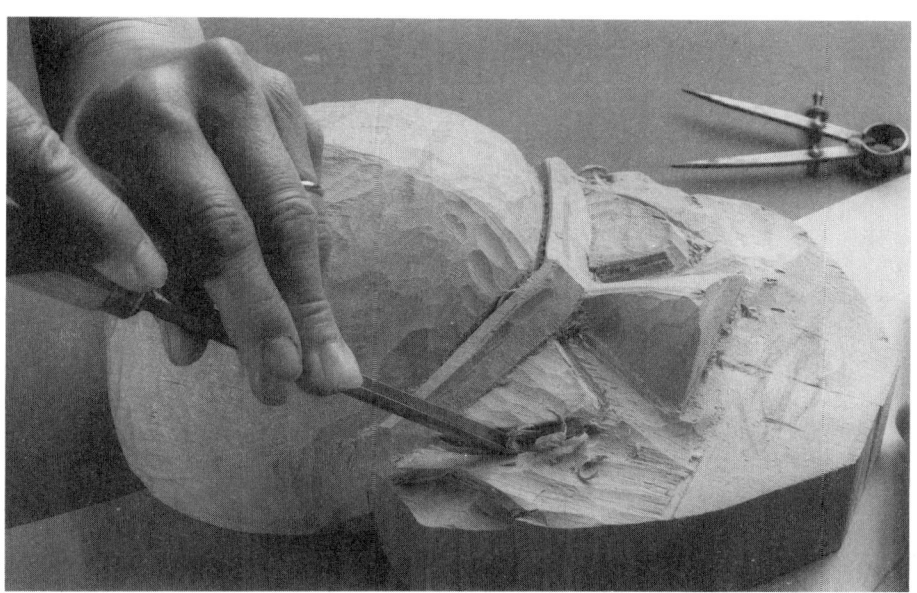

4-10   Use a V-tool or veiner to make the stop-cuts around the eyes.

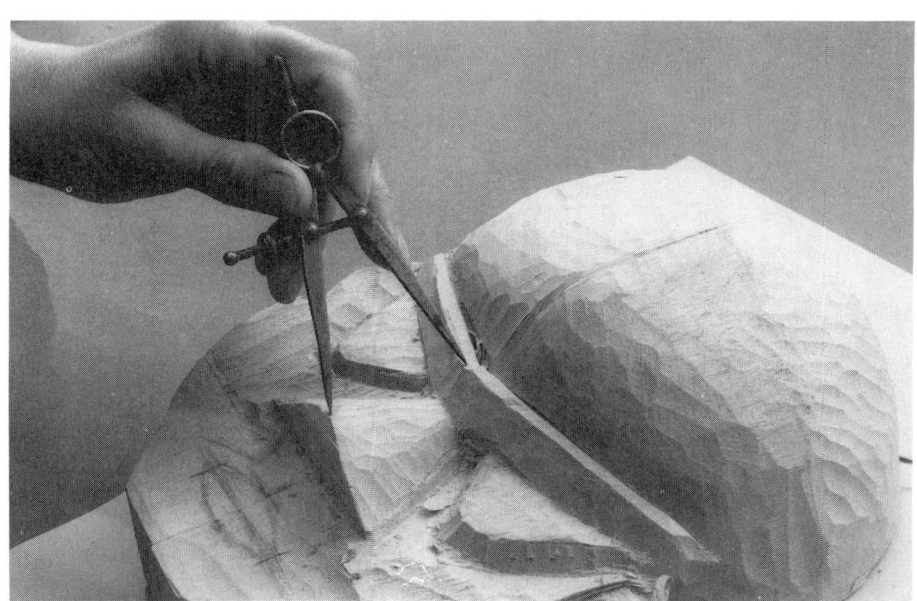

4-11   Make repeated cross-checks with the dividers. Pay particular attention to the overall proportions as well as to the symmetry.

FINISHING

13. Having established the overall shape and position of all the forms, rehone your knife, and then set to work by skimming the gouge marks down to a cleaner finish and cutting-in the teeth (see **4-12**). If you have any doubts as to how to cut the teeth, then try it out on a block of scrap wood. We find that the best way to make a controlled stroke is to use two hands—one hand holding the knife and supplying the energy, and the other hand bracing and limiting the cut.

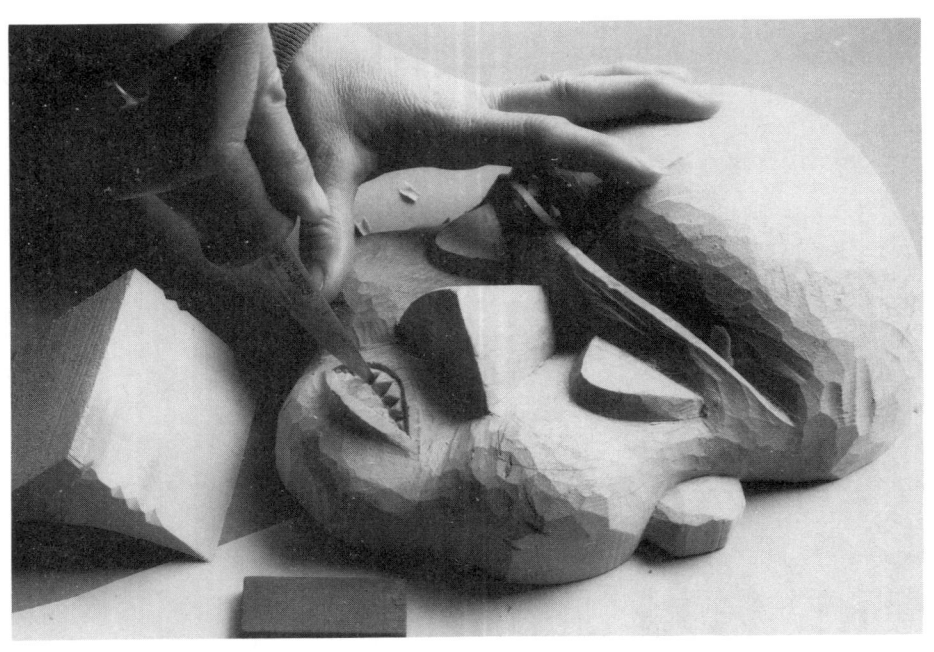

4-12 Keeping in mind that the lips are short-grained and relatively fragile, make a series of carefully placed chip cuts to shape the teeth.

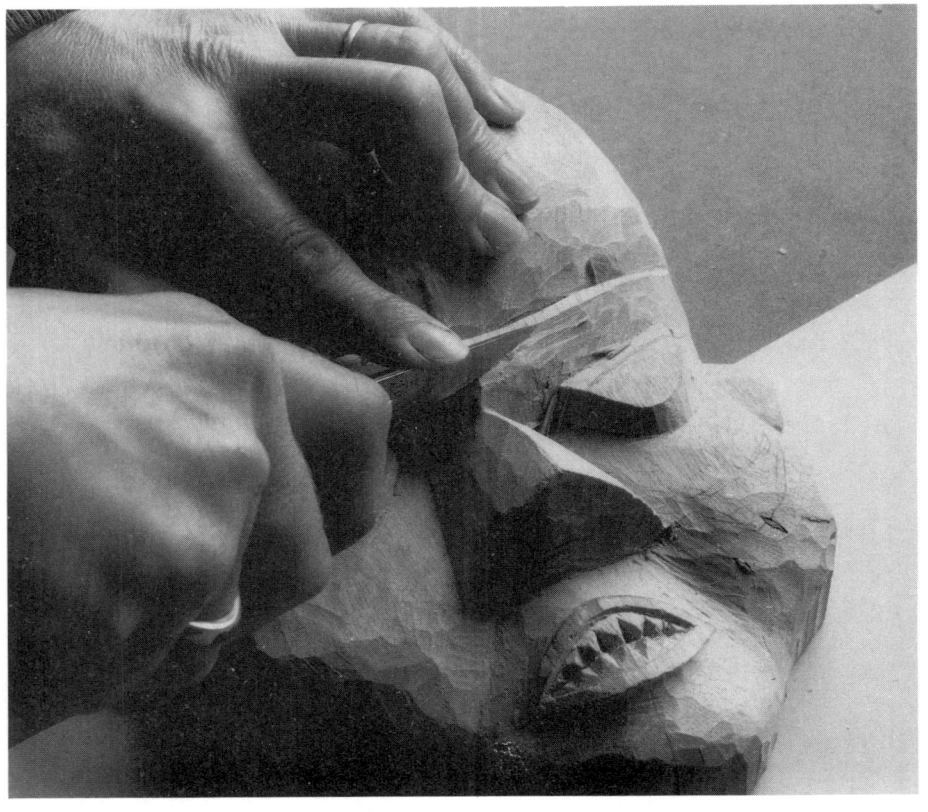

4-13 Use a sharp knife to model the sloping area of end grain that runs down to the eyes. Work with a two-handed restraining cut.

14. Continue using the knife to model the mask to a final shape and finish—shaping the eyebrows, skimming the smooth planes or slopes at either side of the nose, skimming the bulging head, and so on (see **4-13, 4-14,** and **4-15**).

15. Once you are satisfied with the modeling to the extent where you reckon that you have taken the carving as far as it can go, take a scrap of fine-grade sandpaper and rub down the whole workpiece to a smooth finish. Don't go at it so hard that you remove all the tool marks; just make certain that the surfaces are free from rough edges.

Note: If you want to hollow carve the back of the mask, then now is the time. (Refer to *Hollowing* in the "Tools, Techniques & Materials—A–Z Guides.")

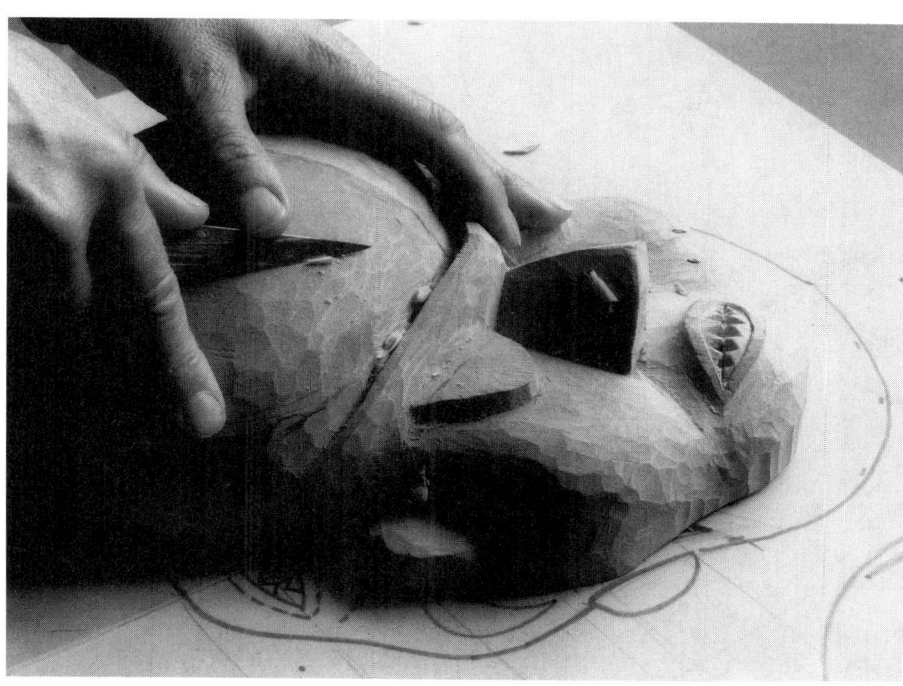

4-14   When you come to modeling the skull and the brow, control the knife with both hands. Have one hand hold and push while the thumb of the other hand braces and guides the blade. This two-handed technique results in a very powerful and well-controlled cut.

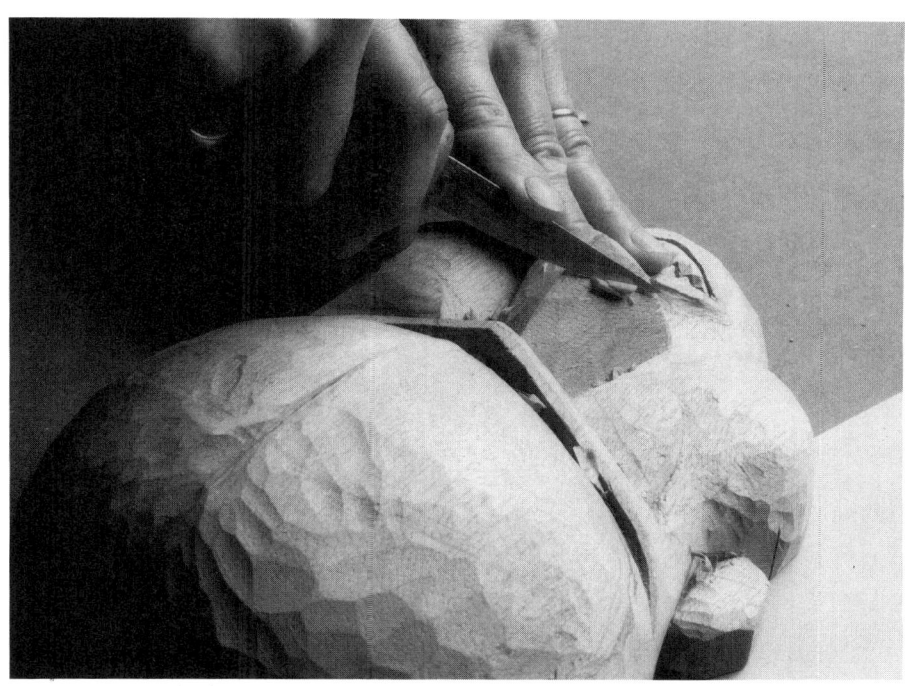

4-15   Model the sides of the nose with a controlled shaving cut.

65

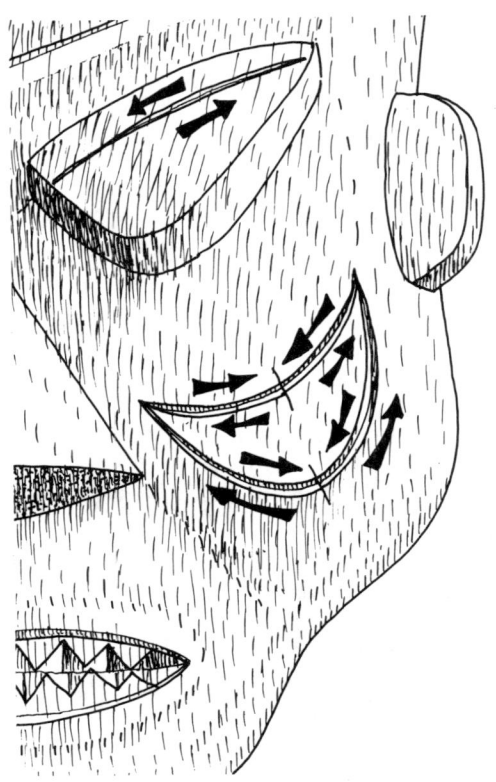
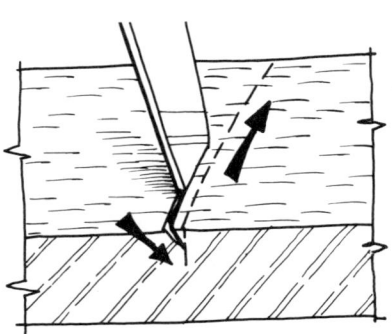
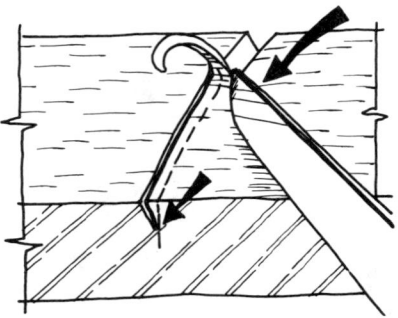

4-16 (Left) The arrows indicate the direction of the knife cuts that make up the incised lines. (Right) Each V-section incised trench is achieved by making two cuts. Note how the direction of the cuts relates to the run of the grain.

16. Finally, having first cut-in the incised tribal marks with the knife (see **4-16**), give the entire workpiece a good wiping over with the black boot polish. Burnish to a dull sheen finish.

Note: If you want to have edge holes, then see *Holes* in the "Tools, Techniques & Materials—A–Z Guides."

Special Tip

If you want the black polish to bleed into the wood, then thin it down with a small amount of white spirits.

PROBLEM-SOLVING

- If you start out on the mask, but reach a stage at some point where you want to change the design, then be brave and follow your fancy.
- Although it's always a good idea to use wood that is well seasoned and dry, this is all the more important when you are carving a mask. Don't be tempted into using green wood; wet or green wood is easy to carve, but it is likely to split and become misshapen as it dries.
- If you are a beginner to carving and wondering how best to equip your workshop, then you can't do better than to get yourself a good-sized band saw. It's great for sawing out blanks, cutting wood down to size, and for all the other sawing tasks.
- If you plan on doing a lot of woodcarving, then we strongly recommend that you use a dust vacuum. For the sake of health and good workshop management, it's important that you keep the mess under control!

·5·
Baule Mask

Ivory Coast, Africa

Of all African masks, the human masks made by the Baule tribe of central Ivory Coast—also commonly named in books and museums as the Côte d'Ivoire—are among the most attractive and the easiest to identify with. This isn't that surprising, because the features and expressions of the Baule masks, and some of those made by neighboring tribes, can simply be interpreted, at one level, as being sweet, jovial, and generally friendly (see **5-1**). Of course, this way of looking at the masks is misguided, because they often represent oppressed individuals like slaves and prostitutes.

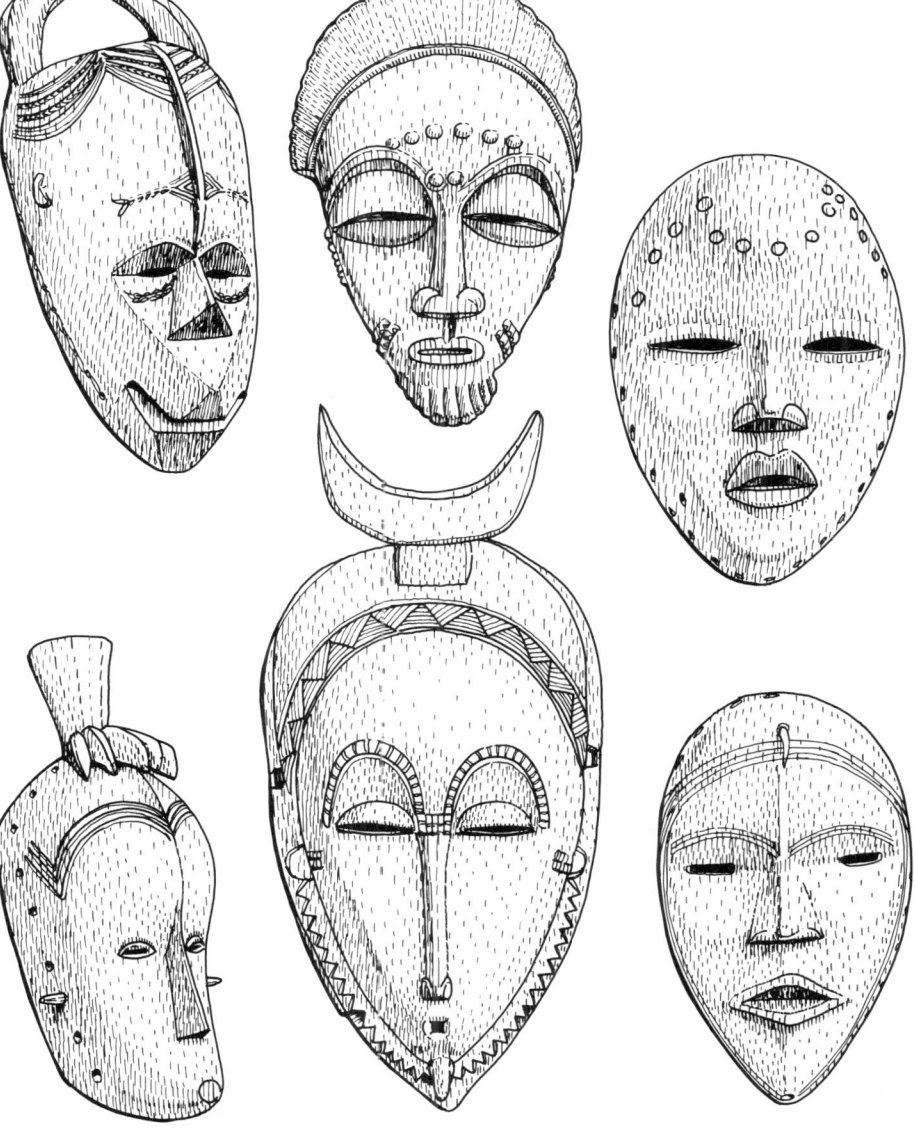

5-1 Inspirational drawings. (Top left) Bete or Guro mask—16in (41cm) high. (Top center) Baule mask—Ivory Coast. Masks of this type and character are very popular in present-day Europe and America because they look to be smooth and serene. Great care is taken with the details and the finish. (Top right) Dan mask of the Poro Society—Liberia. (Bottom left) Guro mask with a leopard claw coiffure—Ivory Coast. Represents Gu, the wife of the powerful Zamble—about 17in (43cm) high. (Bottom center) Baule mask—Ivory Coast. (Bottom right) Dan mask—Liberia. Female mask represents ideal beauty—about 7in (18cm) high.

67

Nevertheless, many outsiders find the characteristic narrow nose, open mouth, round face, zigzag borders, and the smooth brown texture to be most attractive.

Masks of this type (see **5-2**)—meaning specifically masks that are traditionally worn by the Baule men when they attend the "women's" dance—are described variously as being a human personification of the sun and/or moon, or in some instances of a star.

THOUGHTS ON SHAPE, FORM & TECHNIQUE

Have a look at the working drawings (see **5-3**) and see how, at a grid scale of three squares to one inch, the mask measures about 10in (25.5cm) high, 8in (20cm) wide, and 4in (10cm) deep from back to front. We decided to block this mask up from three 4in (10cm) by 4in (10cm) sections, similar to the Ugandan mask of Project 4.

5-2 Project picture—the finished mask.

Special Tip

We find that 4 x 4 wood seems to answer most of our needs; that's why our workshop is full of it. It's a much more flexible option than buying in different thicknesses for each and every project, or even buying a hugely wide 4in (10cm) thick slab. It's much less of a hassle to saw and glue up several 4 x 4 sections—this being the maximum size for our small band saw—than trying to deal with a huge, thick board.

Study the views (refer to **4-3**), and you will note that the step-down border that runs around the edge of the oval form is about 1⅛in (28mm) thick where it meets the face, sloping down at a gentle angle to a thickness of about ⅝in (16mm) at the outermost edge.

As far as technique goes, this mask is much easier than it looks. For example, the primary features—the nose, brows, eyes, and mouth—are not only boldly stylized, but, better still, they are achieved by the simple procedure of carving a smooth egg-like dome, and then selectively lowering the surface to leave the features in relief. The zigzag border may look to be a carving nightmare, but actually it is easily and swiftly managed with a scroll saw, a drill, and a knife.

Having declared that this mask is relatively easy to carve, we must point out that its highly stylized design places tight limits on the carver. If you are to successfully achieve the bold character of this mask, you must stay within the proportions and the forms, not allowing yourself to run loose.

CHOOSING YOUR WOOD

This is one of those projects that calls for a big, generous, no-nonsense chunk of easy-to-carve wood. As usual, we decided to block it up from three 4 × 4 sections, but you might well prefer to go for a single, wide slab. Whatever the case, the chosen wood needs to be smooth textured, straight grained, free from warps and loose knots, as well as easy to carve. If you have a choice, then go for a wood like linden/lime, jelutong, basswood, or even a smooth-grained pine.

Special Tip

When we were beginners to wood carving, we both had a naive notion that a good carver could use just about any wood, and that the carving procedure needed to be a battle between us and the wood. Well, this isn't true. We have come to understand that the quality of the finished carving does, to a great extent, relate to the character of the wood, and you need to go for the best wood that is at hand. We are not talking here necessarily about color, grain, or cost, but more about ease of carving. If a piece of wood is coarse grained and generally a struggle to carve, then this shows in the finished carving. If you don't believe this, then go ahead and try working this project with a piece of maple or a piece of English oak!

Suggested Tools

- workbench with a vise and holdfast
- medium-weight mallet of a size and shape to suit your needs
- good selection of carving gouges and chisels
- a good sharp long-bladed knife—we use a Swedish sloyd knife with a laminated steel blade
- use of a small band saw
- bench drill press with ¼in (6mm) diameter Forstner drill bit
- pencil, ruler, and pair of dividers
- small open-toothed rasp
- one sheet each of workout and tracing paper
- small quantity of dark brown umber oil paint—as used by artists
- small quantity of white spirits
- ½in (13mm) wide brush
- beeswax polish
- typical workshop tools and materials such as sandpaper, oilstone, oil, sharpening slips, Plasticine, a dust mask, and PVA (polyvinyl acetate) adhesive

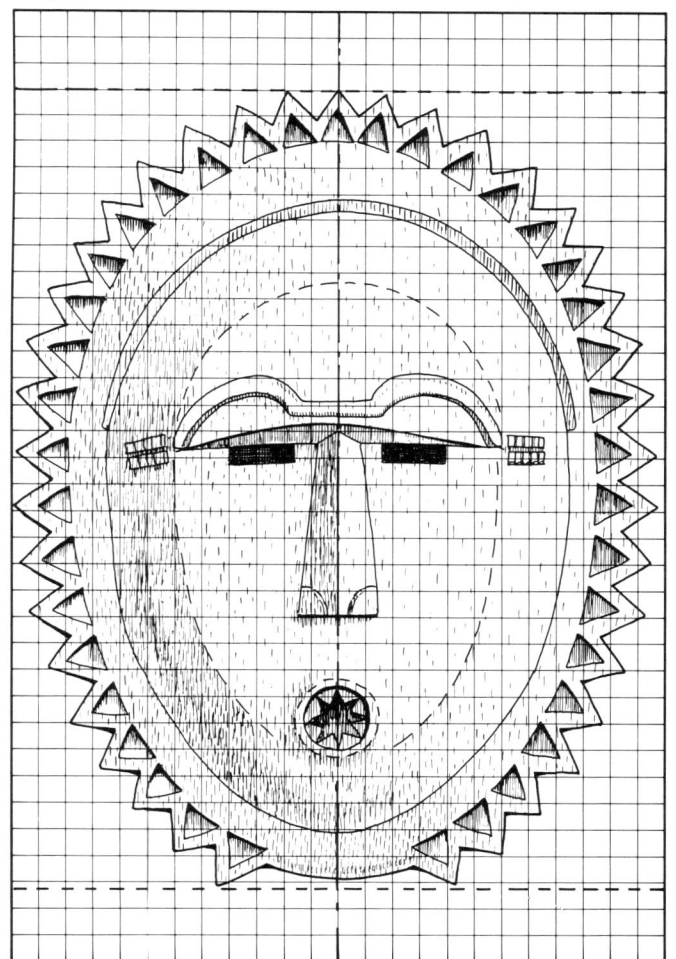

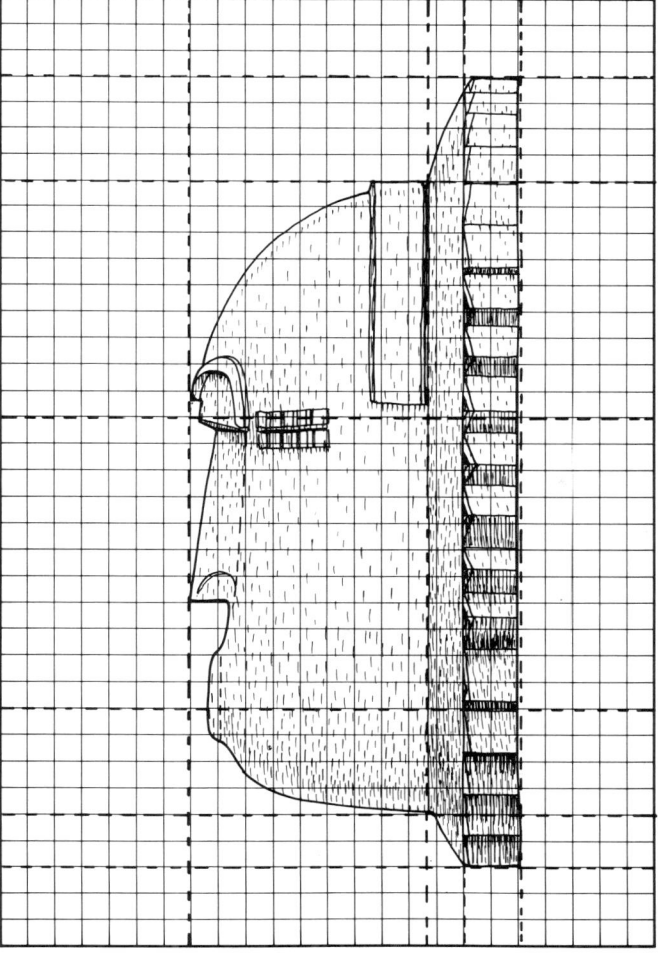

5-3 Working drawings—front and side views. Grid scale equals three squares to one inch. Note the depth of the zigzag collar, and the placing of the stylized scarification marks in relationship to the sides of the eyes.

PROJECT MAKING STAGES

Drawing Out the Design

1. After you have studied the inspirational drawings (refer to **5-1**) and maybe even tracked down various Baule masks in museums and collections, then take a pencil, ruler, and the workout paper, and draw the mask out to size.

2. The easiest procedure with a symmetrical design such as this is to start with a vertical centerline to establish the height and the half-width measurement—meaning the distance from the centerline to one side edge—and then draw half the face. When the half face is complete, you can then fold the paper along the centerline and press-transfer the other half of the image.

3. The dominant feature of this mask is the border or rim. Look at the working drawings (refer to **5-3**), and you will see that this border needs to extend beyond the face by about 1½in (38mm) and to have a cross section that slants from a maximum thickness of 1⅛in (28mm) down to ⅝in (16mm) around the outermost edge.

5-4   Draw out the shape of the zigzag design to see how it relates to the overall form and profile. Note: when our carving was three-fourths finished, we decided to make the zigzag design bigger.

5-5   Use a mallet and gouge to swiftly lower the waste from around the face. Work from the middle side to the ends to avoid cutting directly into end grain.

4. After you have achieved a good, well-visualized design in front view and in side profile—and you might need to make a Plasticine maquette first—then make tracings of the images. Put the working drawings on view out of harm's way in the workshop.

Making the Blank

5. Having chosen a 4in (10cm) thick slab of easy-to-carve wood that measures about 11in (28cm) along the run of the grain, and is 9in (23cm) wide, look it over carefully to make sure that it is in perfect condition.

Special Tip

Although this "look it over carefully" bit of advice might sound like a waste of time, because after all you wouldn't have had your eyes closed when you first selected the wood, it does happen that the wood may start to split and warp once it's in the workshop and/or you notice something like an awkward knot.

6. Once you are happy with the wood, set it out with a vertical centerline, and then pencil-press-transfer the outermost profile and width of the border to the front face.

7. With the primary guidelines in place, move to the band saw and set to work cutting out the profile. It's a good idea at this stage—after you have successfully cut out the profile—to play around with size and shape of the zigzag design just to see how it relates to the overall form (see **5-4**). We make this suggestion because after we drew the small, tight zigzag shown in **5-4**, we decided to go for a bolder option. You might prefer the more delicate version—see what you think!

Roughing Out

8. Having cut out the blank on the band saw, and pencil-labeled the back face, measure 1¼in (3.2cm) up from the back face, and run a line around the cut edge.

9. Secure the workpiece on the bench so that the front face is uppermost—we use a screw-down holdfast—and then use a mallet and straight gouge to cut away the border waste. Work from the middle sides to the end to cut the grain to best advantage (see **5-5**).

10. Once you have achieved a clean cut, square-edged border step 1½in (3.8cm) wide and 1¼in (3.2cm) high, then measure ⅝in (1.6cm) up from the back face of the blank, and run another pencil line around the cut edge of the wood.

11. With the line in place, take a shallow-sweep, straight gouge and trim the step so that it slants down from the inner edge to the outer edge (see **5-6**). The best procedure is to start by slicing the corner down to the line, and then skimming off the waste in between. Once again, make sure that you cut in the correct direction in relation to the grain.

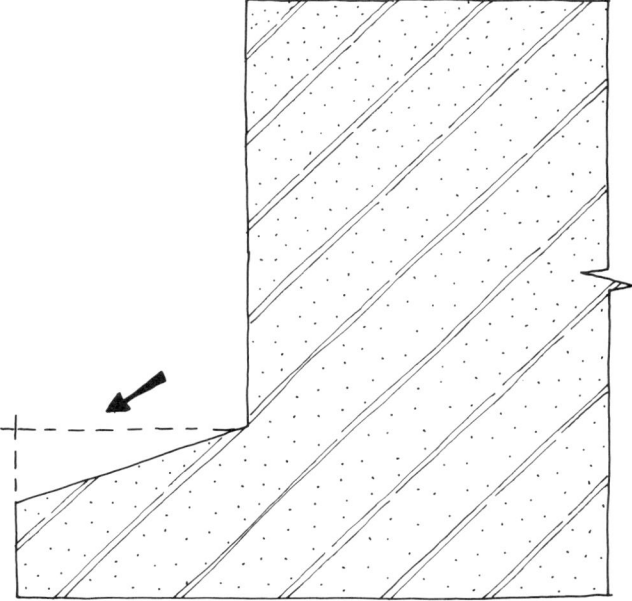

5-6 The cross section of the rim at the roughing-out stage is stepped down and angled.

12. After you have cleaned out the step, established the slope, and cut the face area back to the inner guideline, then comes the swift, easy task of rounding over the edge of the face. Take a large, shallow-sweep, straight gouge, and work systematically around the workpiece, all the while making long cuts that run from the top center of the wood down and around to the top face of the step. It's simple enough as long as you work in relation to the grain by running the cuts either downhill or at an angle to the grain (see **5-7**).

Modeling

13. Once you have achieved the egg-shaped mound, pause and have another good long look at the project picture and the working drawings. Then, with a refreshed, clear picture in your mind, take a soft pencil and draw in the main features of the mask. This project is pretty straightforward —all you need is the centerline, the line of the eyes, the bottom straight line that runs under the nose, the width and angles at the side of the nose, and the mouth. It's important that these lines are well positioned, so use a ruler and dividers to check them off against the working drawings and against each other.

14. With the lines in place, use a small-size, shallow-sweep, straight gouge to lower the wood between the mouth and the underside of the nose. If you have got it right, the surface should angle down from the top of the mouth to the bottom of the nose so that there is a step about ½in (1.3cm) high (see **5-8**).

15. Still working with the gouge, continue lowering the wood so that the surface runs in a smooth sweep from the mouth rim to the underside of the eyes. Establish the depth of the nose where it meets the eye line. While you are establishing the various surfaces around the eyes and nose, draw in the eyebrows. Then take the knife, and very carefully lower the wood between the brows and the eye line (see **5-9**).

16. Having established the height of the nose and the eye line by lowering the wood around the nose, take the knife and very carefully scoop and lower the wood around the mouth. Continue so that the lips stand up like, say, the rim of a volcano. Round over the wood under the mouth so that the chin runs in a full curve from the mouth to the border (see **5-10**).

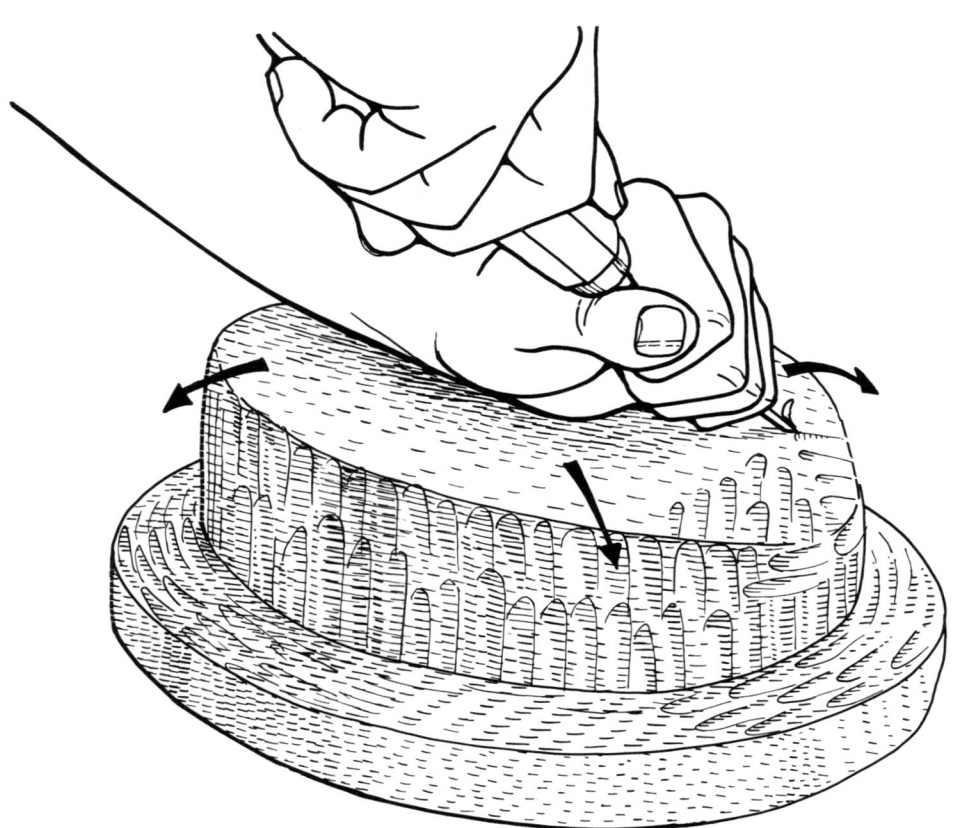

5-7 Run the cuts downhill—from high to low—to cut the wood to best advantage.

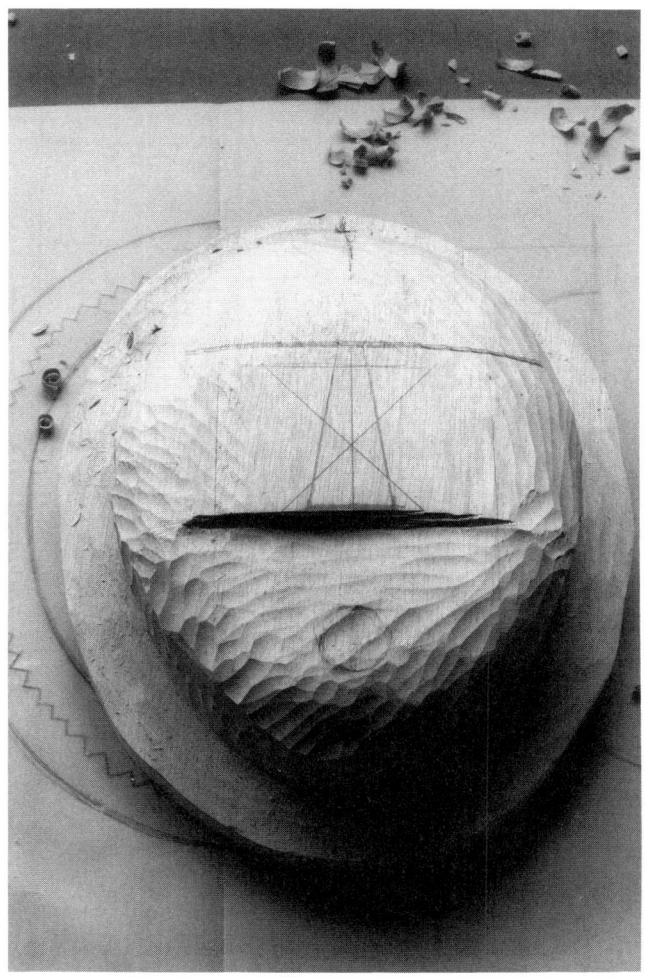

5-8 The surface needs to angle down from the top of the mouth to the bottom of the nose.

5-10 Round over the wood at the underside of the mouth so that the chin runs in a full curve from the mouth to the border.

5-9 Having drawn in the brows, take the knife and very carefully lower the wood between the brows and the line of the eyes. It's a good idea at this stage to draw in the other features such as the position of the scarification marks and the size and placing of the eye slots.

73

17. Still working with the knife, work systematically over the face carefully lowering the marks left by the gouge so that the tribal marks at the corners of the eyes, and the band at the top of the head, stand in relief. Aim to have these features standing by about ¼in (6mm) above the surface of the mask.

18. When you are ready to cut the eye slots, take a ¼in (6mm) wide, shallow-sweep, straight gouge, and work to the waste side of the eye line, chopping down to a depth of about ½in (1.3cm) (see **5-11**). This done, lower the angle of the gouge and clear the waste by running the tool from end to end in the slot. Work in much the same way as you would when cutting a mortise slot in traditional woodworking.

19. To shape the nose, clear the wood at either side of the centerline so that the sides of the nose fall away at a smooth angle. Aim for a long thin ridge that narrows as it gets nearer the eyes.

20. Once you have modeled the overall shape of the nose, line in the shape of the nostrils with a V-section stop-cut. Then use the knife to skim back the wood above the nostril line. Continue until the nostrils stand out in relief (see **5-12**). This is a delicate procedure, so be careful that you don't overrun and slice off a nostril.

21. Having drawn in the shape of the zigzag—the outer edge and the little enclosed triangles—move to the band saw and set to work fretting out the zigzag shape. The best procedure is to work around the rim making a series of straight cuts—first to one side of each zigzag point and then to the other (see **5-13**)

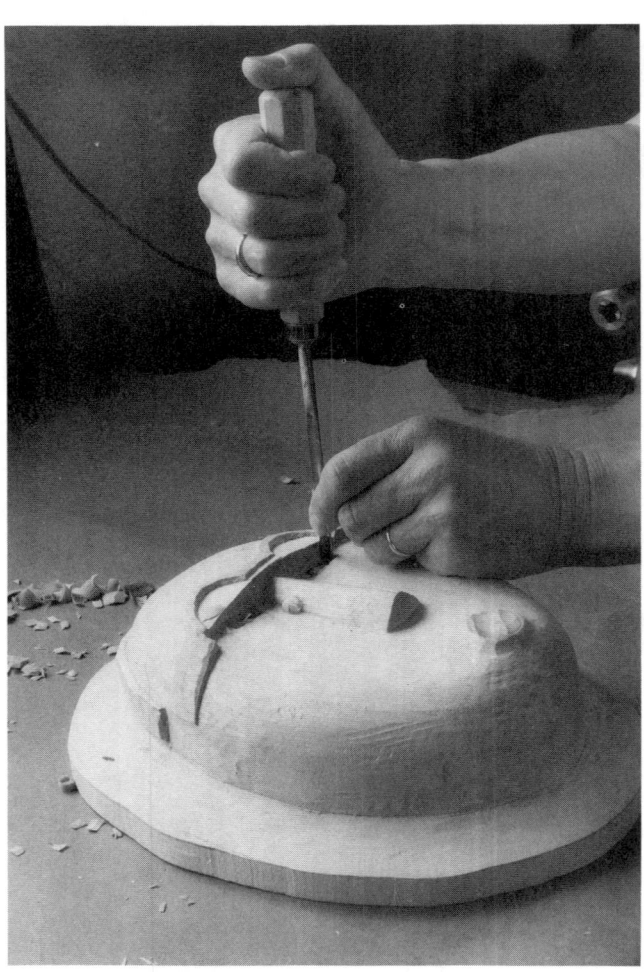

5-11 Work to the waste, or eye, side of the line, and chop down to a depth of about ½in (13mm). Try to achieve a cleanly cut cliff so that there is a crisp angle above the eye.

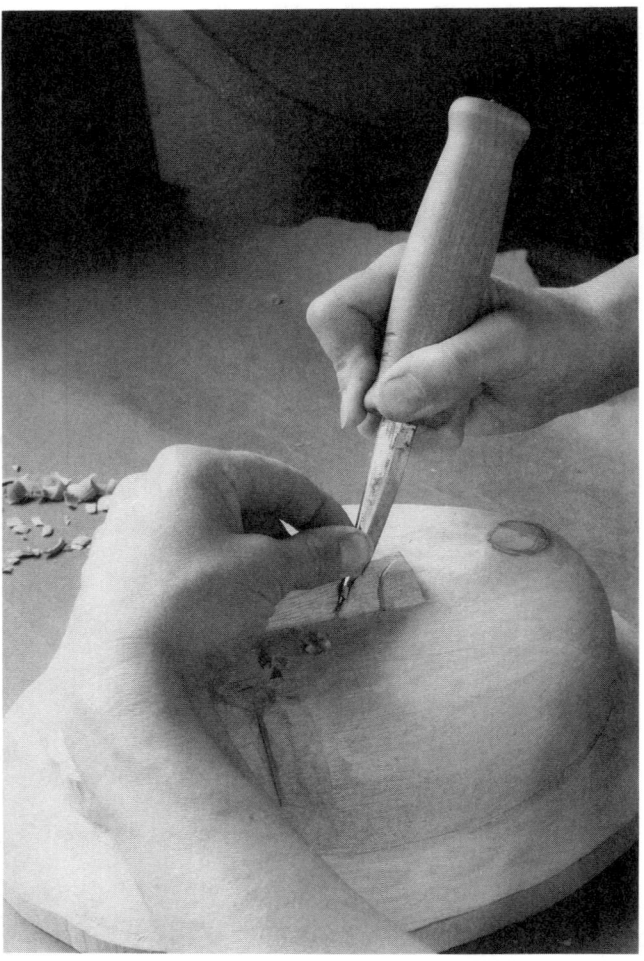

5-12 Modeling the nose: continue until the nostrils stand out in relief. Be sure to hold the knife with a restraining cut to make sure it doesn't overrun and slice off the nostril.

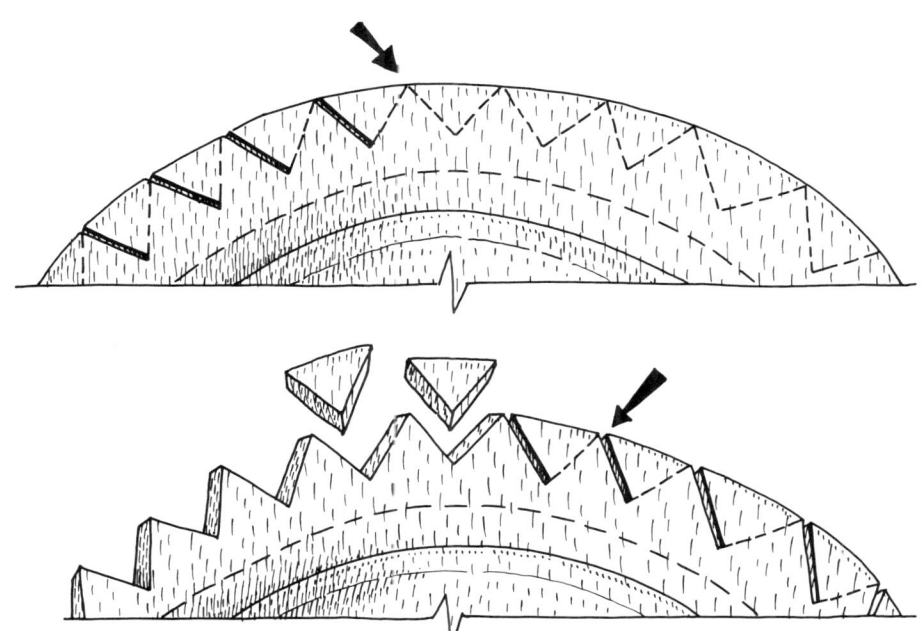

5-13 Work around the rim making a series of straight cuts—first to one side of the zigzag point and then to the other. If you are doing it right, the waste should fall away as little triangles.

22. After you have achieved the zigzag edge, move to the drill press and run a ¼in (6mm) diameter hole into the center of each enclosed triangle. It's a tricky procedure that is best done with a Forstner drill bit. Go at it slowly, all the while being careful not to rush things. Drill down to a depth of about ½in (1.3cm) (see **5-14,** top left).

23. With the drilled holes in place, take the knife—make sure that it's super sharp—and then, one hole at time, make V-section chip cuts that run out from the hole and into the corner of the triangles. Work systematically around the zigzag, until each hole looks to be triangular. Then trim and adjust the outer sawn edge until the ribbon

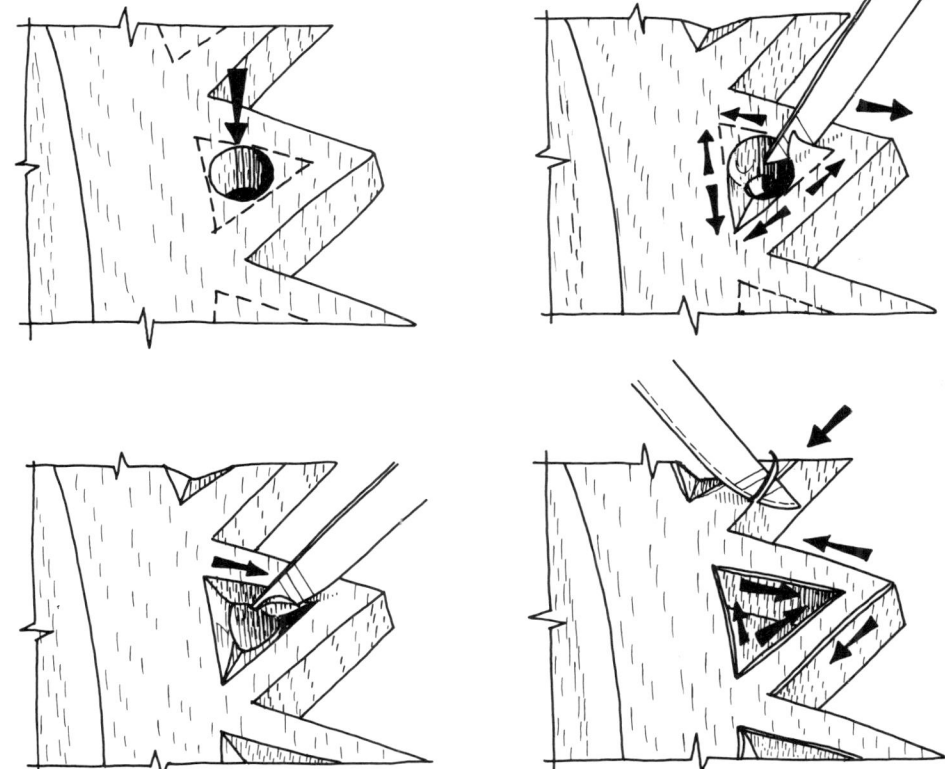

5-14 (Top left) Drill down to a depth of about ½in (13mm). (Top right) Make V-section cuts that run from the hole into the corner of the triangle. (Bottom left) Trim the inside of the triangles to shape. (Bottom right) Trim the outer edges to make the zigzag crisp and even.

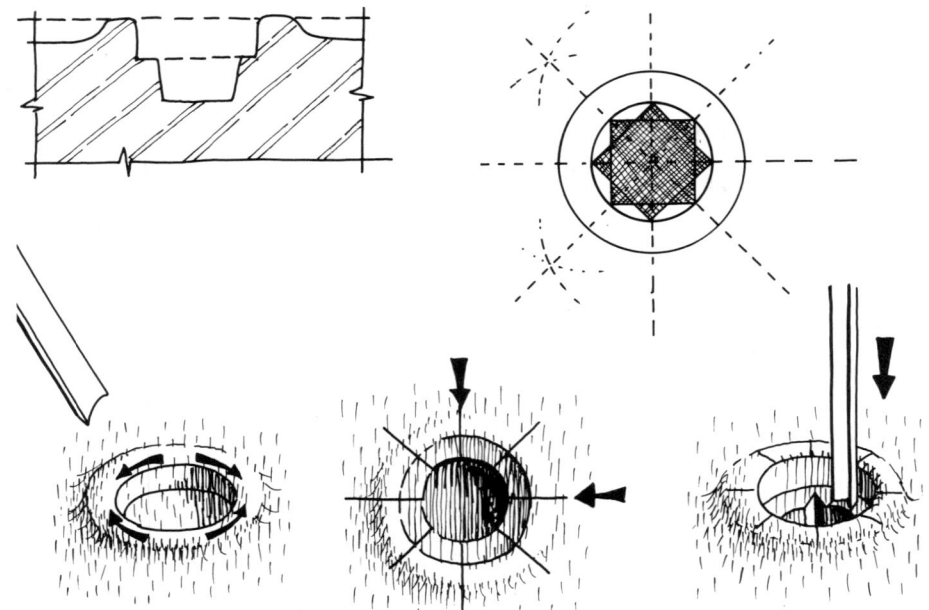

5-15 (Top left) Cut the inside of the mouth down in two stages to create an inner step. (Bottom left) Cut in the direction of the arrows to avoid cutting into the grain. (Bottom center) Divide the mouth circle into eight equal cake-wedge parts. (Right top and bottom) Take the V-section tool and make eight straight-down chopping cuts to create a star-like shape.

that makes up the zigzag looks crisp and even (refer to **5-14**).

24. When you come to modeling the mouth—after first having lowered the inside of the mouth with the knife and a small gouge—take a small V-section tool and work around the inside of the mouth, chopping straight down. Look at the drawing (see **5-15**), and you will see that the eight teeth are created by making eight straight-down chopping cuts. Trim and model the stylized scarification marks in a similar manner.

FINISHING

25. When you consider the mask finished, and you have trimmed up the details, adjusted the edges, and generally brought the carving to order, take a piece of fine-grade sandpaper and rub the whole carving to a good finish.

26. Mix a small amount of burnt umber oil paint with the white spirits, and brush the mix over the entire surface. Let it dry.

27. Finally, wipe the whole surface over with wax polish, and burnish it to a sheen finish.

PROBLEM-SOLVING

- Although overall this mask does need to be symmetrical and sanded to a relatively high finish, this doesn't mean that the symmetry needs to be perfect or that each and ever tool mark needs to be obliterated. We don't want our work to look machine perfect; we like to see tool marks and a little disorder.
- If you want to speed up the project, you could use a large-size Forstner drill bit to clear the waste from the mouth.
- Refer to *Hollowing* in the "Tools, Techniques & Materials—A–Z Guides," if you want to hollow out the back of the mask.
- If you don't have access to a band saw, for cutting the zigzag edge you could use either a large scroll saw or a handsaw.

·6·
Fang Mask

Africa

Keeping in mind that, in the context of Western art, all African masks are considered to be dynamic and inspirational, the masks made by the African Fang tribe are particularly significant in that it was a Fang mask that sparked the "primitive," "tribal," or "modern" art movement.

As the story goes, it was in Paris in the late nineteenth, early twentieth century, when various up-

6-1 Inspirational drawings. (Top left) Lula mask—Zaire—15¾in (40cm) high. A rare mask painted blue and white. (Top center). Fang mask—Gabon—about 12in (30cm) high. Among the Fang, white is the color of death; this white face mask portrays an ancestor or a spirit. (Top right) Mbole mask—Zaire—about 18in (46cm) high. (Bottom left) Kota mask—Gabon—about 12½in (32cm) high. This white face mask was used in funerals and at social functions. (Bottom right) Fang helmet mask—Gabon—about 13½in (34cm) high.

and-coming painters and sculptors were looking to non-European tribal cultures for inspiration... A young artist, Maurice de Vlaminck, on seeing a Fang mask in a bistro (see **6-2**), was so struck by its power and "profound sense of humanity" that he set about collecting similar works. Vlaminck showed the Fang mask to his friend Derain, who in turn showed it to Picasso and Matisse, who showed it to Braque, and so on.

The painters, especially Picasso, were so inspired by the mask that they started to paint and sculpt all sorts of "primitive" and "barbaric" forms. The rest of the story is, as they say, history. Within a space of ten or so years, museums and galleries in London, New York, and Paris were setting up collections of "primitive" art.

Although the term *primitive* is now generally thought of as being offensive, it has nevertheless stuck.

THOUGHTS ON SHAPE, FORM & TECHNIQUE

Have a look at the working drawings (see **6-3**) and see how, at a grid scale of two squares to one inch, the mask measures about 15in (38cm) high, 9in (23cm) wide, and 4in (10cm) deep from back to front.

Note how the mask is built up from three side-by-side 4in (10cm) by 4in (10cm) sections—with the grain running from the top of the crown to the tip of the chin.

Study the side view, and you will see that the total carving—the overall profile and the techniques—can be likened to a shallow dish, with the nose, the mouth, and the various details being achieved by, as it were, lowering the convex curve of the dish.

The overall dish-like form and the minimal details seem to require only easy-to-do procedures—there is no deep carving or undercutting. However, we think it's also fair to say that, while the simple and uncomplicated forms can be carved with the minimum of tools and expertise, this very simplicity makes for a relatively difficult project. Or to put it another way: although you don't need many tools and the techniques are simple enough, it's not so easy to put it all together.

CHOOSING YOUR WOOD

Although our decision to build up the blank from three 4×4 sections has more to do with our supply of wood than anything else, a laminated blank is more stable and less likely to split than a slab of wood straight from the tree. That aside, a relatively large and shallow mask of this character needs to be worked from a smooth-textured, straight-grained, easy-to-carve wood—one free of knots. If you have a choice, then it's best go for a wood like linden/lime, jelutong, basswood, or even a smooth-grained pine.

It's worth noting that even though we fussed around spending a great deal of time and trouble searching out a good piece of wood, the moment we ran the wood through the planer, it was clear to see that it was flawed by a number of small sap holes or insect cavities (see **6-4**).

Special Tip

Although, in the context of making masks, we generally opt for using jelutong, we are gradually

6-2 Project picture—the finished mask.

coming around to consider that it is a bit too loose-grained and fluffy. There is no doubt that it is wonderfully easy to carve, but counter to this, it tends to be a bit crumbly, and it won't take fine details.

Suggested Tools

- workbench with a vise and holdfast
- medium-weight mallet of a size and shape to suit your needs
- good selection of carving gouges and chisels
- a good sharp long-bladed knife—we use a Swedish sloyd knife with a laminated steel blade
- use of a small band saw
- pencil, ruler, and pair of dividers
- one sheet of workout and tracing paper
- two orange-brown, felt-tipped pens—a broad- and a fine point
- beeswax polish
- typical workshop tools and materials such as sandpaper, oilstone, oil, sharpening slips, Plasticine, dust mask, and PVA (polyvinyl acetate) adhesive

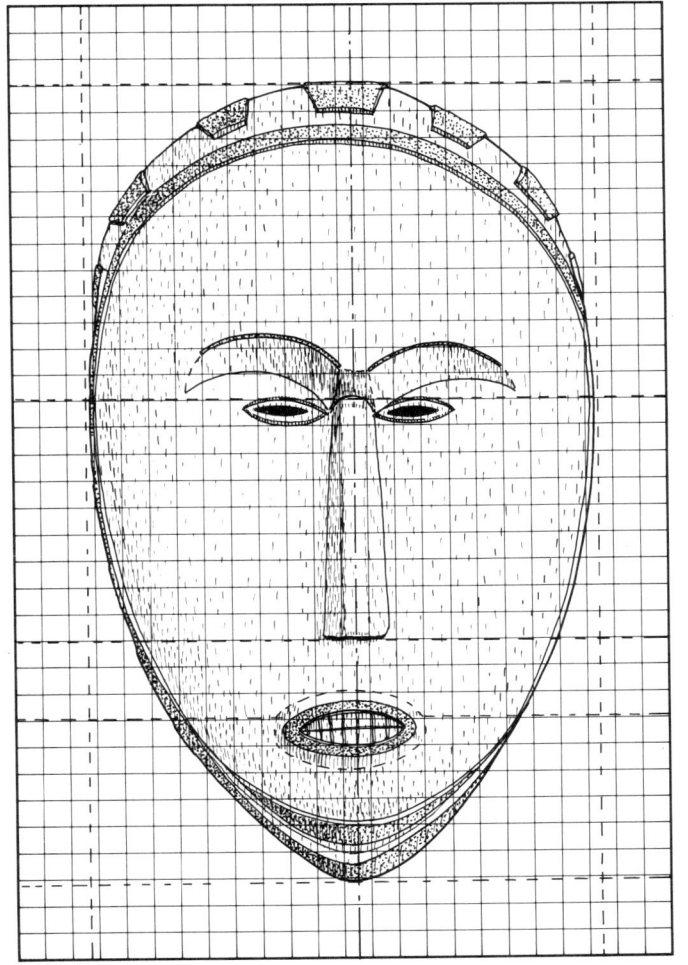
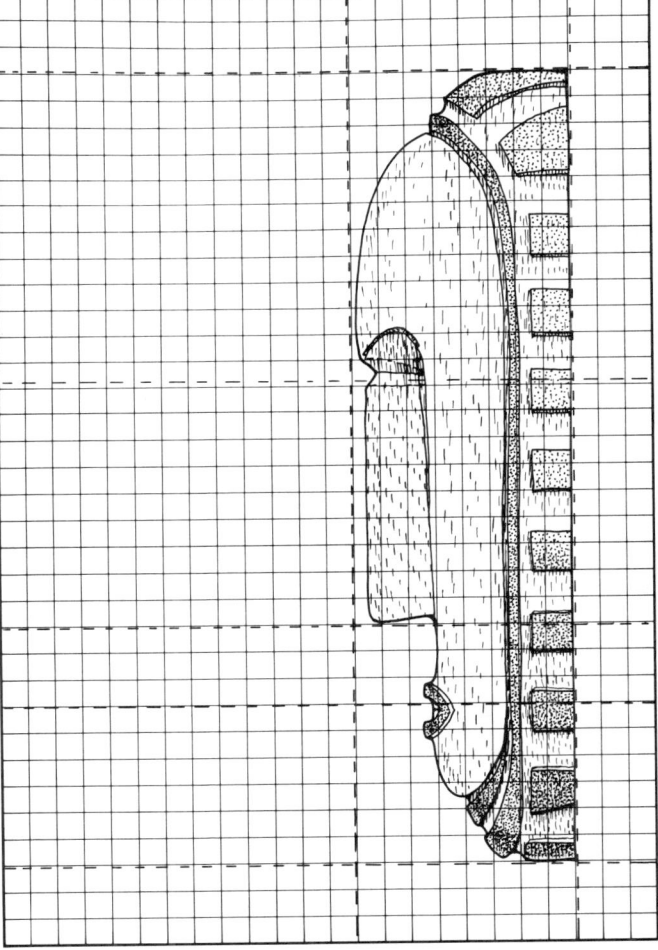

6-3 Working drawings—front and side views. Grid scale equals two squares to one inch. Note, on the front view, the stylized and much simplified proportions, the way the hair design runs down to become a beard, and the strict symmetrical alignment. Note, in the side view, the overall flat dish-like form with the nose marking out the line of the profile, and also the way the hair design is achieved by lowering the wood so that blocks are left in relief.

PROJECT MAKING STAGES

Drawing Out the Design

1. After you have had a good long look at the inspirational drawings (refer to **6-1**) and generally studied Fang masks, take a pencil, ruler, and the tracing paper, and start by setting out a centerline along with the overall height and width parameters of the mask design (refer to **6-3**, front view).

2. With the various guidelines in place, fold the tracing paper down the centerline, and then set to working drawing the imagery on one half of the paper.

Special Tip

If you can't see how the features relate one to another, and/or you're not sure how the mask looks in the round, then make a Plasticine maquette of the whole mask or of particularly bothersome details.

3. Once you are happy with the first half of the front view, trace the imagery to the other half of the fold line. Then draw out the side view (refer to **6-3**).

Making the Blank

4. Having drawn out the designs—on both the workout and the tracing paper—and selected your wood, set the wood out with a vertical centerline, and then pencil-press-transfer the outermost profile, and the primary details that go to make up the face.

5. Make certain that you haven't made any mess-ups, and then move to the band saw and set to work cutting out the profile. Run the line of cut well to the waste side of the drawn line (refer to **6-4**).

Special Tip

If you are new to woodcarving and you want to cut down on unnecessary hard work and sweat, then you can't do better than to get yourself a small benchtop band saw.

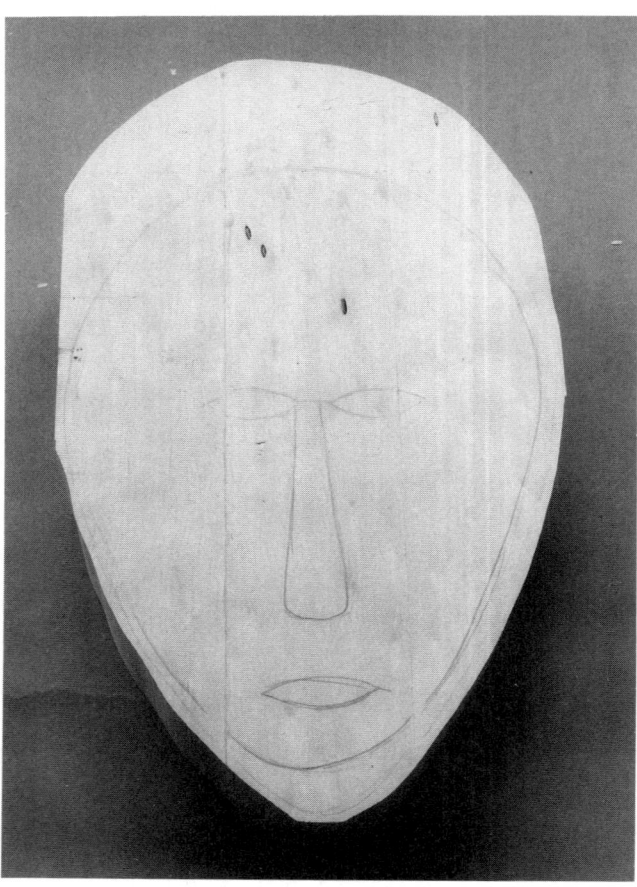

6-4 The laminated blank is shown with the profile cut out and with the main design features drawn in. Note the newly revealed insect/resin cavities.

6-5 Use the deep-sweep gouge to remove the bulk of the waste from under the nose. If the tools are sharp and the wood nice and dry, the waste should come away as uncomplicated crisp curls.

Roughing Out

6. When you have achieved a clean-cut blank and spent time drawing in as many guidelines as you think necessary, secure the workpiece on the bench with the front face uppermost, and use a straight gouge to round over the sawn edge of the profile and to establish the main levels. This done, use a V-tool to make stop-cuts around the nose. Use a deep-sweep gouge to remove the bulk of the waste from under the nose (see **6-5**).

7. Remember to make repeated step-offs with the dividers to check the carved contours against your working drawings. Continue cutting away the rough, until the surfaces run in smooth curves—down from the forehead and down from the sides of the nose (see **6-6**).

8. Aim for an overall dish-like form with a long, straight nose ridge and with the areas around the nose cut away in a depth of 1in (2.5cm) as seen in **6-7**.

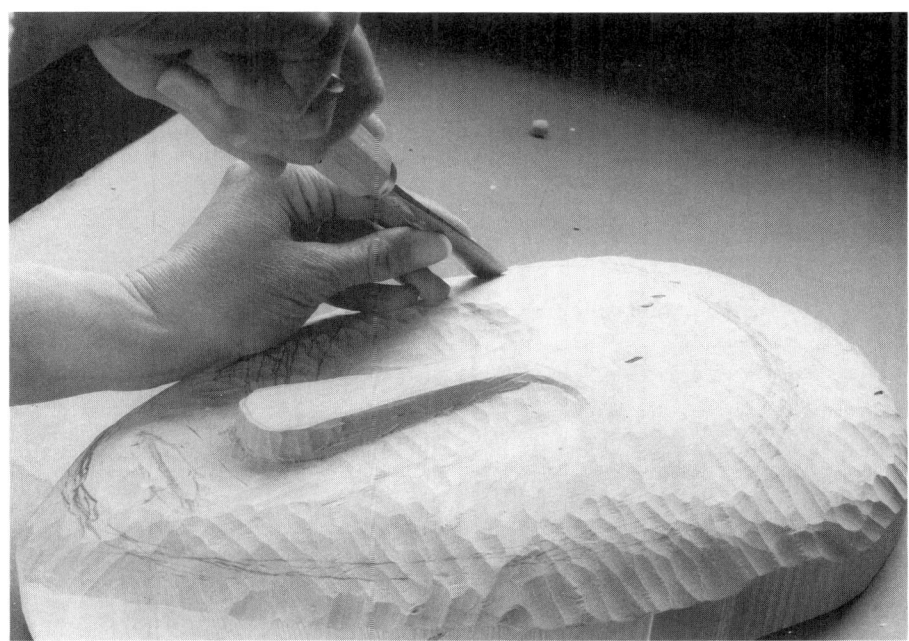

6-6 Remove the waste to create a flattened dome like the underside of a shallow fruit dish. Continue, until the surface runs in smooth curves over the forehead and down from the sides of the nose.

6-7 Side view. Cut away the area around the nose to a depth of about 1in (2.5cm). Note the straight, uncompromising lines.

Modeling

9. Once you have achieved the dish-like mound with the long nose ridge, then set to work drawing in the position of the mouth, the eyes, and the eyebrows. It's important that these details be well placed; use the dividers to step off triangulations against the master design.

Special Tip

Triangulation is a method of using divider step-offs to transfer the precise position of the imagery from the working drawing to the wood. For example, if you want to fix the position of the eyes on the wood, all you do is set the dividers to, say, the distance from the top of the nose to the outer point of the eye (on the working drawing) and then spike the dividers down on the carving—on top of the nose—and make a sweep.

This done, you then fix the dividers to the distance from the bottom of the nose to the outer point of the eye (on the working drawing) and make another sweep on the wood. The intersection of the two sweeps or arcs will fix the position of the outer point of the eye in relation to the nose. The more sweeps you make from various reference points, the more accurate the placing.

6-8 *The arched brow lines slope into the eye sockets, with two lines being drawn for each brow. The ridge of the brow needs to angle down to the level of the eye.*

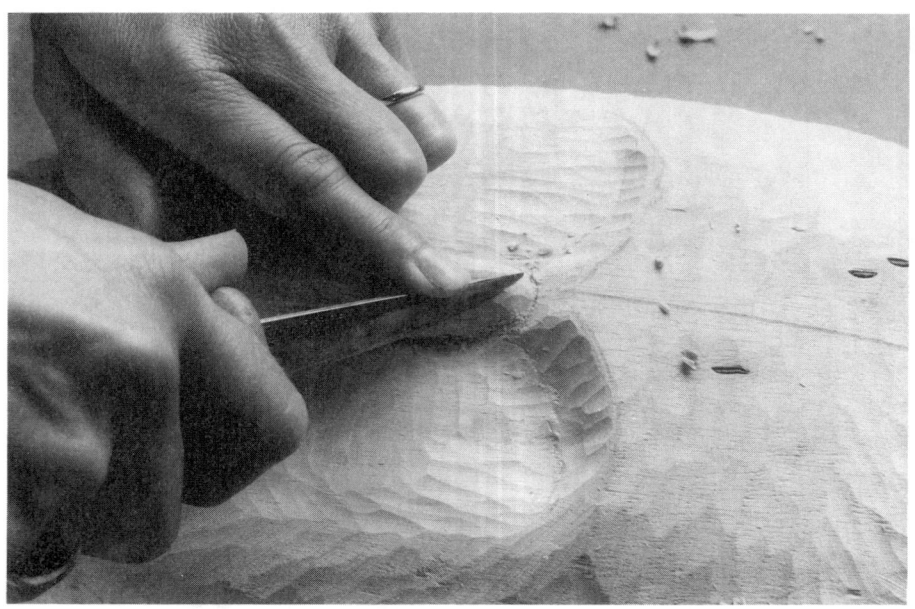

6-9 *Use the knife to slice in toward the curved stop-cut at the top of the nose. Work with small, two-handed controlled cuts to model the sloping planes that run from the top of the nose to the bottom of the brow.*

10. Take the knife, and set out the bottom of the brow line—the second line down from the brow—with a stop-cut. After this, make repeated skims down from the drawn brow line into the stop-cut to achieve the arched brow that slopes into the eye socket (see **6-8**). Repeat this procedure on both eyes, until the eye socket is at a level about 1in (2.5cm) down from the nose ridge.

11. Once you are satisfied with the shape of the brow and the level of the eyes, take the knife and set-in the shape of the top of the nose with a curved stop-cut. Then slice around and down to model both the nose and the brow into the stop-cut (see **6-9**). Aim for crisp, cleanly defined forms.

12. Having first studied the working drawings (refer to **6-3**) and seen how the shape and position of stylized hair is achieved by running a V-trench stop-cut around the mask, draw it with a pencil. Then use a V-tool to set-in the drawn line to a depth of about ¼in (6mm), as shown in **6-10**.

13. To model the mouth, take a small U-section straight gouge and run a trench around the lips (see **6-11**). Then use the knife to lower the level around the mouth. Continue until the mouth

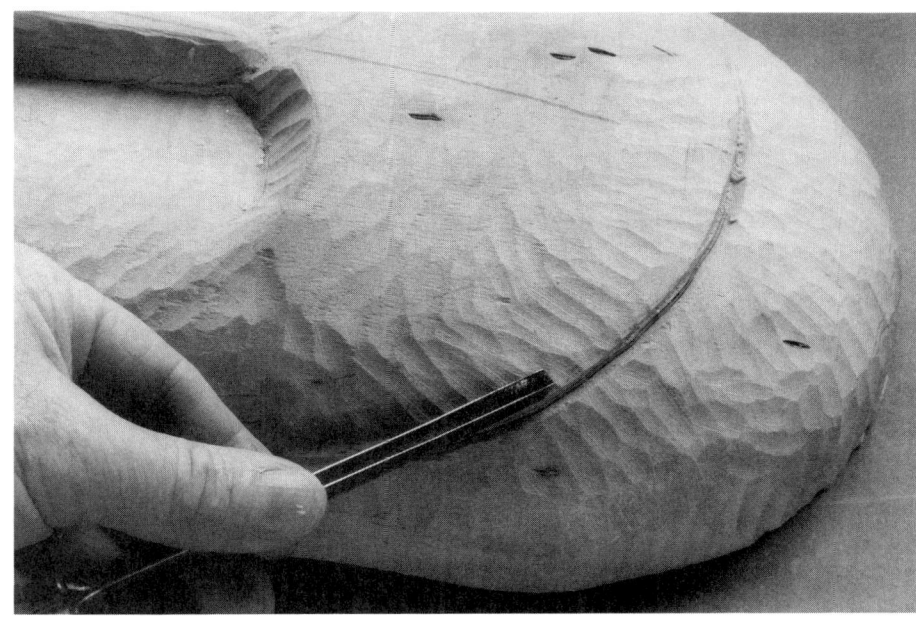

6-10 Use the V-section tool to cut in the hair line. Aim to finish at a depth of about ¼in (6mm). Be sure to work up one side of the trench and down the other to avoid cutting directly into end grain.

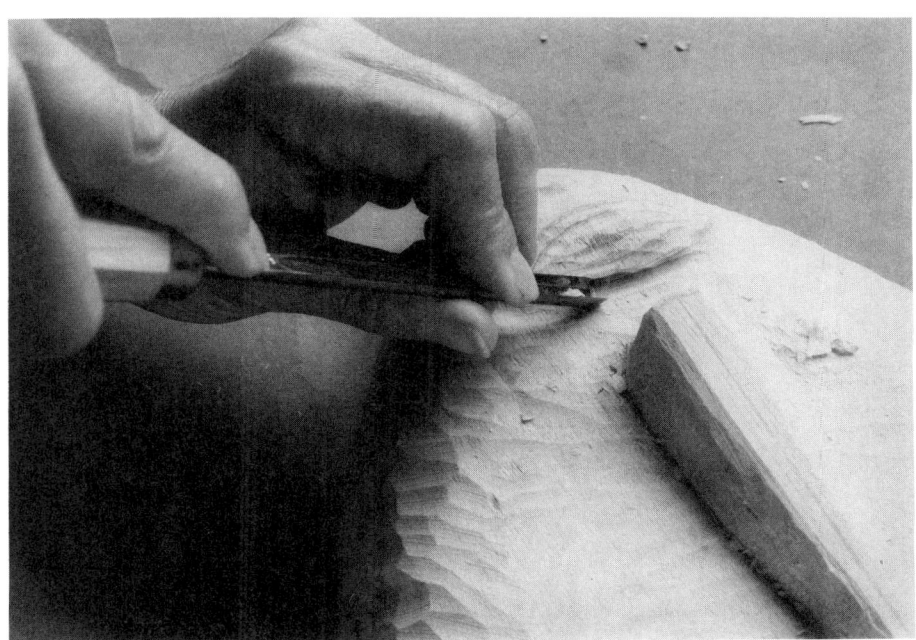

6-11 Keeping in mind the direction of the grain and the direction of the cut, run a U-section trench around the lips to leave the whole mouth area standing in relief. Note that the corners of the mouth are very fragile and short grained.

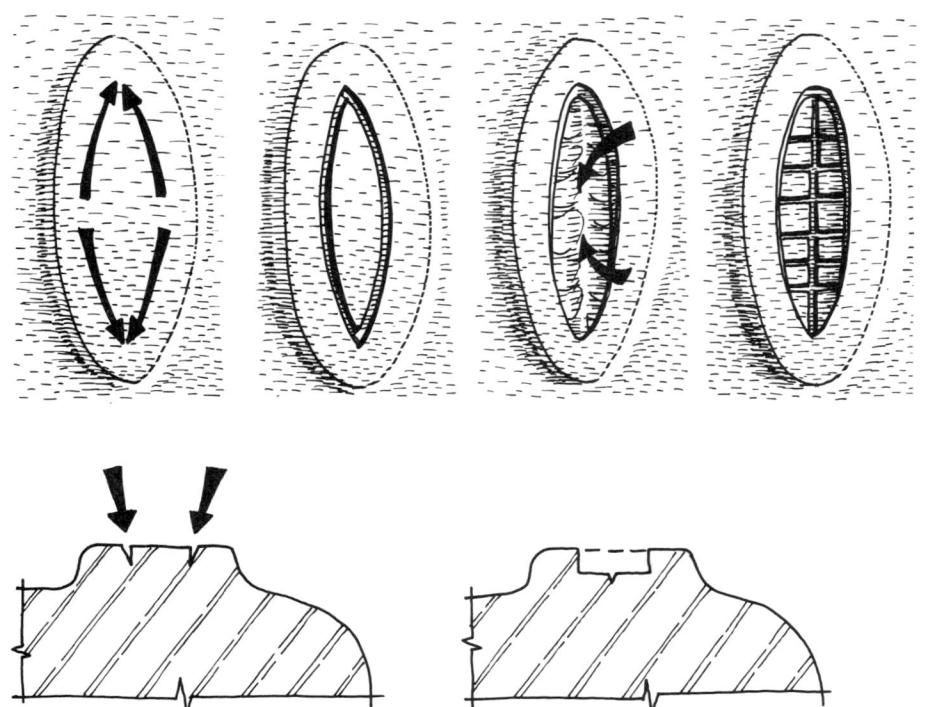

6-12 *Modeling the mouth. First position the mask so that you can work away from the sides—drawing the knife towards your body. (Left) Set-in the line of the inner lip with a V-trench. (Right) Use a small gouge to lower the inner area. (Far right) Use a grid of V-cut lines to create the teeth. (Bottom left) Cross section shows the first cuts. (Bottom right) The finished mouth shown in cross section.*

stands proud like a miniature plateau. Set-in the inner lip line with a knife-cut V-trench, and then use both the knife and the small gouge to lower the inner mouth area by about ⅛in (3mm). Finally, use the knife to set-in the shape of the teeth with a V-cut grid line (see **6-12**).

14. To model the eyes—having first used the pencil, ruler and dividers to fix the precise position of their almond shapes—run a knife stop-cut along the length of each eye from one point to another. Set it in to a depth of about ⅛in (3mm). Angle the knife and run cuts at either side of the initial stop-cut to make a little boat-shaped hole. Repeat this procedure to widen and deepen the hole. Once you are happy with the shape and depth of the eye hole, use the point of the knife to set-in the lid line with an incised V-section cut (see **6-13**).

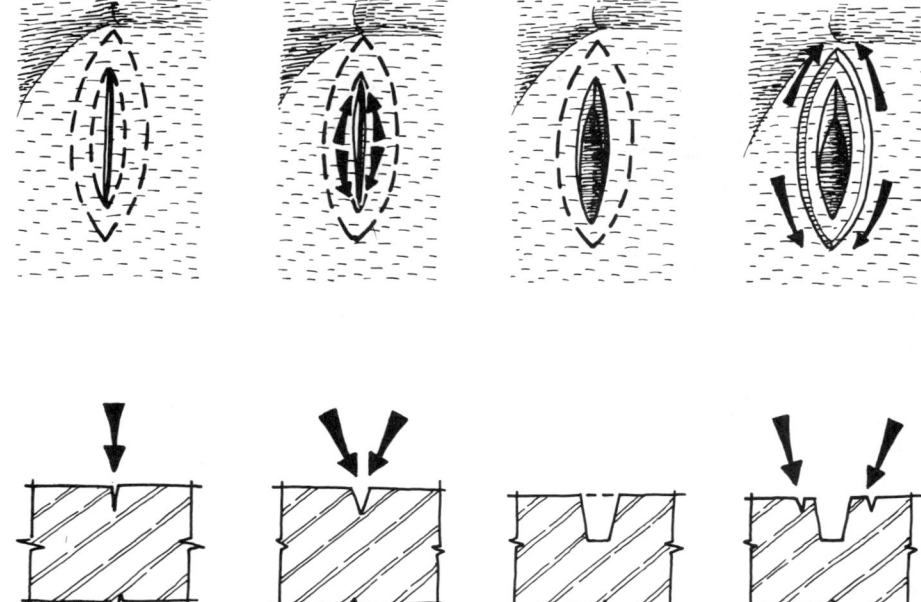

6-13 *Modeling the eyes. First position the mask so that you can work away from the sides—drawing the knife towards your body. (Left to right) Run a stop-cut along the length of the eye, enlarge the cut to form a boat-shaped hole, continue enlarging the hole, and cut-in the lid line with an incised V-section cut. (Bottom) Cross-section stages showing the depth of the cuts throughout the progression.*

15. To model the hair, set the drawn lines in with V-section stop-cuts—after all the shapes of the various raised plateaus, lowered blocks, and V-section grooves have been drawn out (see **6-14**), meaning the shapes that make up the design of the hair. Then lower the waste areas to an overall depth of about 1/8in (3mm). Aim for clean, crisp edges and smooth surfaces for the plateaus, and heavily tooled surfaces for the lowered areas (see **6-15**).

FINISHING

16. Once you are pleased with the overall mask, then it is time to use your full range of tools to bring the mask to a good finish. So you might clean up the creases around the nose with the knife, skim away the tool mark ripples with a flat-sweep gouge, and clean up the right angles with a V-section tool, etc.

Special Tip

The term *good finish* has more to do with your perception of what makes a good finish than with how smooth such and such a surface actually is. One carver's good finish might be heavily tooled; another carver might require that a surface be sanded absolutely smooth.

17. Aim for a smooth sanded surface for just about everything except the lowered areas that make up the hair design. That said, don't overdo the sanding to the extent that you blur the details. Note the slightly rippled areas around the mouth and eyes.

18. Finally, wipe away the dust. Use the brown felt-tipped pens to color the lips, the raised areas of the hair design, and the eyebrows. Then burnish the entire mask to a dull-sheen waxed finish.

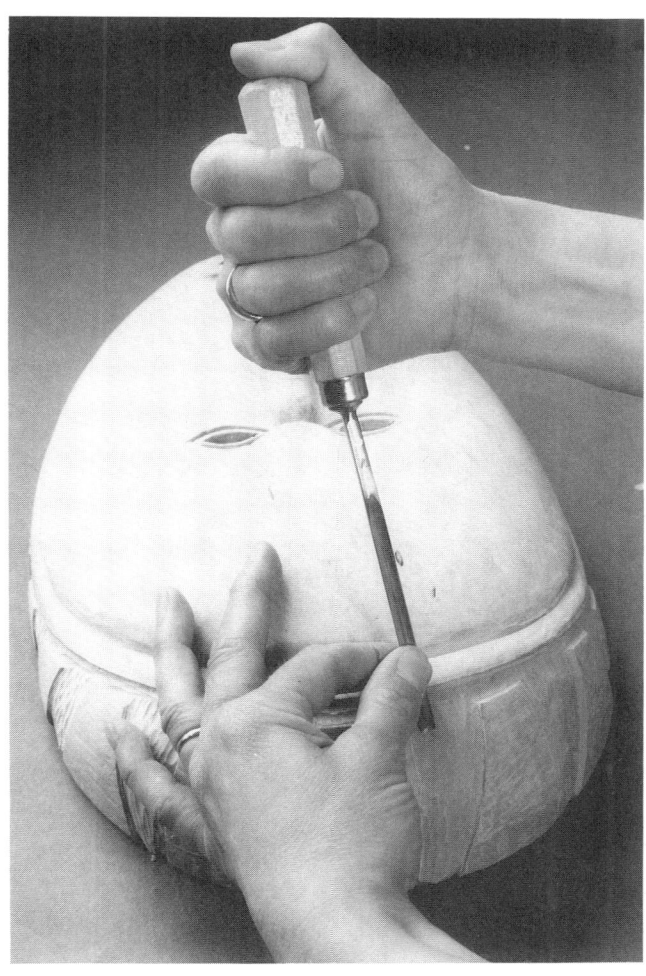

6-15 *Lower the waste so that the blocks of hair stand in relief. Leave the tool marks so that they contrast against the smooth areas.*

6-14 *Draw in the lines of the hair and beard.*

PROBLEM-SOLVING

If you want the mask to be hollow-carved at the back, then see *Hollowing* in the "Tools, Techniques & Materials—A–Z Guides."

- If you don't much like such and such a detail, then always be prepared to go your own way. For example, although traditionally Fang masks tend to be given a swift brush-over with a matt cream/white pigment, we decided to go for a waxed finish.
- We can't know for sure, but we suspect that traditionally the hair of Fang masks was painted an all-over brown color, and then the designs were cut through the color to reveal the pale wood beneath.

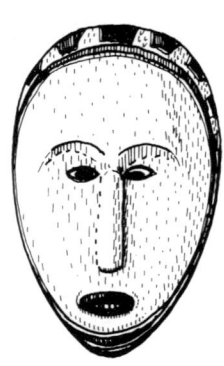

·7·
Bapende Mask

Congo, Africa

Within the African masking tradition, a good number of masks are made to represent animals, or at least beings that are part animal and part human (see **7-1** and **7-2**). The idea is that in a realistic or stylized form the masks or heads of animals have great supernatural power. In most traditional African tribal societies, it is believed that the power is concentrated in the head.

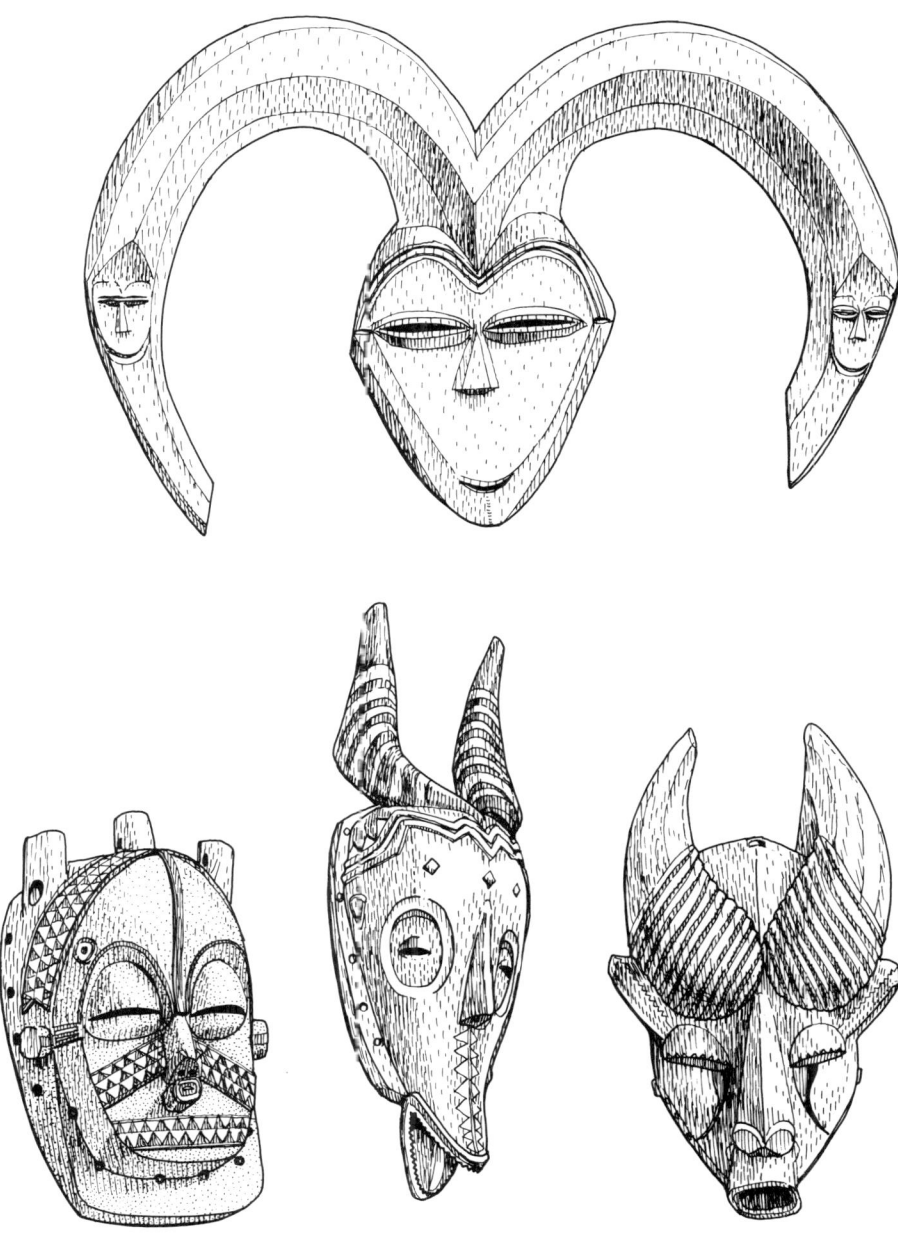

7-1 Inspirational drawings. (Top) Kwele mask—Gabon—about 24in (61cm) high. (Bottom left) Bena-Biombo mask—Zaire—about 15in (38cm) high. (Bottom center) Guro antelope mask—Ivory Coast—used in the Zale Society dances—18¾in (48cm) high. (Bottom right) Igala Ogbodo mask—Nigeria.

When the mask is worn, the wearer dances like the animal in the belief that he will be protected from evil by the power contained in the mask. If the animal has strength, speed, or cunning, then the mask will give him those powers.

THOUGHTS ON SHAPE, FORM & TECHNIQUE

Have a look at the working drawings (see **7-3**) and see how, at a grid scale of two squares to one inch, the mask measures about 18in (46cm) high, 8in (20cm) wide, and 4½in (11.5cm) deep.

One look at this mask is enough to confirm that it is a visually exciting sculptural form in its own right (refer to **7-2**). The large horns, the stylized protruding eyes and mouth, the flat blocks of color, and the patterns all make for a mask that is both dynamic and startling.

In terms of carving technique, the protruding tubes of the eyes and mouth and the horns are something of a dilemma. The problem is whether you carve the basic lump, and then build the mask up from applied bits—separate horns, and dowels for the tubes—or rather you carve the mask from a single lump of wood or laminated blank. Certainly it is easier to carve the horns and the tubes as separate lumps, but, then again, they need to be attached.

If you look to the photographs (see **7-4** and **7-5**) you will see that we laminated up two layers, fretted them out on the band saw, and then glued them together. This operation was a little time-consuming at the gluing stages, but it really speeds up the carving, saves wood, and makes for a strong form. As for hollowing the eyes and mouth, we used the tools at hand and simply bored them out with a drill.

7-2 Project picture—the finished mask.

CHOOSING YOUR WOOD

Although this project calls for an easy-to-carve wood, the unusual shape and form of the mask make it all the more important that the wood be straight grained and relatively strong. We chose to use five lengths of 2½in (6.5cm) by 2½in (6.5cm) square sections of English linden/lime—three lengths for the back, two lengths for the front, and two small offcuts. Have a look at the working drawings for overall size (refer to **7-3**).

Suggested Tools

- workbench with a vise and holdfast
- medium-weight mallet of a size and shape to suit your needs
- good selection of carving gouges and chisels
- a good sharp, long-bladed knife—we use a Swedish sloyd knife with a laminated steel blade
- use of a small band saw
- bench drill press with a good selection of Forstner drill bits
- pencil, ruler, and pair of dividers
- small riffler file
- one sheet each of workout and tracing paper
- small quantity of acrylic watercolor paint—orange-brown, dark umber, and white
- two soft-haired brushes—a broad- and a fine-point—as used by watercolorists
- beeswax polish
- typical workshop tools and materials such as sandpaper, oilstone, oil, sharpening slips, Plasticine, dust mask, and PVA (polyvinyl acetate) adhesive

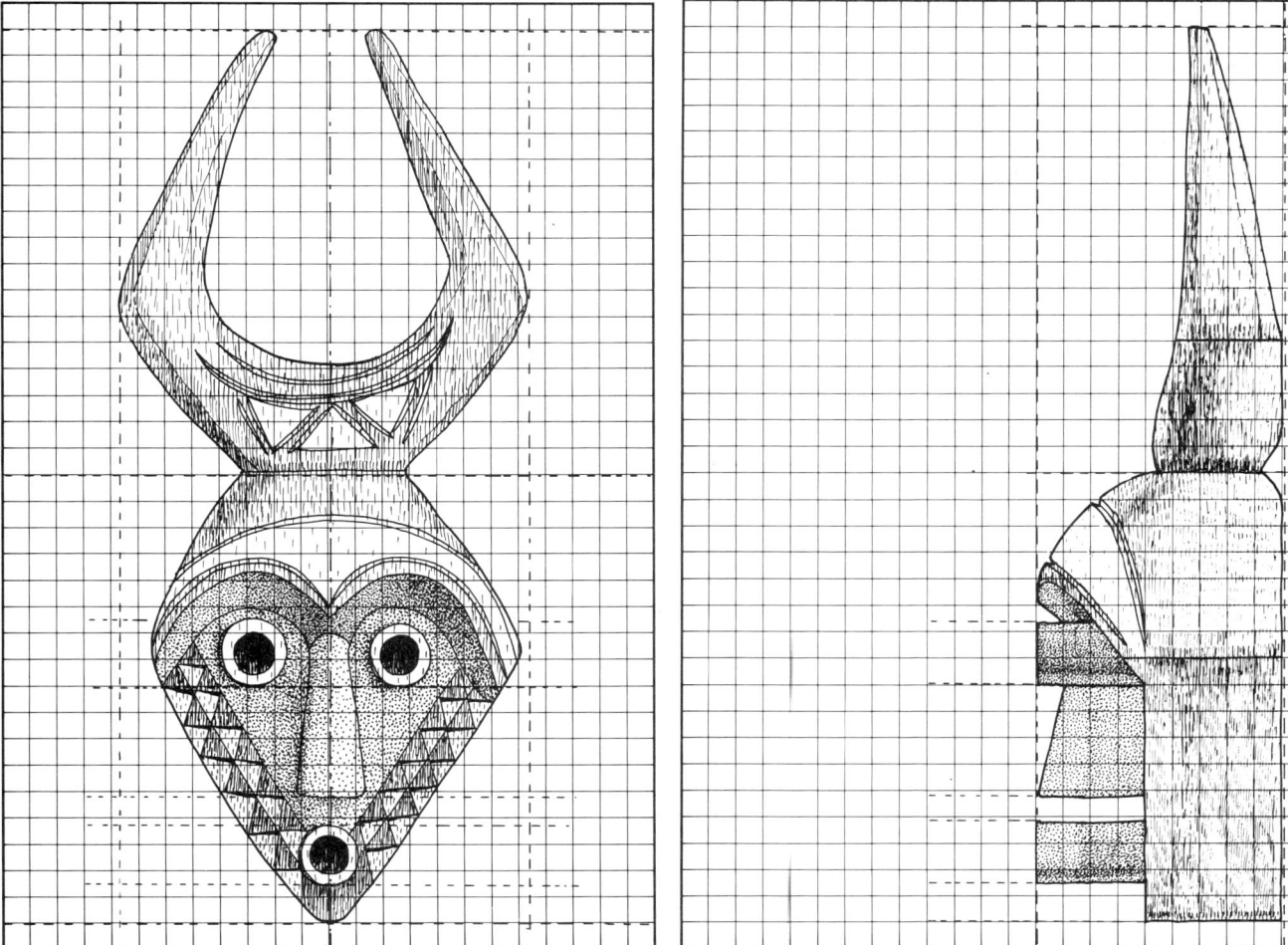

7-3 Working drawings—front and side views. Grid scale equals two squares to one inch. Note the areas of fragile short grain towards the top of the horns. Note, in the side view, how all of the projecting features are cut from the top lamination.

PROJECT MAKING STAGES

Drawing Out the Design

1. Having very carefully studied the inspirational drawings (refer to **7-1**) and the project picture (refer to **7-2**) to the extent that you have a clear picture in mind as to the best way to proceed, then take a pencil, ruler, and the workout paper, and draw the mask out to size.

2. When you are happy with the total front-view image, make a tracing, so that you have two profiles—one of the whole face-and-horns shape, and one of the face up to the bottom of the horns (refer to **7-3**).

3. Draw in the zigzag borders at each side of the mask, and fix the precise position of the three tubes—the two eyes and the mouth.

4. Take clear tracings, and put the working drawings carefully to one side—so that they are in view and yet away from the dust and debris.

Special Tip

Although it's generally easy enough to visualize the front view of a mask, say from a poor reference photograph or from a sketch, it's not so easy to draw out the side view. This being so, we usually draw out the front view and then make a Plasticine maquette that relates to it. We find that by the time we have drawn out the view and built the model, the size and shapes of the side view are self-evident.

Making the Blank

5. Having laminated the five lengths of 2½in (6.5cm) by 2½in (6.5cm) square sections of

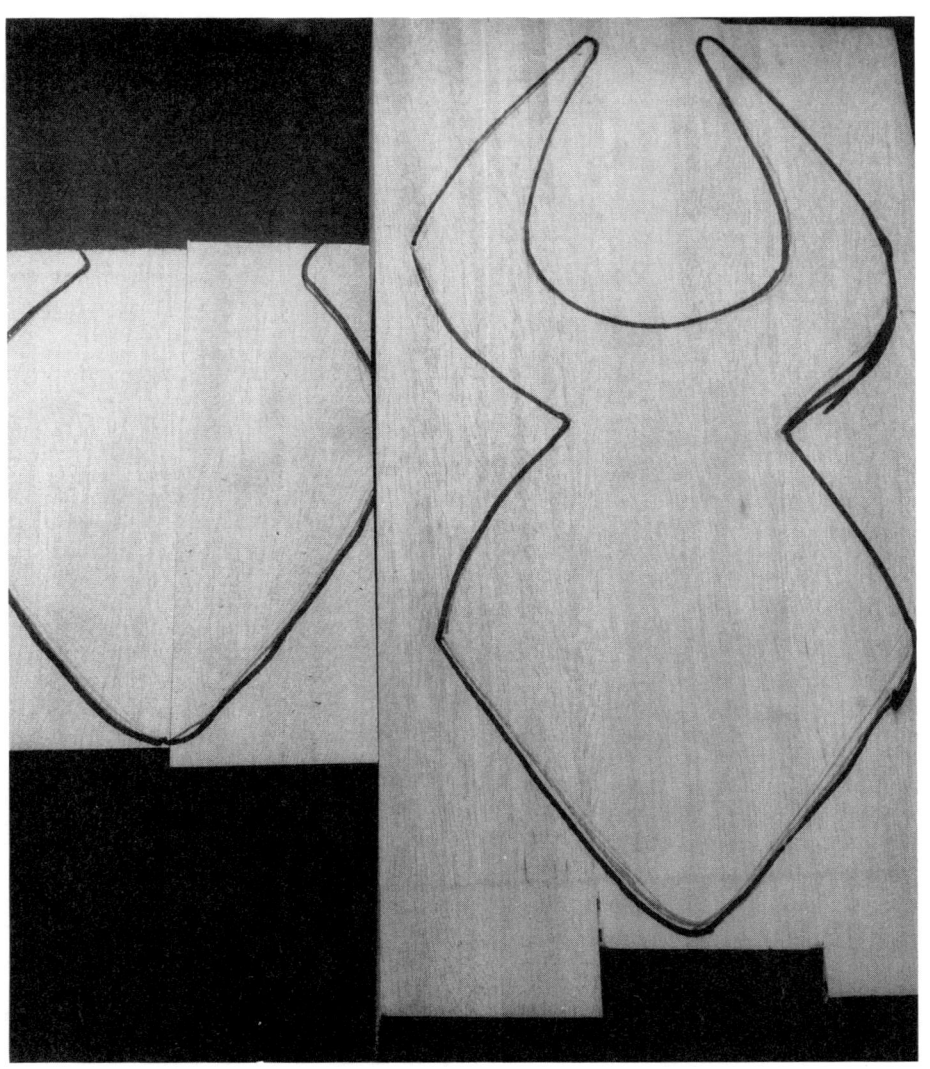

7-4 Transfer the two profiles to the wood—the front face part to the top lamination, and the outline with horns to the lower section.

7-5 *When you are happy with the cutouts, smear a generous amount of PVA glue on the mating surfaces, and clamp them together.*

wood—two for the front and three for the back—take the tracing, and press-transfer the imagery to the wood (see **7-4**).

6. With the two profiles set out so that there is no doubting the line of cut, then fret them out on the band saw.

7. Rub down the mating faces until the two profiles come together for a close fit—you could do this with a plane and/or sandpaper. Then smear glue on the mating faces. Bring the two components together, making sure they are well aligned, and put them to one side until the glue is set (see **7-5**).

8. Having noted that there are now two little steps—one at either side of the face—take a couple of small offcuts, smear them with a generous amount of glue, and clamp them in place (see **7-6**). Make sure that the grain is aligned so that it runs from top to bottom.

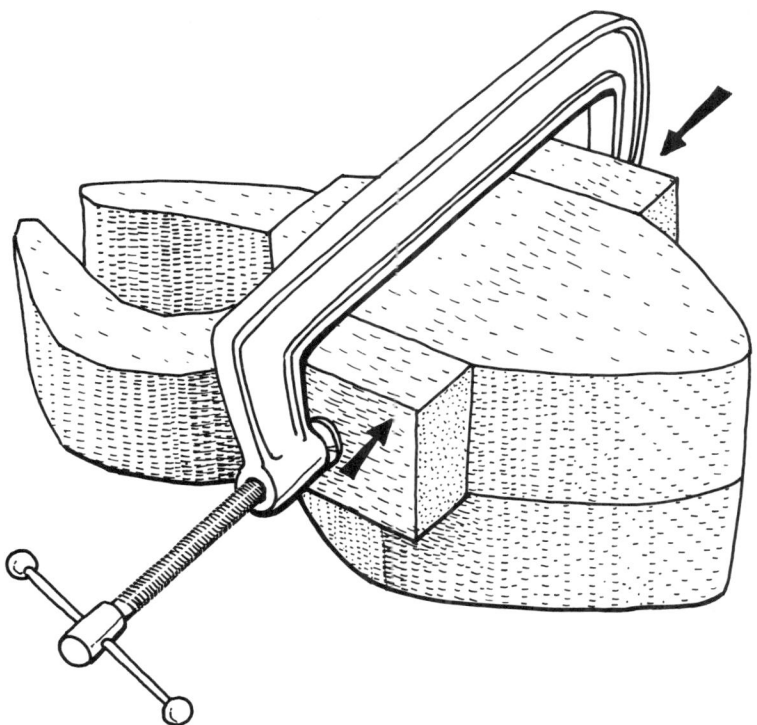

7-6 *Build up the width by gluing small offcuts at either side.*

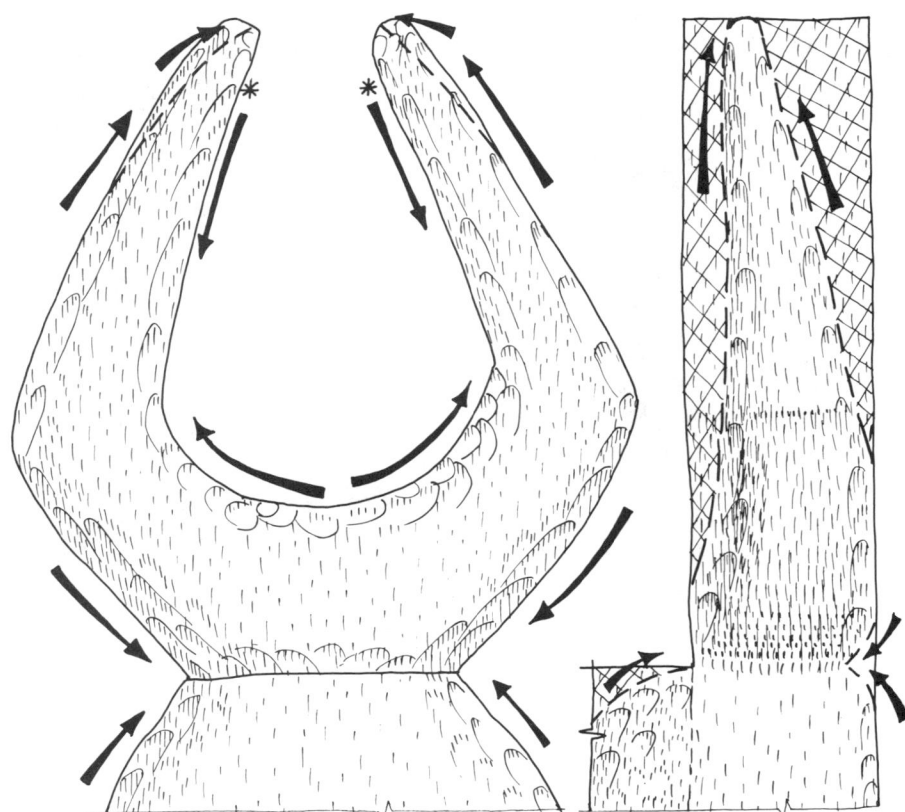

7-7 (Left) When you come to using the knife to carve the horns to shape, work in the direction of the arrows to avoid cutting into the grain. Note that the areas towards the top of the horns—marked with the asterisks—are especially short grained and fragile. (Right) If you want to speed up the procedure, then it's best to start this stage by using a saw to rough out the shape of the horns as they appear in side view.

Roughing Out

9. Make certain that the glue is good and dry, and then use the tools of your choice to cut away the rough and to generally round over the sawn edges.

10. Being careful not to slice directly into end grain (see **7-7**), use the knife to cut the horns to shape, and to round over the forehead (see **7-8**). Continue, until the curves of the horns and head

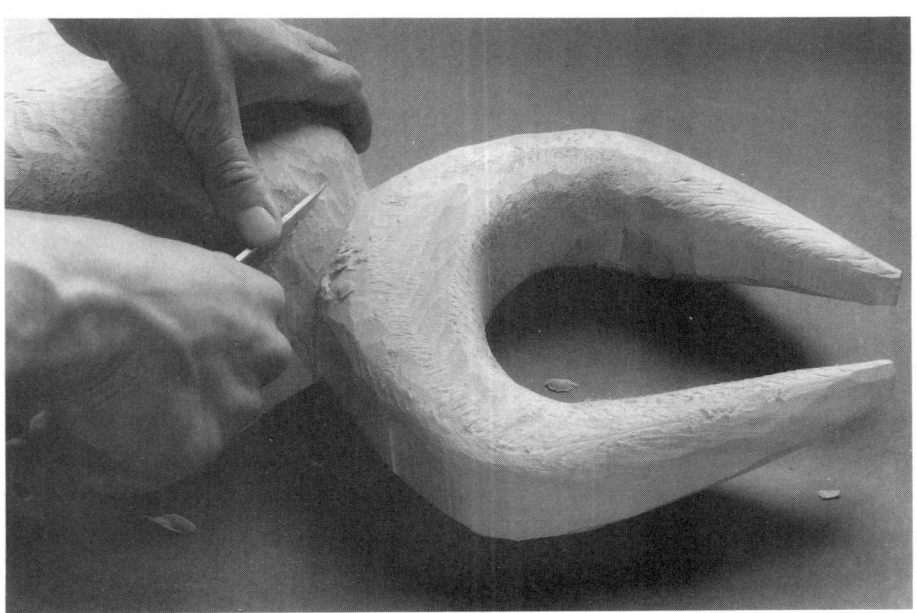

7-8 Use the knife and a two-handed levering hold when you come to carving the difficult end-grain area at the top of the forehead. The best procedure is to hold and guide the knife in one hand, while pressing and levering with the other.

meet in a sharply defined valley or crease. The horns need to look as if they have been carved as a separate component and then attached (see **7-2**).

11. Move to the drill press, and use the various size Forstner bits to systematically bore the waste out to an overall depth of about 2in (5cm). Be sure to allow for a good amount of all-around waste. If you are doing it right, the nose, mouth, and eyes should be left standing like some sort of "Wild West" canyon landscape in miniature (see **7-9**).

Modeling

12. With the overall shape of the mask roughed out, and with the bulk of the waste removed, take the knife—you might prefer to use the chisels and gouges—and work around the forms tidying up the grooves and chimneys left by the drill bits. Aim for crisp blocks that stand up in relief on a level ground (see **7-10**).

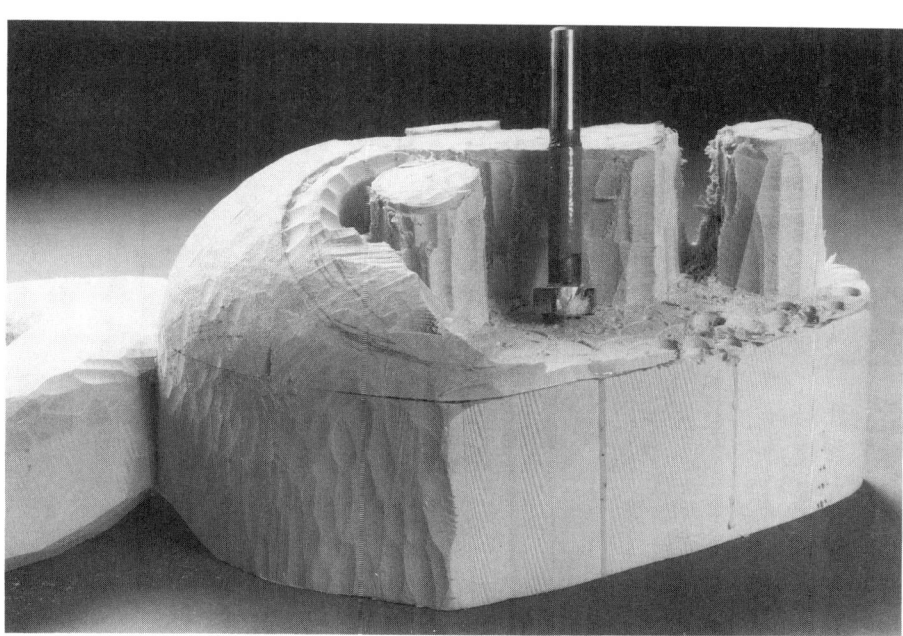

7-9 Although we used the Forstner drill bit to clear the bulk of the waste, notice how we also left a good amount of waste to be worked with a knife.

7-10 Use the knife to tidy up, working with a careful tight stroke, all the while aiming for a positive angular profile.

Special Tip

In the context of this project, when we use terms like *tidy* and *crisp*, we don't mean that you should aim for forms and surfaces that look to be precision engineered, but rather, we have in mind that the forms should look ordered, with the working procedures and the tools leaving their own characteristic "footprints."

13. Carve the shape of the inner eyelid, so that it runs in a smooth curve from the line of the brow down to the base of the eye tube. There needs to be a clearly defined crease where the two planes meet.

14. Being mindful that the eyes are doubly fragile—they are short grained with a glue line at the base—so be very careful not to lever against them with the tools. We found that the back-bent gouge was the best tool for this task (**7-11**).

15. With the modeling complete, move back to the drill press, and use a Forstner bit to bore out the eye and mouth holes. We used a ⅞in (22mm) diameter bit and drilled down to a depth of about 1¼in (32mm).

Special Tip

The eye and mouth holes have to be right—there is very little room for error. It's best to work on a drill press and to use a Forstner bit at low speed. Bore the holes out, little by little—down and up, down and up—to clear the waste.

16. With the holes in place, take the knife and slice the V-section incised lines that make the peaked design at the front of the forehead—meaning the eyebrow lines that arch over each eye, and the single, curved line that arches over the brows to define the top of the cap-like shape. Each V-section trench is achieved with three cuts—a single cut to mark out the depth of the V, and then a slanting cut at each side to remove a sliver of waste. Work with a careful thumb-braced dragging cut (see **7-12**).

7-11 Be very wary when you are clearing the waste that you don't lever against, and do the damage to, the eyes. If you have such a tool, then use a shallow-sweep, back-bent gouge.

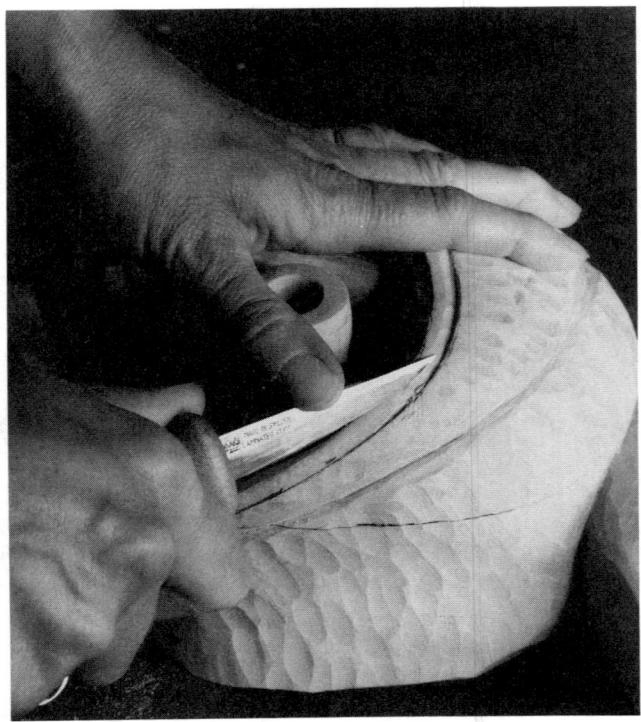

7-12 Bearing in mind that cutting the decorative V-section brow lines is a bit tricky, you should go at it nice and slowly—one hand guiding and the other pushing and bracing. Watch out for the changing direction of the grain.

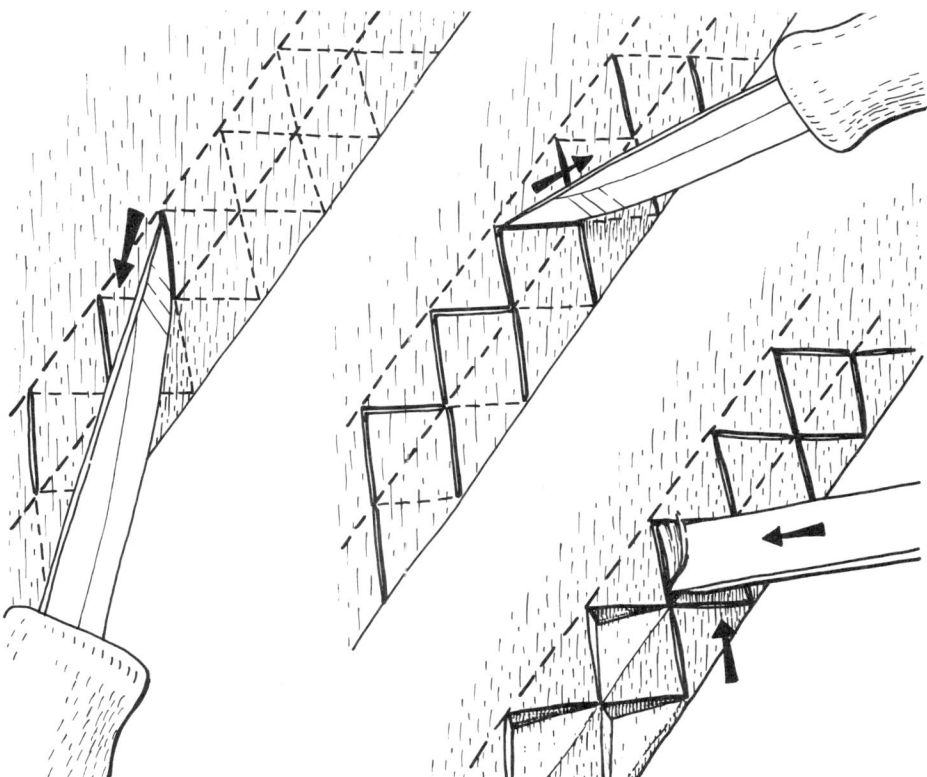

7-13 Carving the zigzag motifs. (Left) Make stop-cuts with the knife—stab the knife into the point or deepest part of the triangle, and then draw the knife out of the wood—to make a sloping cut. (Center) Repeat the procedure and make another stop-cut on the other side of the triangle. (Right) Use the chisel to make two low-angle cuts to remove a wedge-slice of waste.

17. To carve the zigzag motifs, draw in the two lines of zigzag triangles at each side of the face, use the knife to sink stop-cuts—two for each triangle—and then skim out the waste with a straight chisel (see **7-13**). This is a wonderfully swift and easy procedure as long as the stop-cuts are crisply and cleanly defined, and as long as you use the chisel so that the bevel is facing the wood with the flat side uppermost. Work with a restrained two-handed hold—one hand holding and pushing, and the other hand guiding the cutting edge (see **7-14**).

While the knife is at hand, cut in the incised line pattern on the front of the horns (refer to **7-2** and **7-3**).

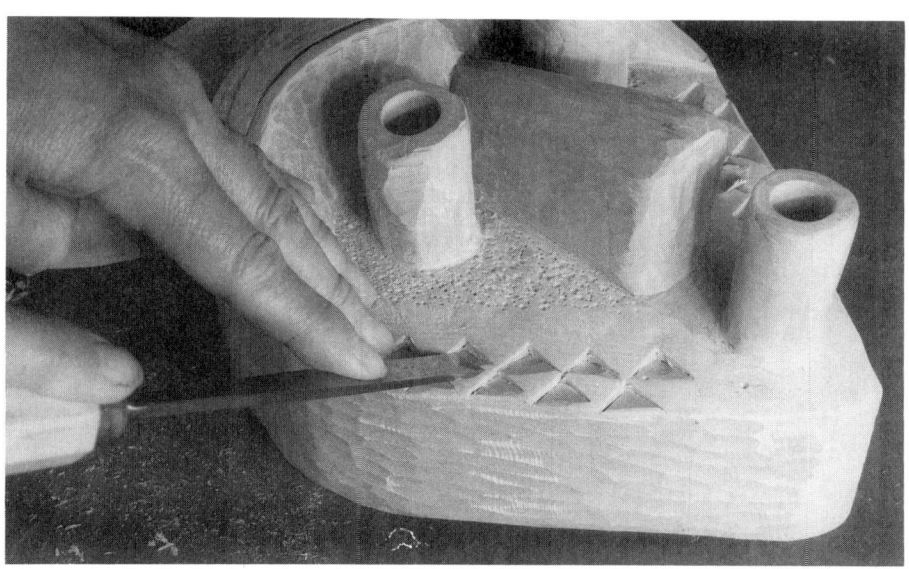

7-14 Work with a restrained two-handed hold—one hand pushing and the other guiding while ready to brake.

FINISHING

18. When you have taken the carving as far as you want it to go, and when you have generally sanded and cleaned up the dust and debris, take a pointed tool and systematically punch-texture the whole area in and around the eye tubes (see **7-15**). Continue jabbing until the surface begins to break up and take on a uniform, pecked texture. Work hard up against the base of the eye and mouth tubes to emphasize their smoothness.

19. Having textured the lowered area, take the acrylic paints and paint in the blocks of flat thin color—burnt umber for the horns, the sides of the mask, and the raised part of the zigzag design; orange-brown for the flat part of the face, the nose, and around the sides of the tubes; and white with just a touch of brown for the ends of the tubes, the cap shape on the forehead, and the zigzag motif at the front of the horns.

20. Finally, once the paint is completely dry, use a scrap of fine-grade sandpaper to cut through the color at wear areas, brush away the dust, give the whole works a rubdown with the wax, and burnish to a good finish.

PROBLEM-SOLVING

- Being mindful that the eye and mouth tubes are short grained and so consequently relatively fragile, it might be a good idea to adjust the thickness of the two layers that go to make up the blank so that the glue line is at a lower level than the bottom of the tubes.
- If you want to hollow out the back of the mask, then see *Hollowing* in the "Tools, Techniques & Materials—A–Z Guides."
- If you have a mess-up, splitting off one or other of the tubes—and this is easily done—then either glue the part back on again, or adjust the order and method of work so that the tubes are glued doweled additions.
- The pecked texture is done for two good reasons; first, it sorts out areas that would be difficult to reach if you wanted to go for a smooth finish; and second, the pecked texture takes up more color, to the extent that the darker tone emphasizes the tubes.

7-15 Peck-texture the difficult-to-reach areas in and around the nose, eyes, and mouth. Continue until the surface takes on an all-over texture.

Haida mask, Northwest coast of North America (project 9).

Fool mask, Europe (project 3).

Kwakiutl mask, Northwest coast of North America (project 8).

Bapende mask, Congo, Africa (project 7).

Ugandan mask, Africa (project 4).

D

Fang mask, Africa (project 6).

Lombok mask, Java, Indonesia (project 12).

Tsimshian beaver mask, Northwest coast of North America (project 10).

Flour spout mask, Alsace, Europe (project 2).

Green man mask, Britain (project 1).

Baule mask, Ivory Coast, Africa (project 5).

Barong mask, Bali, Indonesia (project 11).

·8·
Kwakiutl Mask

Northwest Coast of North America

The native Indians who lived on the Pacific Northwest Coast of North America—the Tlingit, Haida, Tsimshian, Kwakiutl, and one or two other tribes besides—lived in what can only be described as a "woodcarver's paradise." Not only were they blessed by being surrounded by forests of easy-to-carve, fine-textured, straight-grained cedar, but, better yet, the seas and forests were so abundant

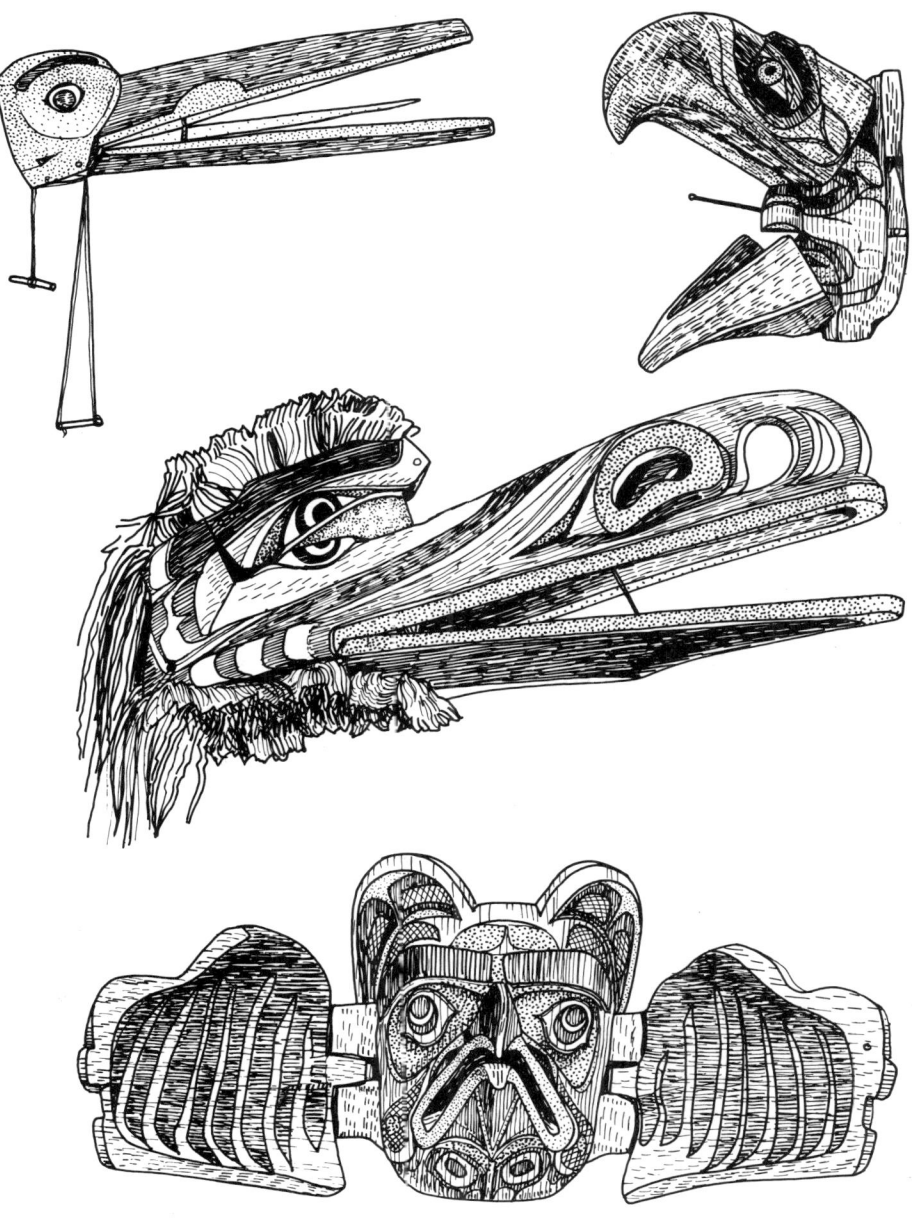

8-1 Inspirational drawings. (Top left) Tsimshian bird mask with movable jaw, tongue, and eyes—about 28in (71cm) long. (Top right) Haida bird mask that opens to reveal a human portrait mask. (Middle) Kwakiutl crooked-beak-of-heaven mask worn by the women during the Hamatsa dances. (Bottom) Transformation mask that opens to reveal a bird of prey—about 30in (76cm) wide when opened.

that in just a few months of hunting, gathering, and preserving, they had enough food put by for the rest of the year.

Once the food was stored away, the Indians withdrew into their houses, into themselves, and into a supernatural period. At this time, names were changed, masks were worn, long dance dramas and rituals were performed, and, of course, various carvings were made. This whole state of affairs—the easy-to-carve wood, the abundance of food, and the ceremonies and dance dramas—gave rise to a culture that was more or less dedicated to woodcarving. Using archetypal tools—the crooked knife, the adze, and various bone and stone scrapers—they created woodcarvings of incomparable size, beauty, variety, quantity, and color. They made totem poles well over 70ft (21m) high, canoes carved all-of-a-piece, steamboat boxes, houses, dishes, hats, rattles, and, of course, masks. All of these were carved and finished to a high degree, and all decorated and painted with stylized motifs and symbols that told of the name of the clan, the wearer's lineage, and the various hereditary entitlements.

The helmet-mask type—as featured in this project—was worn during the "supernatural" dance dramas. The masked cannibal bird spirit would jump out of the shadows and into the firelight, and, then, with much biting and clacking, and by means of various backup tricks and illusions, blood would appear to flow, the dead would rise, and the whole group would join in with whistles, hammering, and with set initiation responses.

THOUGHTS ON SHAPE, FORM & TECHNIQUE

Have a look at the working drawings (see **8-3**) and see how, at a grid scale of two and half squares to one inch—or better said, five grid squares to two inches—this mask-helmet measures about 14in (36cm) long from the back of the head to the point of the beak, 4in (10cm) wide, and about 4in high—that is, from the underside of the beak to the top of the head.

Be mindful that as we have carved this mask at half size, the original Indian mask that inspired this project measures 28in (71cm) long, 8in

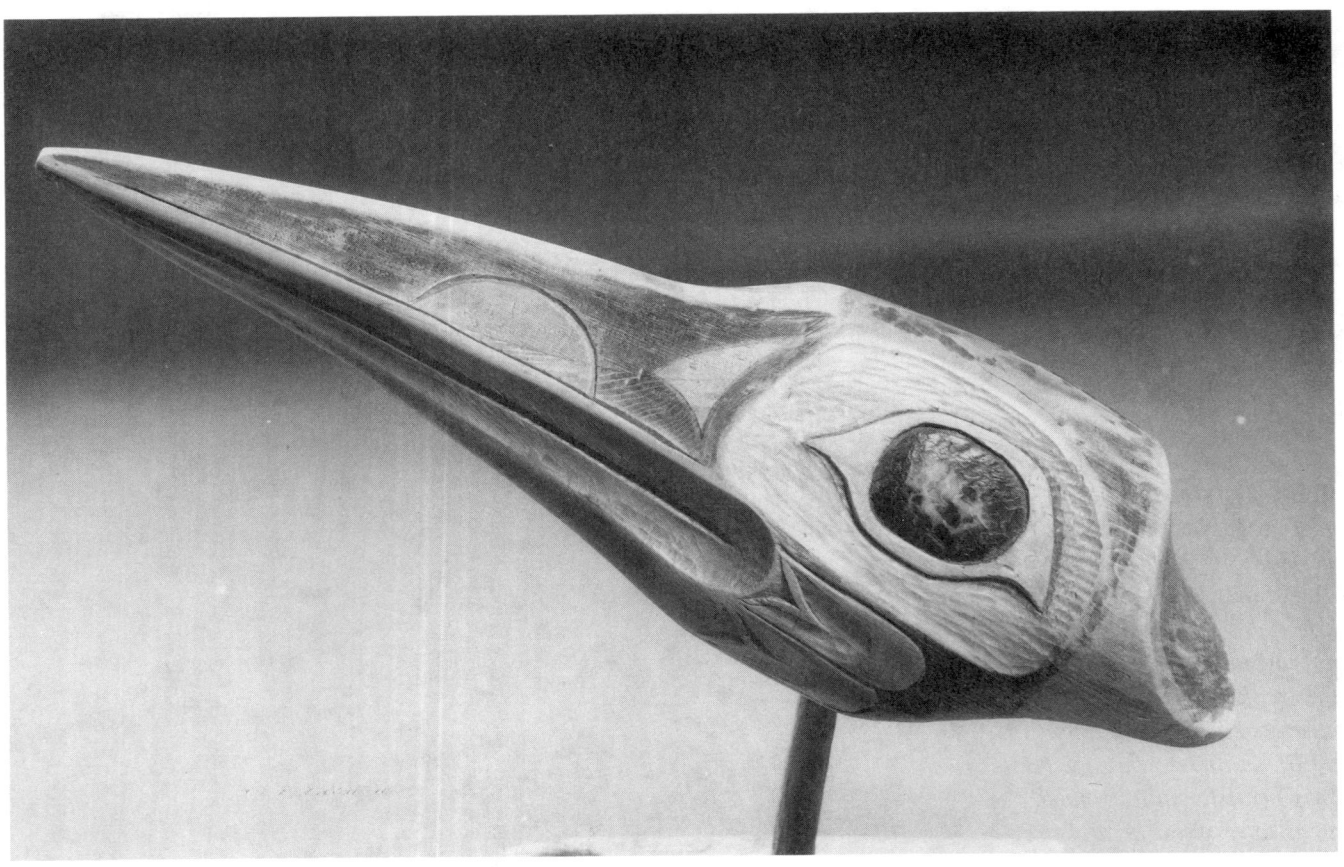

8-2   *Project picture—the finished mask.*

(20cm) wide, and 8in deep—big enough to sit on the average head like a helmet.

See how the mask is characterized by being stylistically carved in the round, and then surface-decorated. The important point to note is that the flat, almost graphic, designs and images all relate to a set way of working—almost comprising a set of rules. For example, all bird eyes are more or less the same shape. This being the case, it's most important that you do your best to stay with the imagery, as illustrated. And the same goes for the symmetry, the colors, and the overall crispness of the designs—they all relate to a traditional way of working.

CHOOSING YOUR WOOD

Of all these projects, we think that this one really needs to be worked in an easy-to-carve, dynamically grained wood—so, what better than to use the traditional cedar!

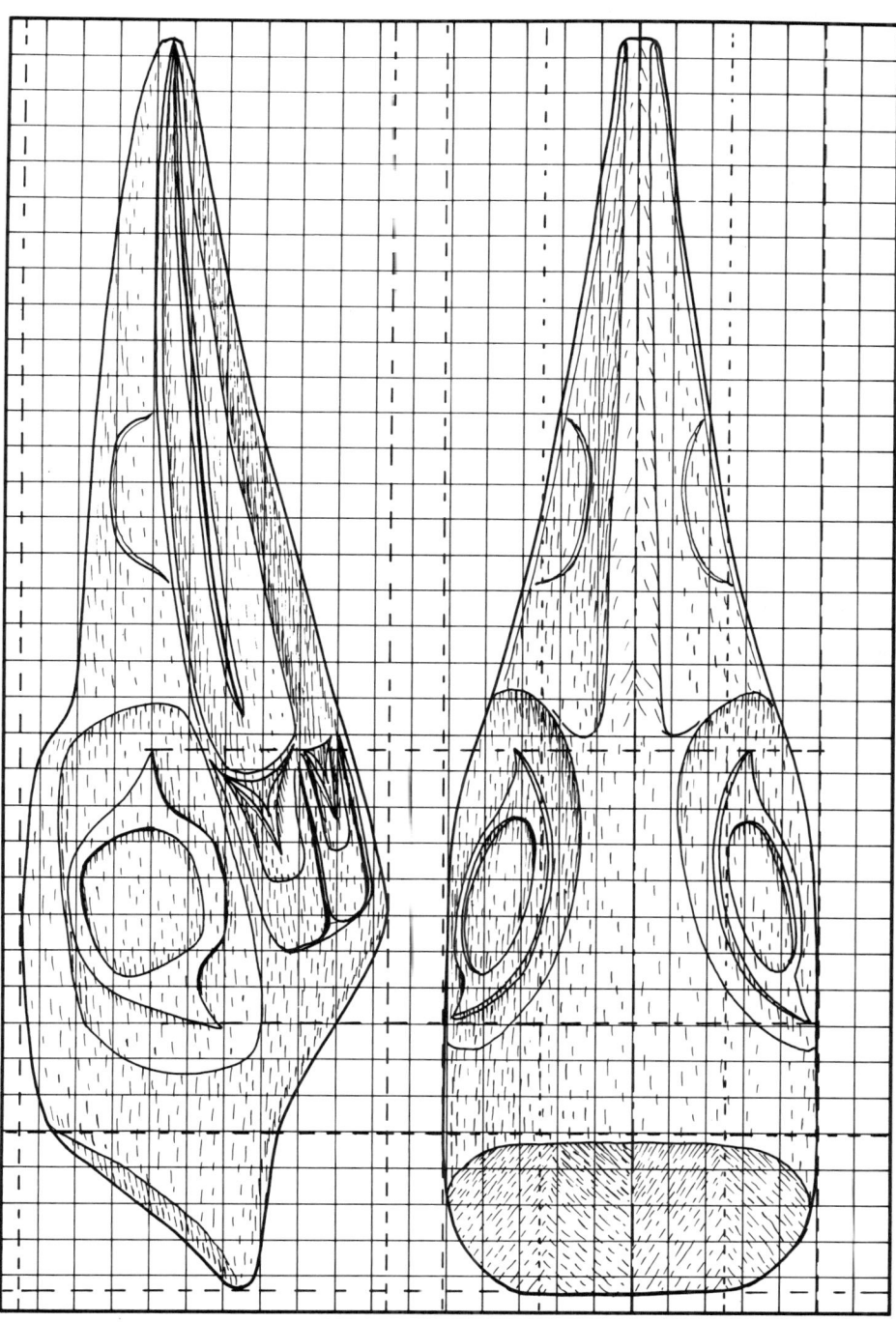

8-3 A Working drawings—side and plan views, design grid. Grid scale equals 2½ squares to one inch. Note the dotted lamination lines on the plan view.

Our wood supplier only had prepared 1in (2.5cm) thick boards in stock, so we decided to laminate the blank from four thicknesses. Laminating isn't ideal, and it does present problems when you come to figuring out the direction of the grain, but, then again, on the plus side, the laminating makes for a strong and stable structure.

Have a look at the working drawings for the length of plank needed (refer to **8-3**).

Suggested Tools

- workbench with a vise and holdfast
- medium-weight mallet of a size and shape to suit your needs
- good selection of medium-size carving gouges and chisels
- a good sharp, long-bladed knife—we use a Swedish sloyd knife with a laminated steel blade
- crooked knife (refer to **8-7**)

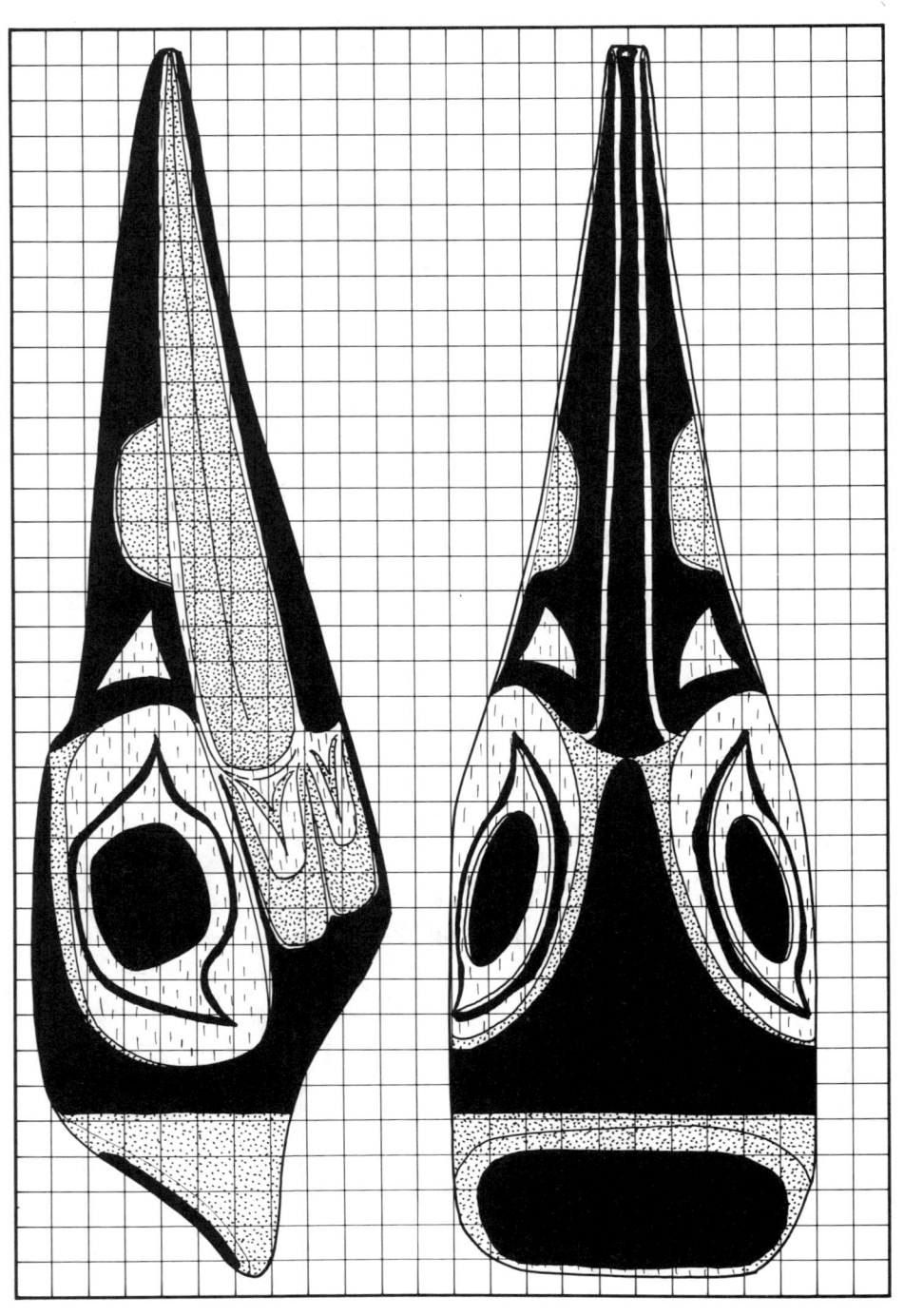

8-3 B Working drawings—side and plan views, painting grid. Grid scale equals 2½ squares to one inch.

- use of a small band saw
- pencil, ruler, and pair of dividers
- sheet each of workout and tracing paper
- fine cardboard for the template
- craft knife and cutting board
- watercolor paints in the colors brick/ochre red and black
- two soft-haired brushes—a broad- and a fine-point—as used by watercolorists
- pure beeswax furniture polish
- typical workshop tools and materials such as sandpaper, oilstone, oil, sharpening slips, Plasticine, dust mask, and PVA (polyvinyl acetate) adhesive

PROJECT MAKING STAGES

Drawing Out the Design

1. Study the inspirational drawings (refer to **8-1**), the working drawings and painting grids (refer **8-3**). This done, take a pencil and ruler, and set to work drawing the mask out to size.

2. After you have drawn out both the front and top views, plus the imagery to fit the views, then trace and press-transfer the primary motifs to the thin cardboard—that is, the long beak shape and the eye (see **8-4**). Still don't cut the image out, however, because you will almost certainly have to change it slightly.

Special Tip

If you like the notion of this project, and want to know more about Northwest Coast Indian carving, then, with due modesty, we must say that you can't do better than read our book *Carving Totem Poles & Masks*—also published by STERLING.

Making the Blank

3. When you have finalized the imagery, and made a master copy and a tracing, then use the tracing to press-transfer the total side-view profile to the best face of the plank wood. If you are using 1in (2.5cm) thick plank wood, as described, then repeat the procedure four times or as many as are needed to make up a total 4in (10cm) thickness.

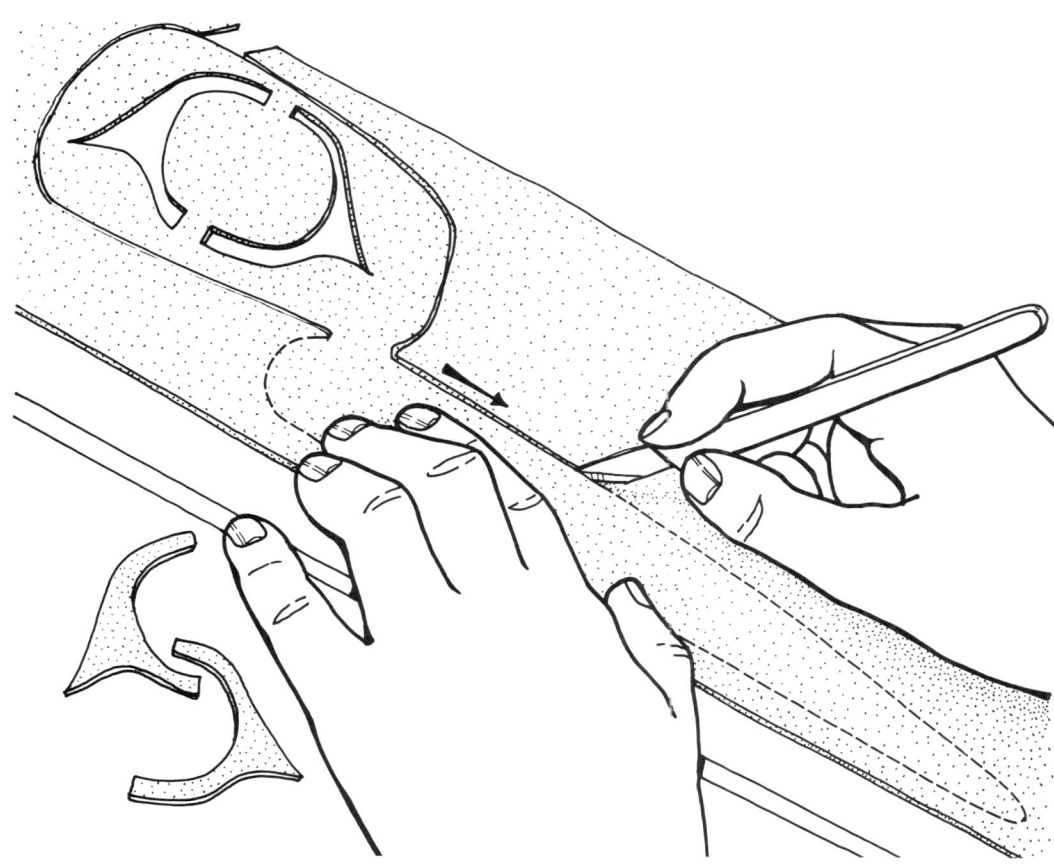

8-4 Draw the cardboard template to size. Leave the cutting out to a later stage—just in case you need to modify the lines slightly to fit your carving.

8-5 Having drawn the image out in side view, use a band saw to cut away the waste. If you don't have access to a band saw, then you might use a scroll saw to cut the individual layers before lamination.

4. Once you have achieved the correct number of profiles to make up the total 4in (10cm) thickness, carefully cut them on the band saw. Run the line of cut well to the waste side of the drawn line, so that there is a good amount of all-around waste.

5. Smear glue on the mating faces and clamp up.

6. Wait until the glue is good and dry, then rework the drawn profile line on the topmost lamination so that there is no doubting the line of cut. Then cut the image out using the band saw (see **8-5**).

7. With the "side" view cut out, press-transfer the "top" profile to the top of the workpiece, and cut this out in the same way (see **8-6**).

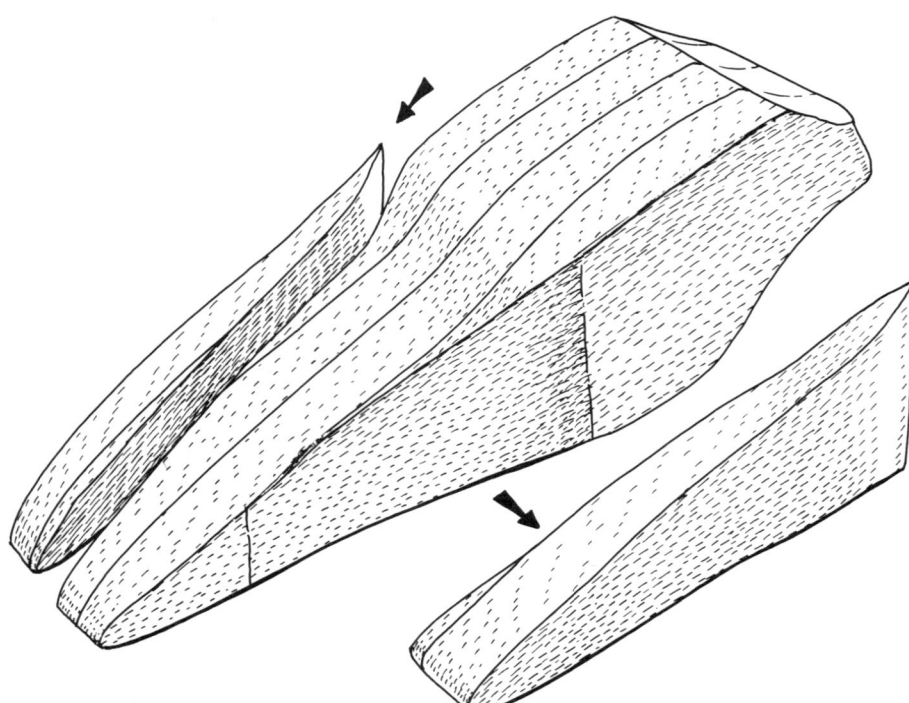

8-6 Transfer the plan view to the top of the cutout, and then cut away the waste as seen in the top view. As always, be sure to run the line of cut a little to the waste side of the drawn line.

Roughing Out

8. First refresh your eye by having another look at the project picture (refer to **8-2**) and at any other research pictures or books that you have collected along the way. Then use the two knives to round off the sawn faces and edges (see **8-7**).

9. When you have brought the main head lump to order (see **8-7**), redraw the main guidelines so that you know how you want to proceed, and whittle the beak to shape (see **8-8**).

In broad terms, the procedure is one of repeatedly shaving away the waste and redrawing the guidelines.

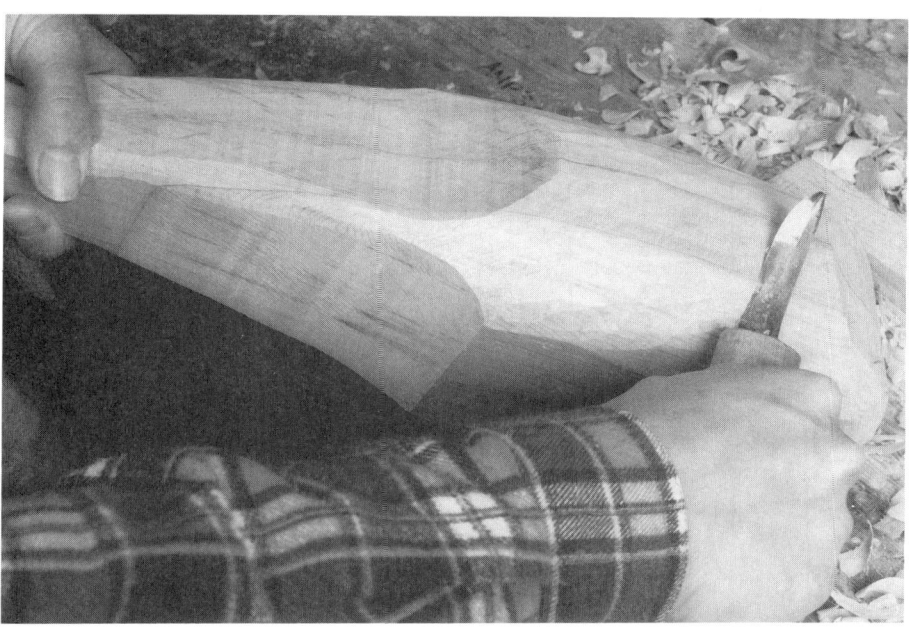

8-7 Work with a tight, controlled slicing cut—all the while being mindful about the hand that is holding the wood.

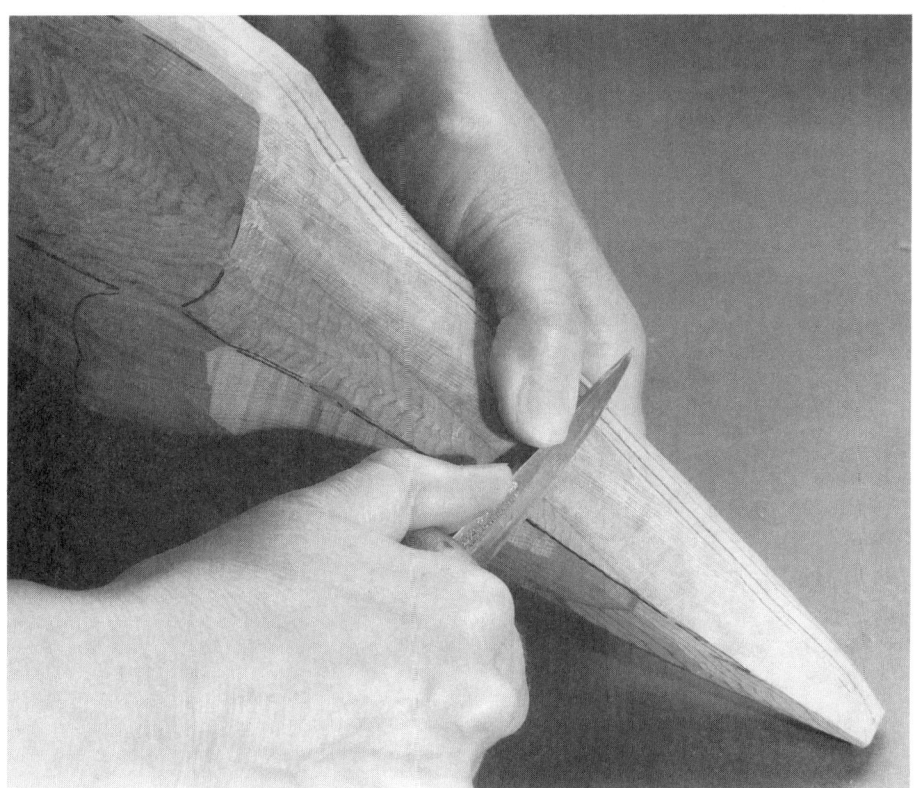

8-8 The whittling procedure is wonderfully easy—as long as the wood is smooth grained and the knife razor sharp.

10. Although, overall, the roughing-out state is pretty straightforward, the curve at the back of the head is tricky, simply because it is all end grain. We found that the best procedure was to chop out the bulk of the waste with the mallet and gouge, and then shape up with the knives (see **8-9**). Use the gouge to scoop out the whole eye socket area —not too deep, just a shallow depression.

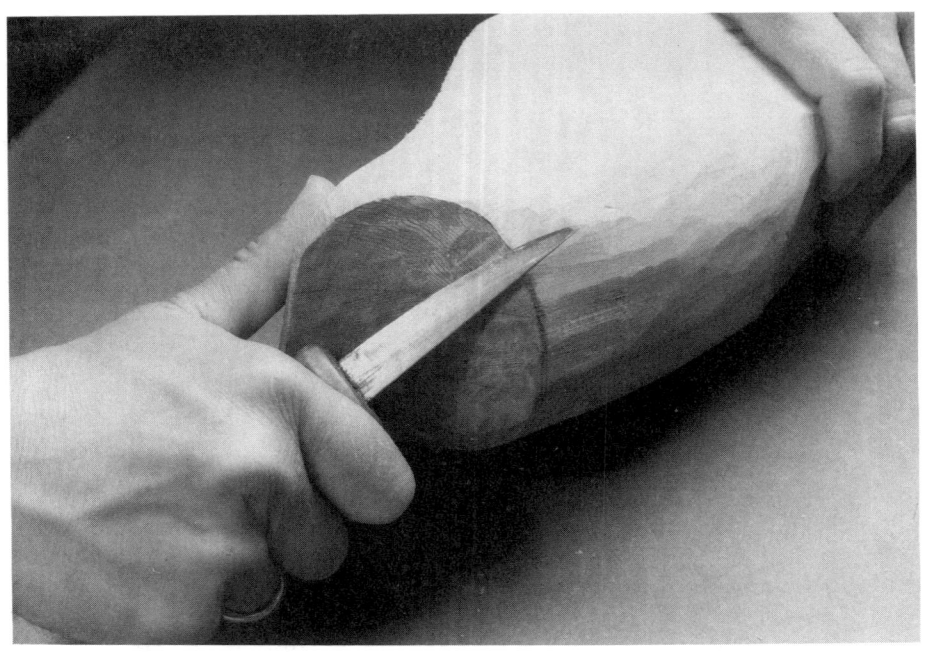

8-9 Having chopped out the bulk of the end-of-head waste with a gouge—or, perhaps, you might use a coping saw—then use the knife to shape the curve. Work with a tight, controlled, thumb-braced paring cut.

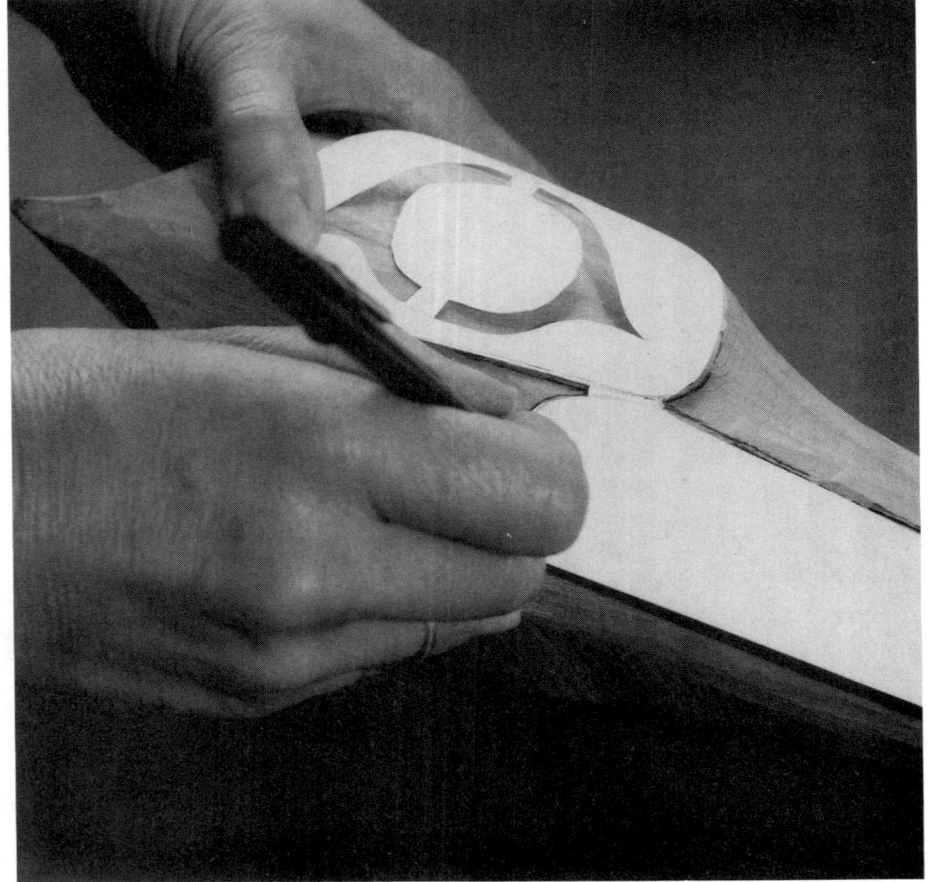

8-10 Modify and cut the cardboard template to fit the size of your carving (refer to 8-4), and then use it to establish the shape of the eyes and beak. Do your best to ensure that the drawn imagery is set equidistant from the centerline—so that the head is symmetrical.

Modeling

11. Having achieved what you consider is a good, roughed-out form, reestablish the various guidelines—the top-of-head centerline and the top-of-beak lines—then trim the cardboard templates to fit the carving (refer to **8-4**).

12. Set the templates down on the workpiece, and use them to draw the main lines that make up the design (see **8-10**). Spend time making sure that the drawn imagery is well placed and symmetrical—from one side of the head to the other.

13. With all the guidelines in place, use a shallow-sweep, straight gouge and a knife to carve the long, curve-sided trench that runs along at either side of the beak. The easiest procedure is first to establish the middle-of-beak line with the knife, then to rough out the trench shape with the gouge, and next to deepen the line with the knife, and so on, until the depth and profile are right (see **8-11** and **8-12**).

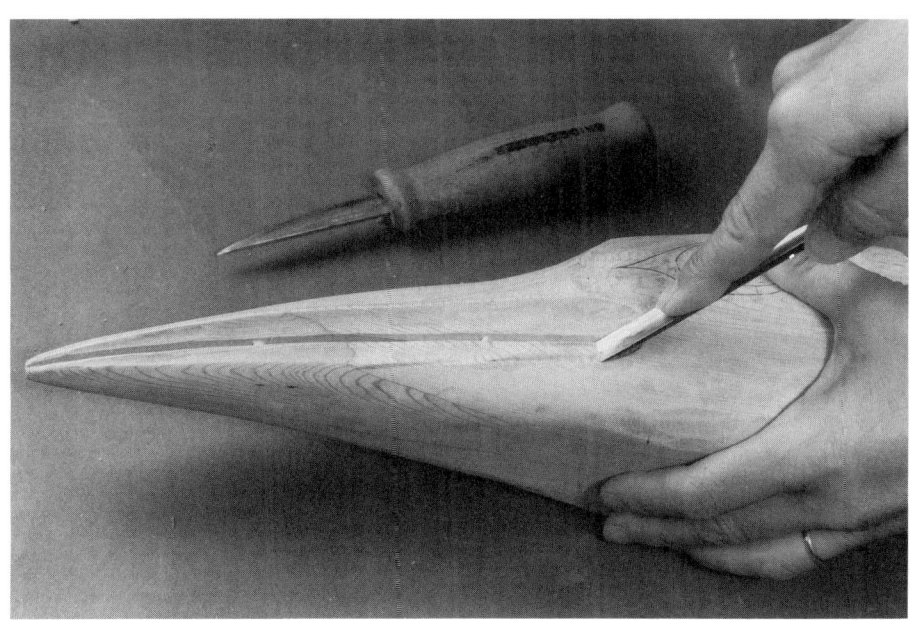

8-11 Use a straight gouge to carve out the shallow U-section trough at the side of the beak. Do this on both sides of the head. Aim to keep a crisp line at the top and bottom of the trough.

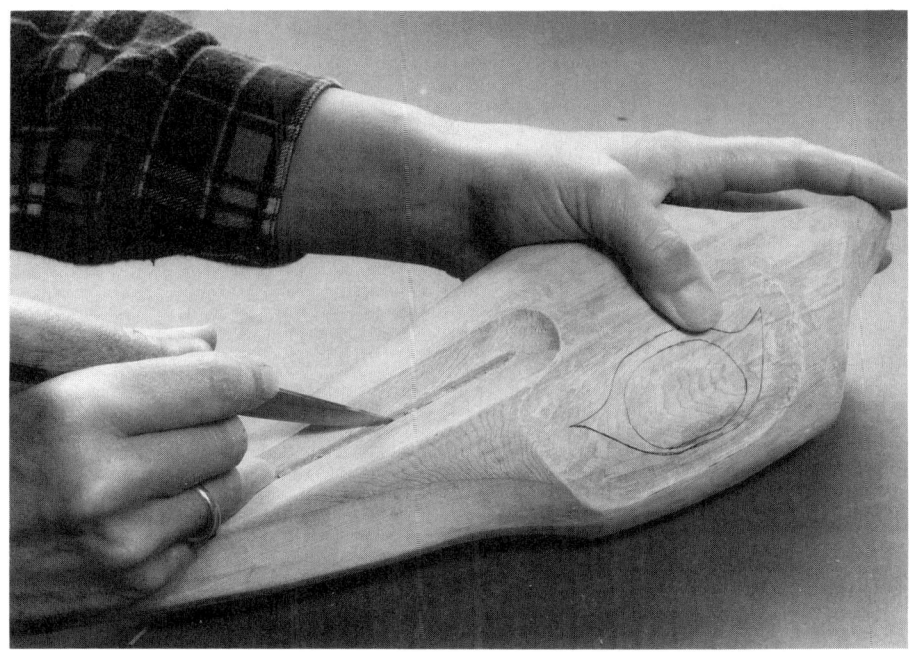

8-12 When you are happy with the depth and shape of the beak trough, set the beak line in with a V-section cut. Keep the line crisp so that it follows the line of the beak.

14. To model the eyes: after first trimming the outer edge of the eye socket to shape (see **8-13**), then crisply and cleanly define the shallow curve that runs around the socket (see **8-14**). Take the knife, and set-in the lines that make up the design of the eye.

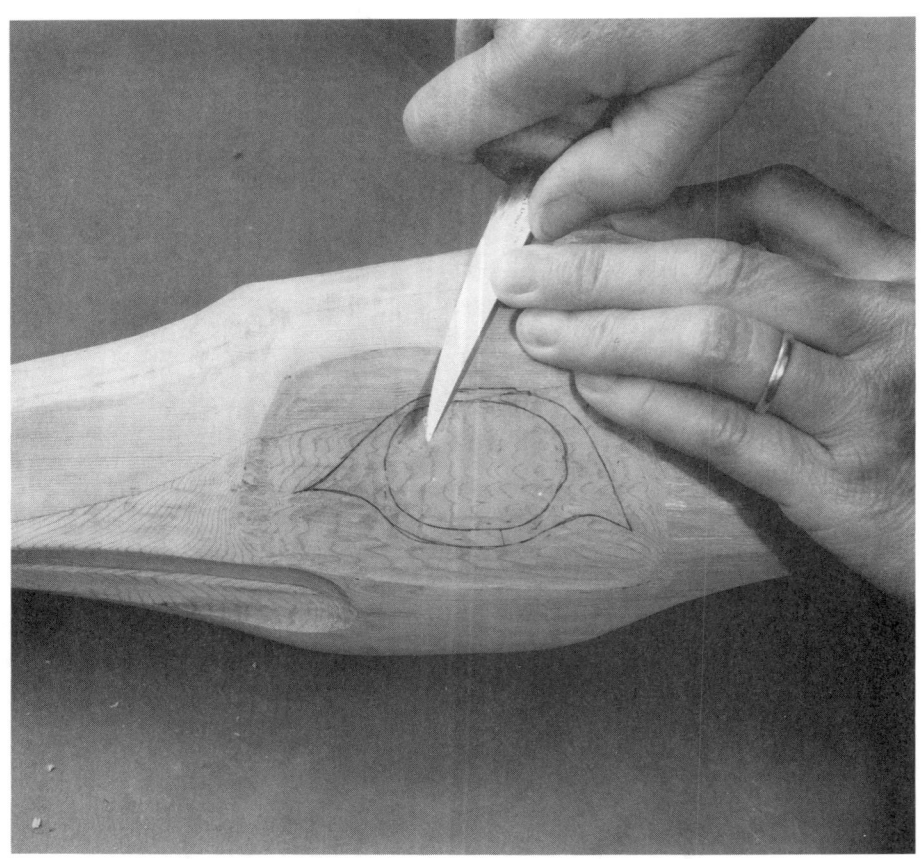

8-13   Having established the overall shape of the eye socket, and dished out the center, and drawn in the shape of the eye, use the knife to skim the socket profile to shape. If you have it right, the socket should be outlined with a slight ridge.

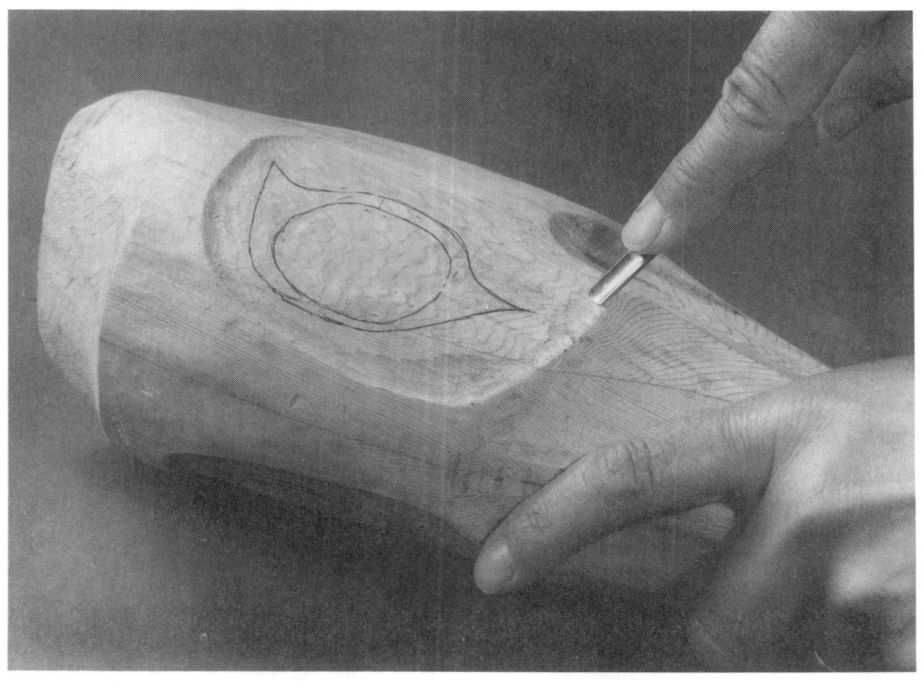

8-14   As necessary, deepen the ground to the socket side of the line so that the outline is left in relief and there is a moat around the inner-eye shape.

15. Set in the lines with stop-cuts, and then scoop out the waste so that the overall shape stands in relief (see **8-15**). Aim for having the central eye shape sliced in at the edges so that it is slightly domed.

16. When you have established the shape of the eye and the socket—for both eyes—take one or other of the small gouges and tidy up the edges and dips (see **8-16**).

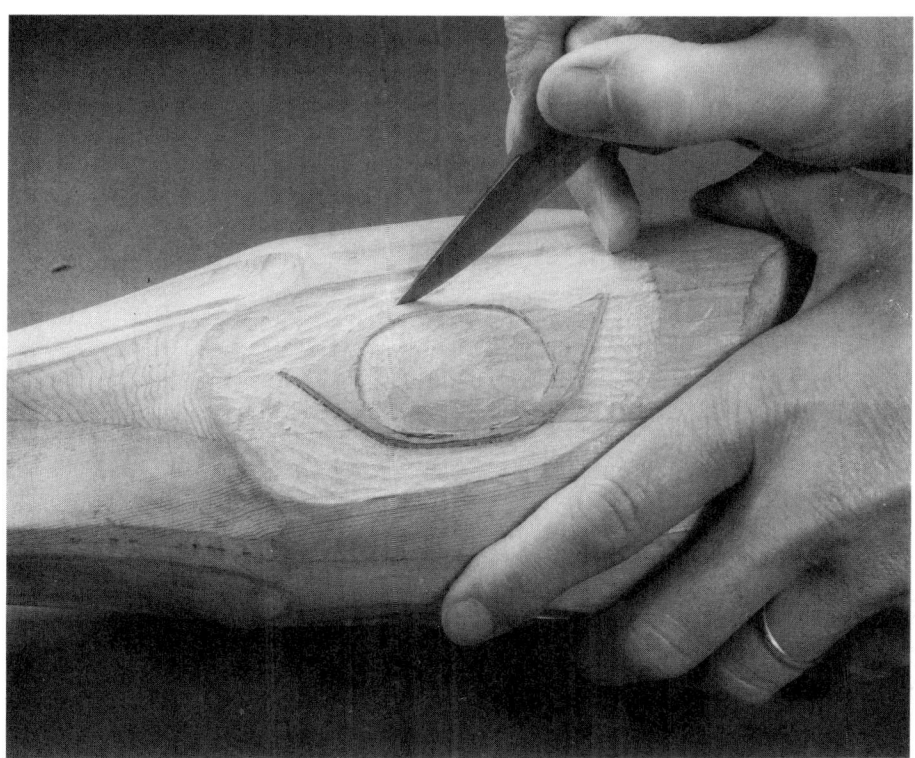

8-15 Use the knife to make a stop-cut around the eyeball and around the outer eye. Lower the waste so that the eyeball is slightly domed and so that the white of the eye stands in relief.

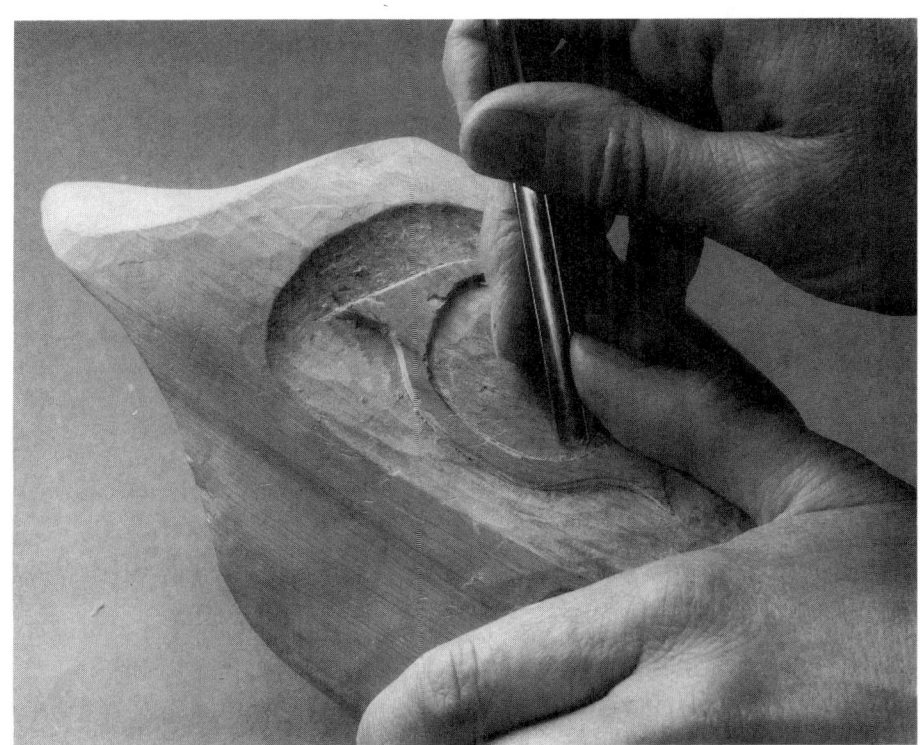

8-16 Be very wary when you are lowering the waste; be watchful that the tool doesn't overrun and do damage to the short-grained area that is left standing in relief.

17. To model the clan motif: first use the point of the knife to set in the outer and the inner V-line with stop-cuts (see **8-17**). Rework the outer line at the point where it meets the centerline, so that the total form is divided into two round-ended lobes.

18. Still working with the knife, scoop out the waste so that the V-shape stands in relief. If you have done it right, the relief V will look as if it is standing in a U-shaped dip or depression (see **8-18**).

FINISHING

19. When you are pleased with the overall carving, take a scrap of fine-grade sandpaper, and rub down all the surfaces to a smooth finish—everything needs to be smooth and crisp.

20. Mix the water paints to a thin wash, and then block in the center of the eye, the back of the head, and the underside of the beak with black, and the beak sides and raised part of the clan motif with red—all as shown in the painting grid (refer to **8-3**).

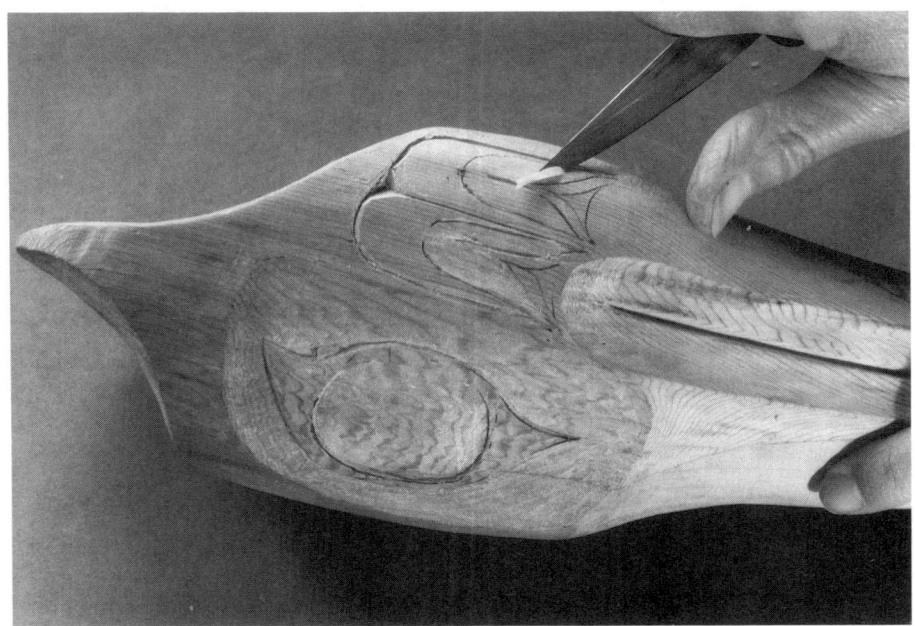

8-17 Set-in the lines of the clan motif with stop-cuts, and then skim down to the stop-cut so that the inner area is slightly dished and the stylized feather-like shape is left standing in relief.

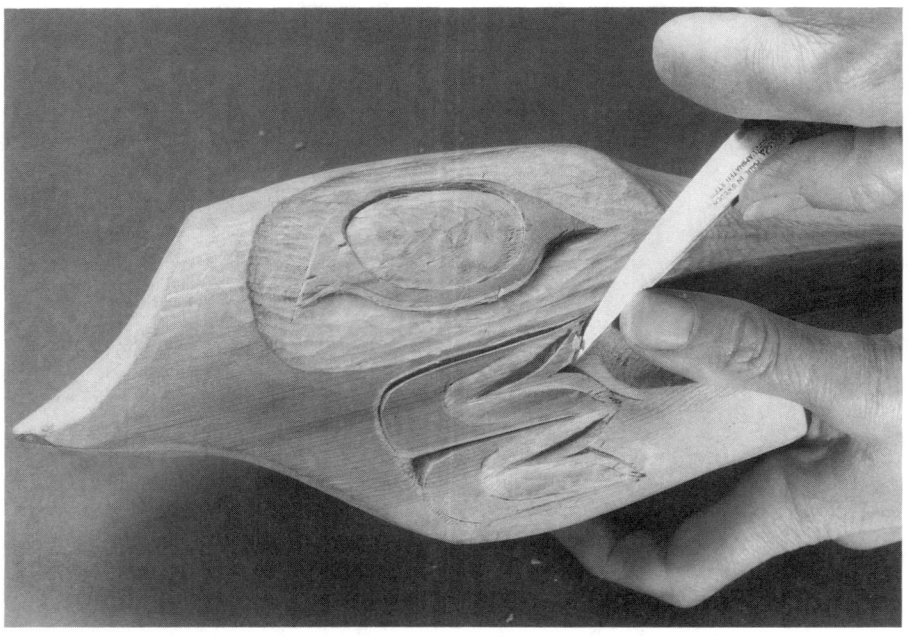

8-18 Make repeated stop-cuts, and then skim down until the lines are crisp. Be very wary that the knife doesn't slip—work with a delicate, thumb-braced action.

21. Wait until the paints are good and dry, then rework the whole carving with the fine-grade sandpaper to abrade and rub through all the painted surfaces. Aim for a finish that looks as if it is much worn and handled (see **8-2**).

22. Finally, wipe the entire carving over with the beeswax polish and burnish it to a rich, dull sheen finish.

Special Tip

Although this carving could be hung on the wall, we decided to mount it on a stand. All we did was search out a nice heavy slab of driftwood for the base, whittle a short length of plum for the stem, and then drill the base and the underside of the head and link them with the stem. If you intend to make a stand, be careful not to create a structure that is going to compete with the carving.

PROBLEM-SOLVING

- Northwest Coast carvings are characterized by being crisp, clean lined, and formalized, so it is especially important that you know your subject. Our best advice is to visit a museum and get to see some of the carvings close-up.
- To a great extent the success of this project hinges on your choice of wood and the sharpness of your tools. Our advice is to use a smooth-grained cedar, and to spend a good time honing your tools to a razor-sharp edge.
- One of the problems with this project is how to hold the workpiece! Although we tried in the first instance to use clamps, the vise, the holdfast, and so on, you will see from the photographs that we found that the best way to proceed was to hold the beak in one hand—with the head end butted up against a bench stop—and then to use the knife and the gouge in the other hand.
- If you do decide to make a full-sized carving—one that can be worn, with a hollowed-out underside—then you might consider drilling holes around the underside rim and adding streamers of fiber or rope, so that the wearer is hidden from view.

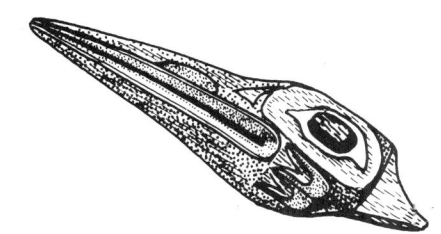

·9·
Haida Mask

Northwest Coast of North America

When the Native Americans of the Northwest Coast of North America had a difficulty—a war, disease, dispute, or whatever—they traditionally worked out the problem through a shaman intermediary.

The shaman's power had a great deal to do with his dramatic showmanship and his use of sleight-of-hand tricks. In the case of certain fevers, the shaman would play out a masked drama that involved him in pleading with the spirits for the

9-1 Inspirational drawings. (Top left) Kwakiutl portrait mask—9in (23cm) high—made about 1850. (Top right) Kwakiutl mask—10¾in (27cm) high—made about 1850. (Middle left) Tlingit shaman's mask—7⅝in (19.5cm) high—made about 1820. (Middle right) Kwakiutl Bokwus or wild-spirit-of-the-woods mask. (Bottom left) Kwakiutl(?) mask—made about 1850.

tribal member's lost soul. Like an actor, or, perhaps, we might say a modern psychotherapist, the shaman would work through a carefully staged performance.

Imagine a firelit room with a sickbed and friends and relatives gathered around. Backstage the shaman is beating a drum, singing, and tapping his rattle and staff. The chanting gets louder and louder, and then suddenly there is total silence. With a flurry of curtains, the shaman enters the room—he is wearing a masked headdress of feathers, bones, and amulets, and he is carrying a "soul-catcher" tube. The masked figure goes into a trance and travels into the other world—a dangerous supernatural world where troubled spirits and demons are on the loose. The shaman does battle, and successfully entices the lost soul into the tube. Finally, the shaman comes out of his trance, blows the captured soul back into the patient, and dramatically makes an exit.

THOUGHTS ON SHAPE, FORM & TECHNIQUE

Have a look at the working drawings (see **9-3**) and see how, at a grid scale of four squares to one inch, the mask measures about 9in (23cm) from crown to the tip of the chin, about 8in (20cm) wide, and 4in (10cm) thick from back to front. Note how the form of the mask—the clean-cut, crisply worked eyes, eyebrows and mouth—is characteristic of the mid- to late nineteenth century Haida Indian style. See, also, how the features are naturalistic interpretations of life, which, while somewhat stylized, in general terms make this a portrait mask.

Our best advice, if you really want to get into the mood of this project, is to study our inspirational drawings (see **9-1**), and visit a museum and spend time studying Northwest Coast portrait masks.

9-2 *Project pictures—the finished mask, front and side views.*

CHOOSING YOUR WOOD

Keeping in mind that the detailing on portrait masks needs to be crisp and tight, we decided to make it up from three layers of lime/linden. We appreciate that lime/linden isn't a traditional Northwest Coast wood, but, then again, as the mask is to be painted, we felt that it didn't matter too much anyway.

Our timber supplier only had prepared 1 3/8 in (35mm) thick boards in stock, so that is what we used to laminate the blank.

Special Tip

As you may already have gathered, a woodcarver's life has to do with being able to make the most of the wood that comes to hand. Building a blank up from laminated pieces is a bit of a nuisance, but, then again, the advantage is that the narrow sections can be worked easily on the band saw, or even on a large scroll saw.

Suggested Tools

- workbench with a vise and holdfast
- medium-weight mallet of a size and shape to suit your needs
- good selection of medium-sized carving gouges and chisels
- a good sharp, long-bladed knife—we use a Swedish sloyd knife with a laminated steel blade
- a crooked knife
- use of a small band saw
- pencil, ruler, and pair of dividers
- one sheet each of workout and tracing paper
- watercolor paints in the colors brick/ochre red, black, green-blue, and umber
- two soft-haired brushes—a broad- and a fine-point—as used by watercolorists
- pure beeswax furniture polish
- typical workshop tools and materials such as sandpaper, oilstone, oil, sharpening slips, Plasticine, dust mask, and PVA (polyvinyl acetate) adhesive

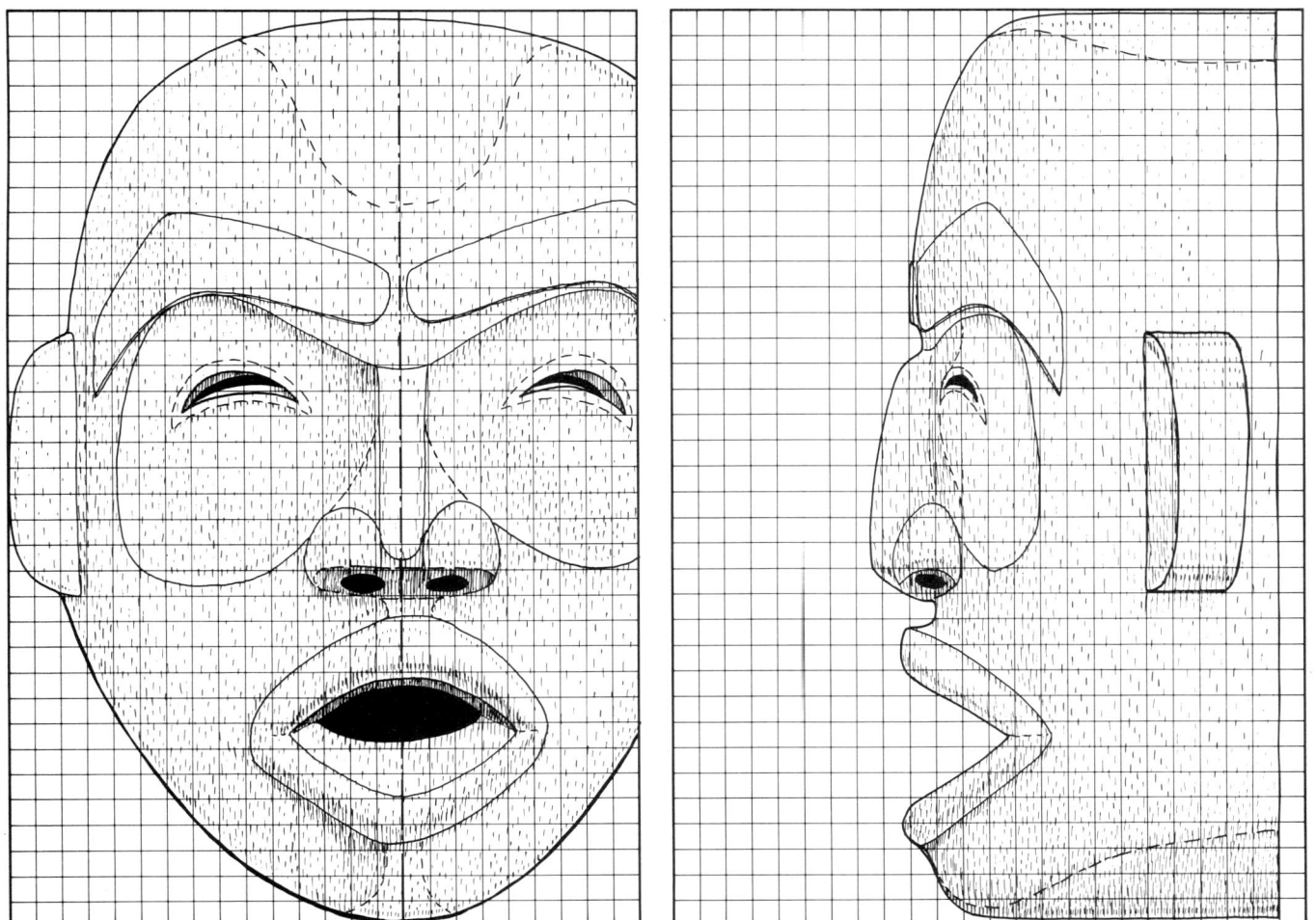

9-3 Working drawings—front and side views. The grid scale is four squares to one inch.

PROJECT MAKING STAGES
Drawing Out the Design

1. Start by having a good long look at the project pictures (see **9-2**), the working drawings (see **9-3**), and the painting grids (see **9-4**). When you have a clear picture in mind of how the project needs to be worked, take a pencil and ruler, and draw the mask out to size. Draw a front and side view.

2. Once you are happy with the imagery, make clear tracings, and put the master copies safely to one side.

Making the Blank

3. Take your pieces of prepared wood—our wood is 1⅜in (35mm) thick—stack them together so that you have a total thickness of slightly more than 4in (10cm), and generally spend time making sure that the stacking order uses the wood to best advantage.

4. When you have achieved what you consider is a good arrangement, pencil-label the stack—so that you know what goes where—then smear a generous amount of PVA glue on mating faces, and clamp the pieces together.

5. Having waited for the glue to dry, carefully pencil-press-transfer the traced imagery to the best face of the stack. Rework the pressed lines with a soft-tipped felt pen, so that there is no doubting the position of the lines that make up the design.

6. Last, take the wood to the band saw and cut out the total profile shape. Try, in this instance, to cut as close as you can to the waste side of the drawn line (see **9-5**)

Roughing Out

7. Have a good long look at your master drawings, and at any other reference material that you have collected along the way. Then take a

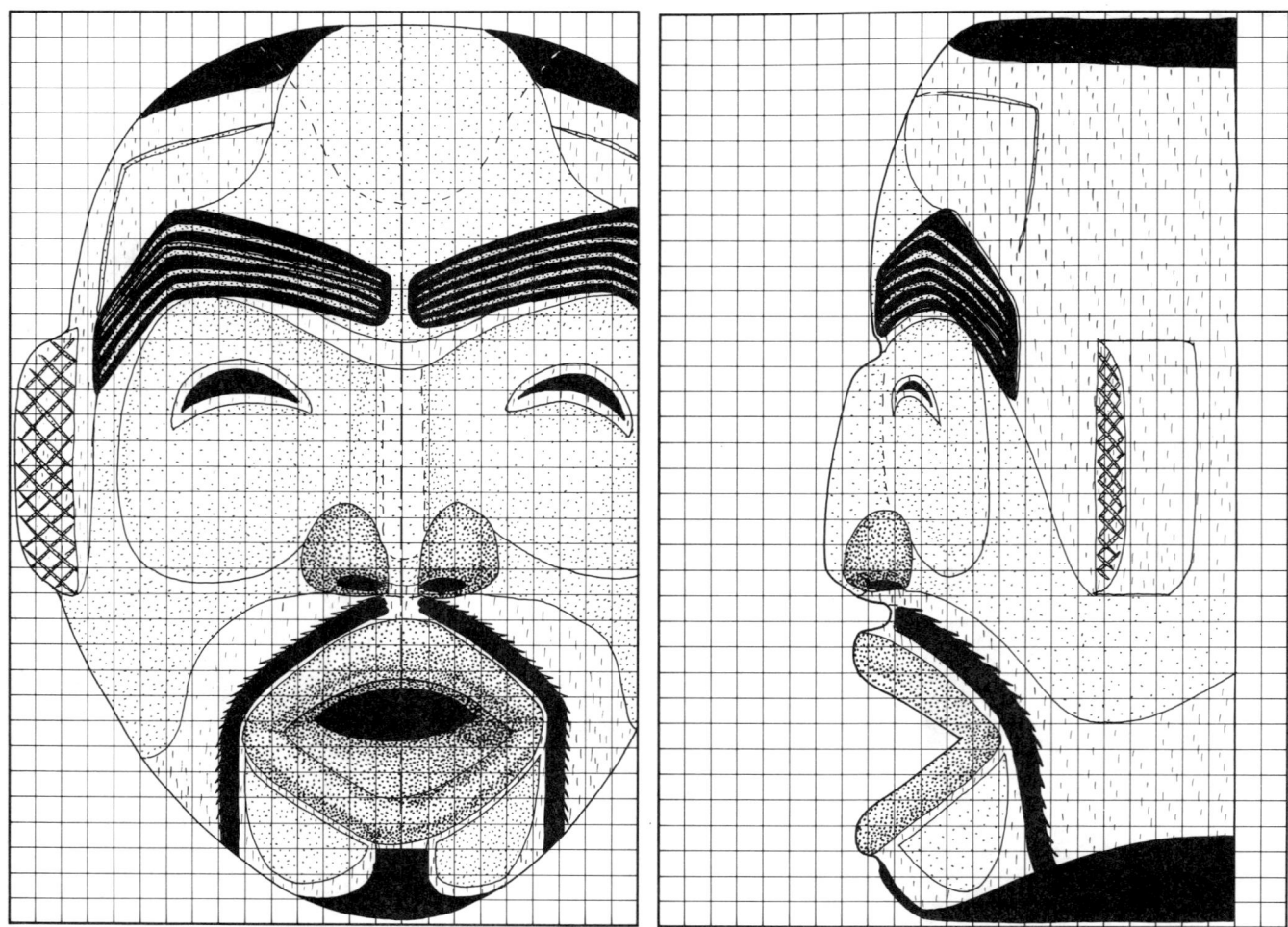

9-4 *Painting grid—front and side views. Grid scale equals four squares to one inch.*

medium-sized straight gouge, and lower the whole area around the nose and the mouth. Cut down to a depth of about ¼in (6mm).

8. Lower the waste at the side edges of the profile so that the side of the mask curves down towards the level of the ears. Aim, at this stage, to lower the ears by about 1⅜in (35mm) (see **9-6**). Continue this procedure at the chin and side cheeks (see **9-7**).

9. When you have achieved the overall curve of the front of the mask, run a centerline down the nose and the mouth, and then set to work cutting away the sides of the mouth so that the lips follow the curve of the face (see **9-8**). Repeat this lowering of the side face and the lips, until the sides of the face fall away from the nose—to the extent that the nose stands up in high relief.

Special Tip

Though the roughing out is generally rather straightforward, the end grain at the crown and the chin tends to be relatively hard going. The best procedure is to cut the end grain straight down with the mallet and gouge, and to settle for a textured finish (refer to **9-2**).

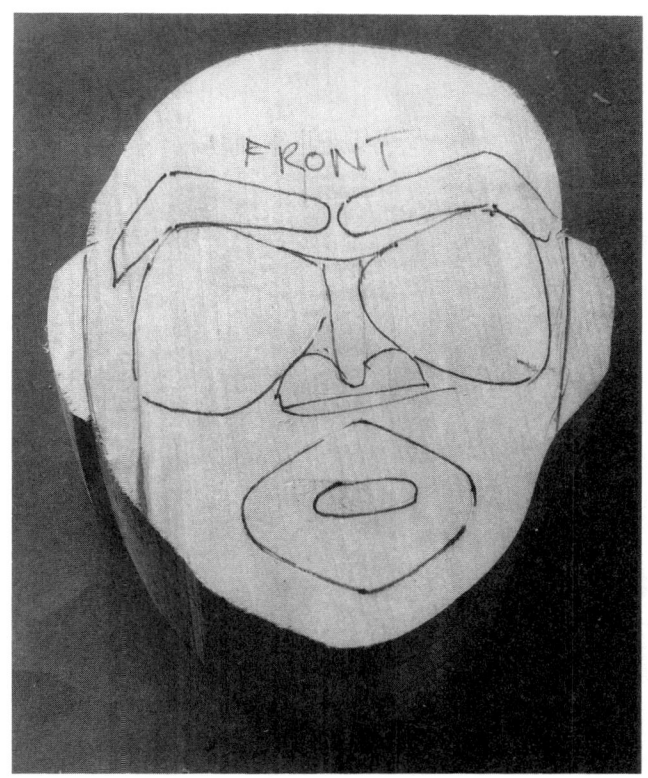

9-5 Cut out the profile on the band saw, and double-check that all the lines are accurately and clearly established.

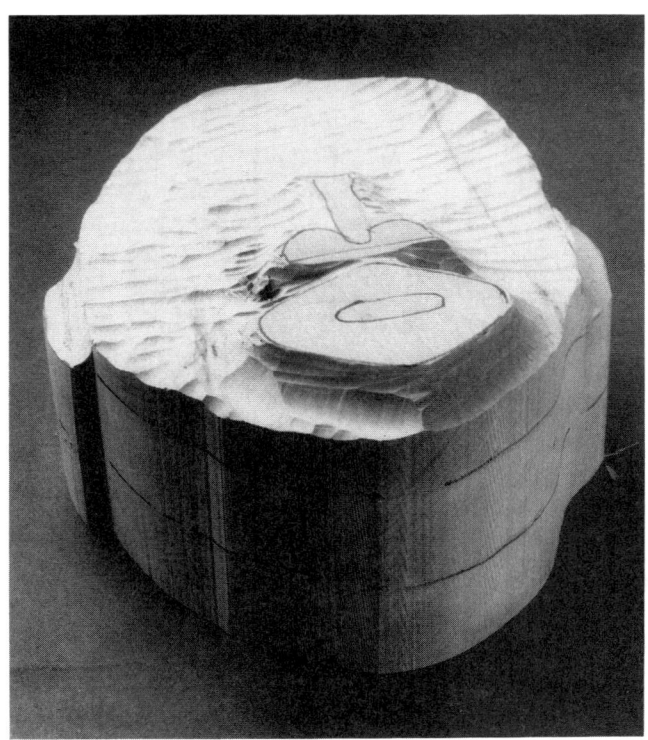

9-6 Lower the waste wood so that the nose and mount details stand in relief.

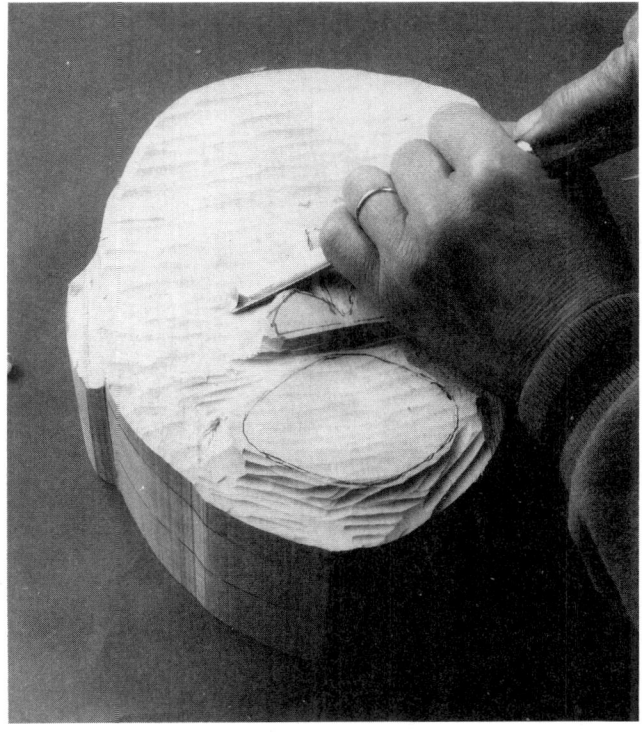

9-7 Round over the sides of the face, and systematically reduce the wood from around the profile.

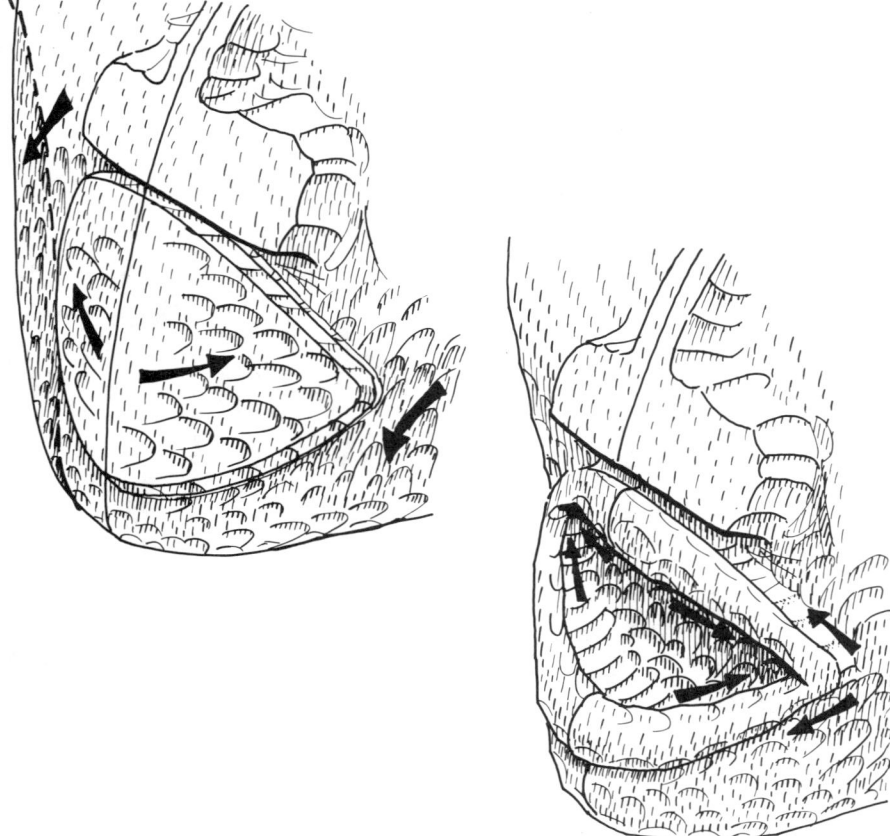

9-8   Draw in a centerline, and roughly sketch in the eye socket. Then round over the lips so that they fall down at the sides to follow the curve of the face. (Left) Draw in the center guideline—through the nose and mouth—and reduce the waste so that the mouth follows the curve of the face. The arrows indicate the best approach to the run of the grain. (Right) Hollow out the mouth cavity, and shape the lips so that they are curved in cross section and so that they run in a smooth curve through the face. Note that each quarter of the mouth—the lips, top left, top right, bottom left, and bottom right—needs to be approached from a different direction and angle. See the photo above.

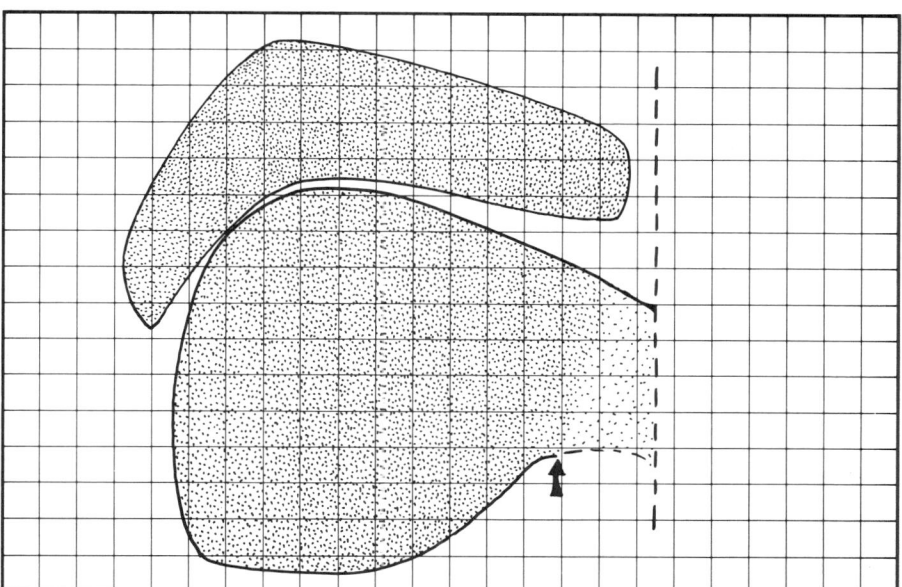

9-9 Template guide—the grid scale is four squares to one inch. Note the centerline and the arrow marking the point where the eye socket meets the nostril.

Modeling

10. Rough out the whole front of the face so that the surfaces curve and undulate down from the nose centerline; then use the tracings to make paper templates of the eye sockets and eyebrows (see **9-9**).

11. Set the templates down on the front of the mask, and draw in the shape and position of the eye sockets and brows.

12. With all the guidelines in place, use a shallow-sweep, straight gouge and a knife to lower the area around the brows, and to dish and lower the eye sockets. Aim for crisp sharp-edged brows, and dished or moated sockets (see **9-10**).

13. To model the mouth: after you have lowered the sides of the mouth—so that they fall back sharply from the centerline—lower the waste within the lips to a depth of about 1in (2.5cm).

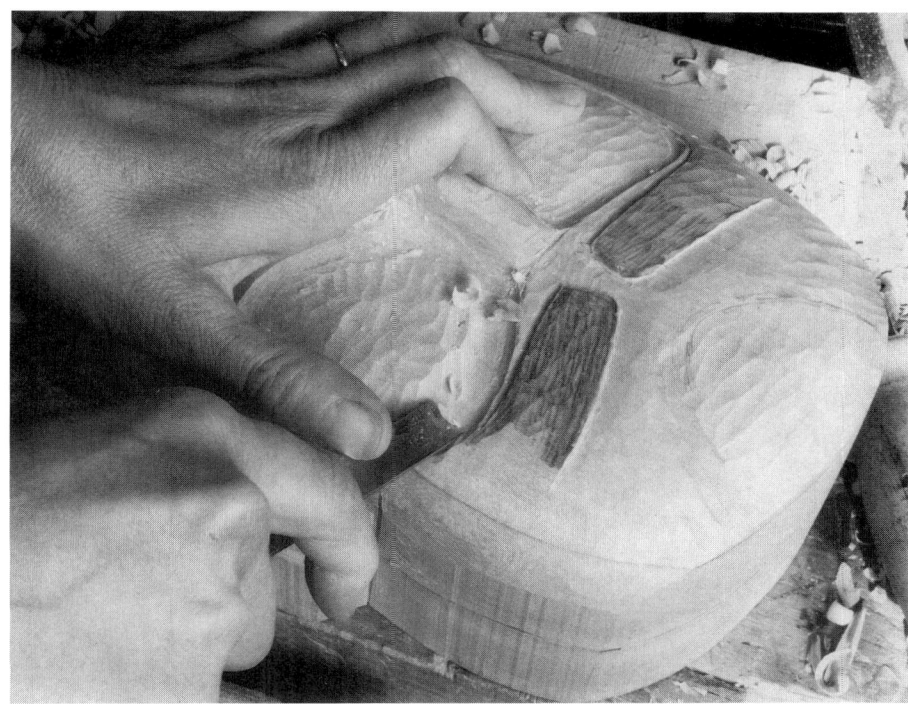

9-10 Create a moated area around each eye—making controlled cuts using your thumb as a lever.

14. Use a narrow U-section gouge to lower the area around the lips and under the nose so that the edge-of-lip line runs down in a "sensitive" curve to the face (see **9-11**).

15. With the curve of the mouth nicely established, move to the drill press, and use the biggest Forstner bit to sink a hole at the back of the mask. Run the drilled hole through to meet your carved hole. Model the surface between the underside of the mouth and the chin and the top of the mouth and the eye sockets so that the stylized beard is marked out by the line of a ridge and so that there is a smooth, curved fall-away from the sides of the nostrils to the cheeks and the sides of the outer profile (see **9-12**).

16. To model the nose: after studying the nose in detail, and seeing how it is, in essence, made up from three forms—a round-sided ridge, with two nut-like nostril bulges—take the knife and round over the "nuts" and the end of the central ridge (see **9-13** top). Be very wary when you come to carve the short-grain areas at the sides of the nostrils that you don't catch and split the grain.

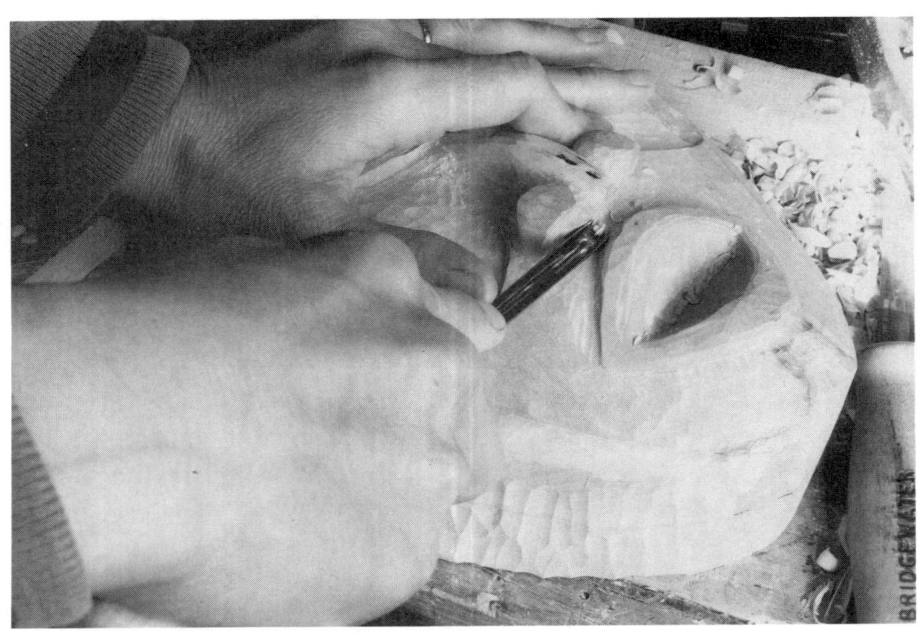

9-11 Use the small U-section gouge to lower the area around the lips and under the nose.

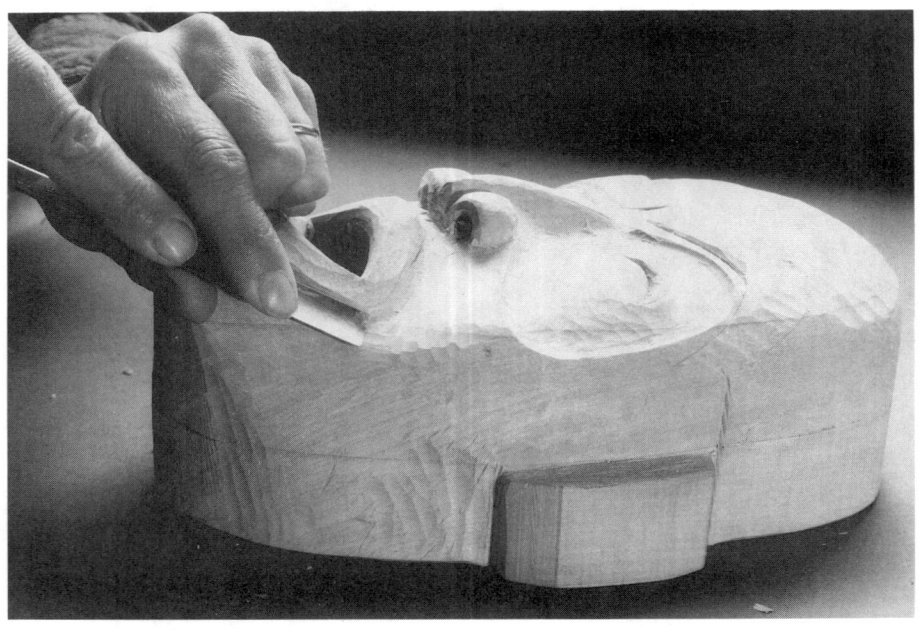

9-12 Continue to reduce the wood and model the smooth curves—from the sides of the nostrils to the cheeks.

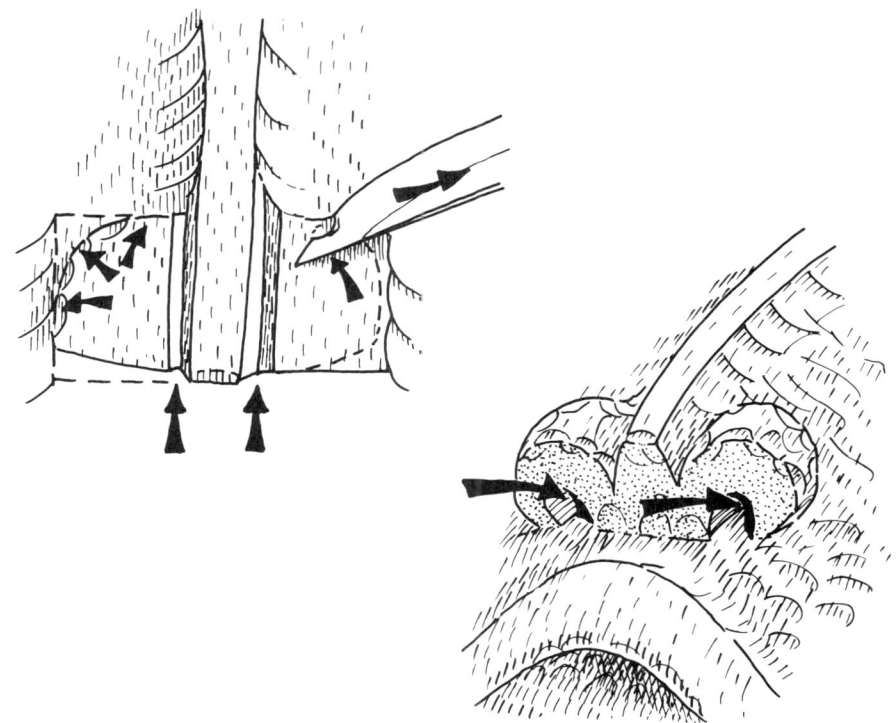

9-13   (Top) Modeling the nose. Cut a V-section trench at either side of the nose—then, working with a small, tightly controlled cut, pare and round over the nostrils.

Special Tip

If you are not too happy using a knife to skim and round over the sensitive end-grain areas on each nostril, you might prefer using a scrap of fine-grade sandpaper.

17. When the end of the nose ridge and the nostril bulges are rounded, take a small spoon gouge and set to work scooping out the nostril holes. This stage isn't easy, so go at it very slowly, all the while being exceedingly careful not to lever against the sides of the nostril holes (see **9-13** bottom). Aim for a wood thickness at the rim of the nostril hole of about 1/8in (3mm).

18. To model the eyes and the brows: first use the paper templates to establish the position of the eye holes—the two crescents—and the arched brows.

19. The procedure for cutting the eye holes is beautifully straightforward; all you do is repeatedly pare out the shape of the outline to make a little sharp-bottomed hollow—like the inside of a small bent rowboat.

20. Once you have fixed the basic shape and position of the eyebrows at the roughing-out stage, use the point of the knife to clean up the stepped outlines. Aim for a step-down from the surface of the brow to the forehead of about 1/16in (1.5mm) (see **9-14**).

9-14   Clean up the edges and creases with the knife. Press down on the back of the blade with your index finger to increase the leverage.

FINISHING

21. After you have modeled the lips, nostrils, nose ridge, eyes, brows, ears, and all the other features and details that make up the design, use the gouge (see **9-15**), knife, and sandpaper to fine-tune the whole surface. Aim for clearly stated crisp-edged lines and smooth ridges, peaks, and hollows. Use a small gouge to scoop-texture the short-grained areas at the chin and forehead.

22. When you are happy with the imagery and finish, take a scrap of fine-grade sandpaper, and rub down all the rounded surfaces to a smooth finish.

23. Wipe away the dust and move to the area set aside for painting. Mix the water paints to a non-runny consistency, and paint the lips and nostrils red, the beard and brows black, the areas in and around the eyes, beard, and forehead blue, and the grid markings and lines on the ears and brows umber (refer to **9-4**).

24. Wait until the paints are good and dry, then rub down all the surfaces to remove all the rough areas and nibs of grain.

25. Finally, wipe the whole carving over with the beeswax polish, and burnish it to a rich, dull-sheen finish.

Special Tip

Although this carving could be hollowed out at the back (see *Hollowing* in the ''Tools, Techniques & Materials—A–Z Guides'') and as we decided to display this mask on the wall, we opted instead simply to sink two large-diameter drilled holes at the back—one for wall mounting and the other for the mouth.

PROBLEM-SOLVING

- As with all of the projects, if you really want to get in tune with the culture that made the mask, then visit a museum and get to see the masks firsthand.

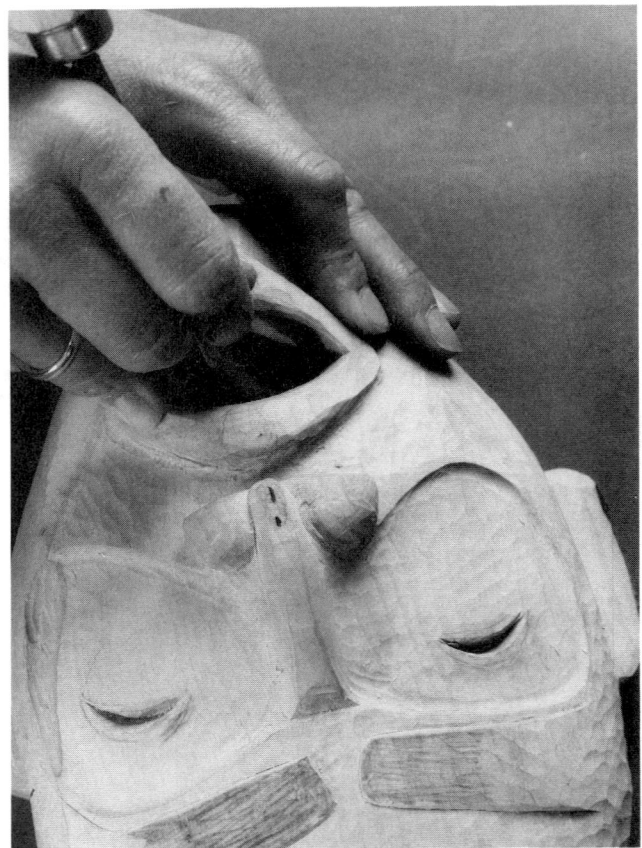

9-15 Use a small gouge—in a single-handed pickling hold—to scoop out the waste from inside the mouth cavity.

- Since the success of this project hinges on the modeled details being crisp and cleanly worked, a lot depends on your tools and the choice of wood. The wood needs to be smooth grained and easy to work, and the tools need to be sharp.
- If you have doubts about your choice of wood, have a tryout on a small scrap to see how it works.
- If you can't quite figure out how such and such a detail looks in the round, then it's best to make a maquette from modeling clay, Plasticine, or even soap.

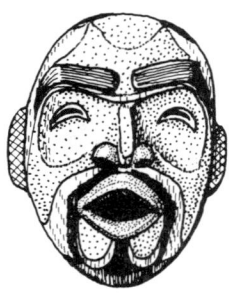

·10·
Tsimshian Mask

Northwest Coast of North America

The traditional ceremonial life of the native Indians living on the Northwest Coast of North America was, in many ways, symbolized by the wearing of masks (see **10-1**). Masks were worn primarily at the potlatch feasts—a time when presents were offered, and various society status claims and crest entitlements were requested, confirmed, and proven. At this time, children were named, mar-

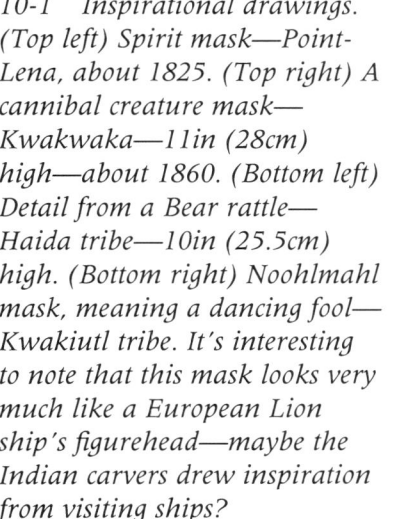

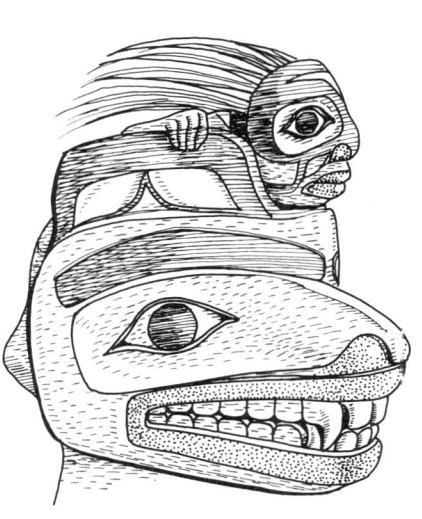

10-1 Inspirational drawings. (Top left) Spirit mask—Point-Lena, about 1825. (Top right) A cannibal creature mask—Kwakwaka—11in (28cm) high—about 1860. (Bottom left) Detail from a Bear rattle—Haida tribe—10in (25.5cm) high. (Bottom right) Noohlmahl mask, meaning a dancing fool—Kwakiutl tribe. It's interesting to note that this mask looks very much like a European Lion ship's figurehead—maybe the Indian carvers drew inspiration from visiting ships?

riages and deaths were celebrated, and all the other tribal, clan, and family matters were set right.

Masks were all part and parcel of the concept of clan crests and family symbols, the individual mask types representing mythical creatures that were considered to be spirit helpers. The various families, clans, and societies donned specific masks—such as the beaver mask (see **10-2**)—and then performed night-long dance dramas, during which they acquired status and reenacted the various myths and legends that related to rank and clan.

THOUGHTS ON SHAPE, FORM & TECHNIQUE

Have a look at the working drawings (see **10-3**) and see how, at a grid scale of three squares to one inch, the mask measures about 10in (25.5cm) from the top of the ears down to the underside of the chin, about 8½in (21.5cm) wide, and 6in (15cm) thick from the flat back through to the front of the nose.

Consider how this mask type is characteristic, in that the features are expressed in semi-human form with the overall human face being stamped as "beaver" by the instantly recognizable beaver teeth. Compare this mask with the other two Northwest Coast types (see Projects 8 and 9), and note how it also has clean-cut, crisply stylized eyes, eyebrows, and nostrils—in more or less the same shape and design.

When we began to search out wood for this particular mask, we faced a heap of problems, not the least being that since the mask was 6in (15cm) from front to back, it needed to be carved from a smooth, easy-to-carve wood, and our supply of

10-2 Project picture—the finished mask.

wood was limited to bits and pieces. We solved this problem by planing many little pieces of lime/linden to the same size and thickness, then planing selected edges and laminating a large block. If you look over all of the project photographs, you will see that, generally speaking, this method works pretty well. There are one or two cracks and joins that get in the way at the early stages, but, then again, they aren't very important, because they either get to be cut away in the waste or covered in paint.

Special Tip

Our problem with finding suitable wood points to the comforting fact that even the most frustrated carver—not much money, not many tools, and working in a small space—can manage by using pieces of wood that many suppliers are glad to give away!

CHOOSING YOUR WOOD

Since the detailing on this mask needs to be crisp and tight, we decided to go for lime/linden. It's a beautiful wood—creamy white, easy to carve, sustainable, easy to paint, and relatively inexpensive—just perfect for this project. You could, however, go just as well for a traditional wood like red cedar, or even some species of straight-grained, easy-to-carve pine.

The most important question to ask yourself is: Will the bit of wood that you are turning over in your hands take the depth of carving without splitting? Keep in mind that the areas around the beaver's nose, nostrils, and mouth are difficult to carve, so you will need to use a wood that is hard and smooth grained.

If you have any doubts, then it's best to go for maximum control by building the blank up from several layers—as we did.

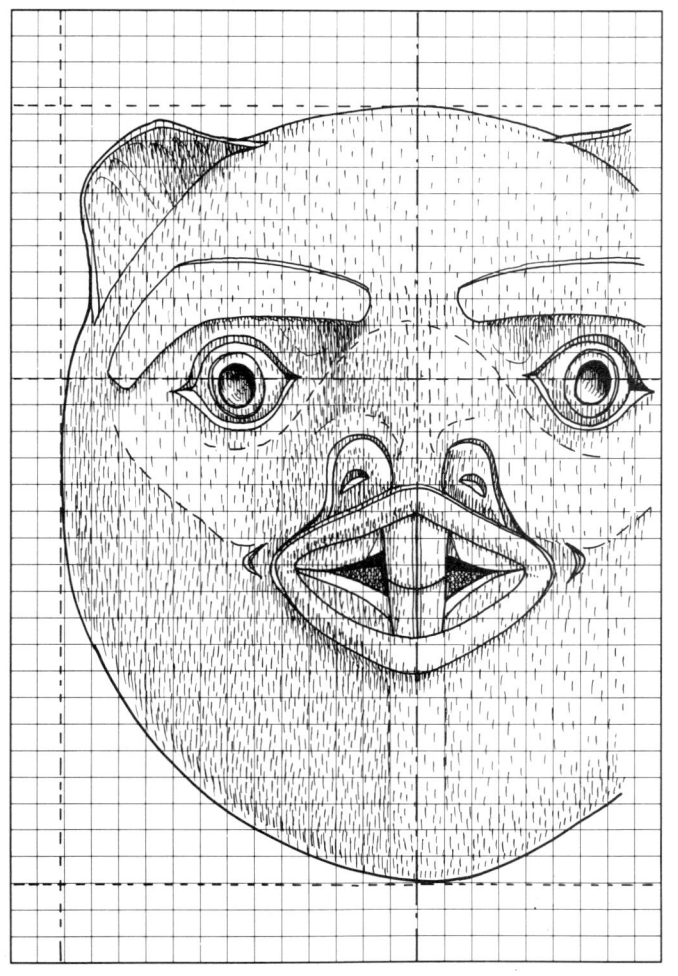 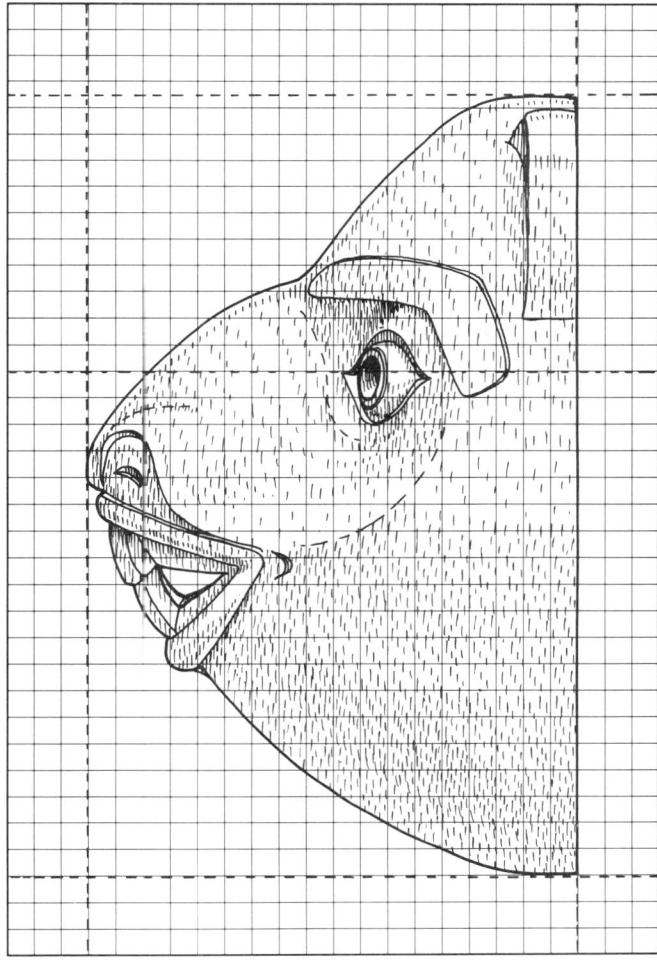

10-3   Working drawings—front and side views. The grid scale is three squares to one inch.

Special Tip

We feel it bears repeating that a woodcarver's life has to do with being able to make the most of the wood that comes to hand. Building up a blank from lots of small pieces is certainly a bit of a chore, and in many ways it is much more fun to carve wood straight from the tree, but at the end of the day a laminated block is less likely to split, warp, twist, or generally let you down.

Suggested Tools

- workbench with a vise and holdfast
- medium-weight mallet of a size and shape to suit your needs
- good selection of medium- to large-sized carving gouges and chisels
- a good sharp, long-bladed knife—we use a Swedish sloyd knife with a laminated steel blade
- crooked knife
- small benchtop band saw
- drill press with a 5/8in (16mm) diameter Forstner drill bit
- small bench planer
- pencil, ruler, and pair of dividers
- one sheet each of workout and tracing paper
- watercolor paints in the colors brick/ochre red, black, blue-green, and white
- two soft-haired brushes—a broad- and a fine-point—as used by watercolorists
- small quantity of pure beeswax furniture polish
- typical workshop tools and materials such as sandpaper, oilstone, oil, sharpening slips, Plasticine, dust mask, and PVA (polyvinyl acetate) adhesive

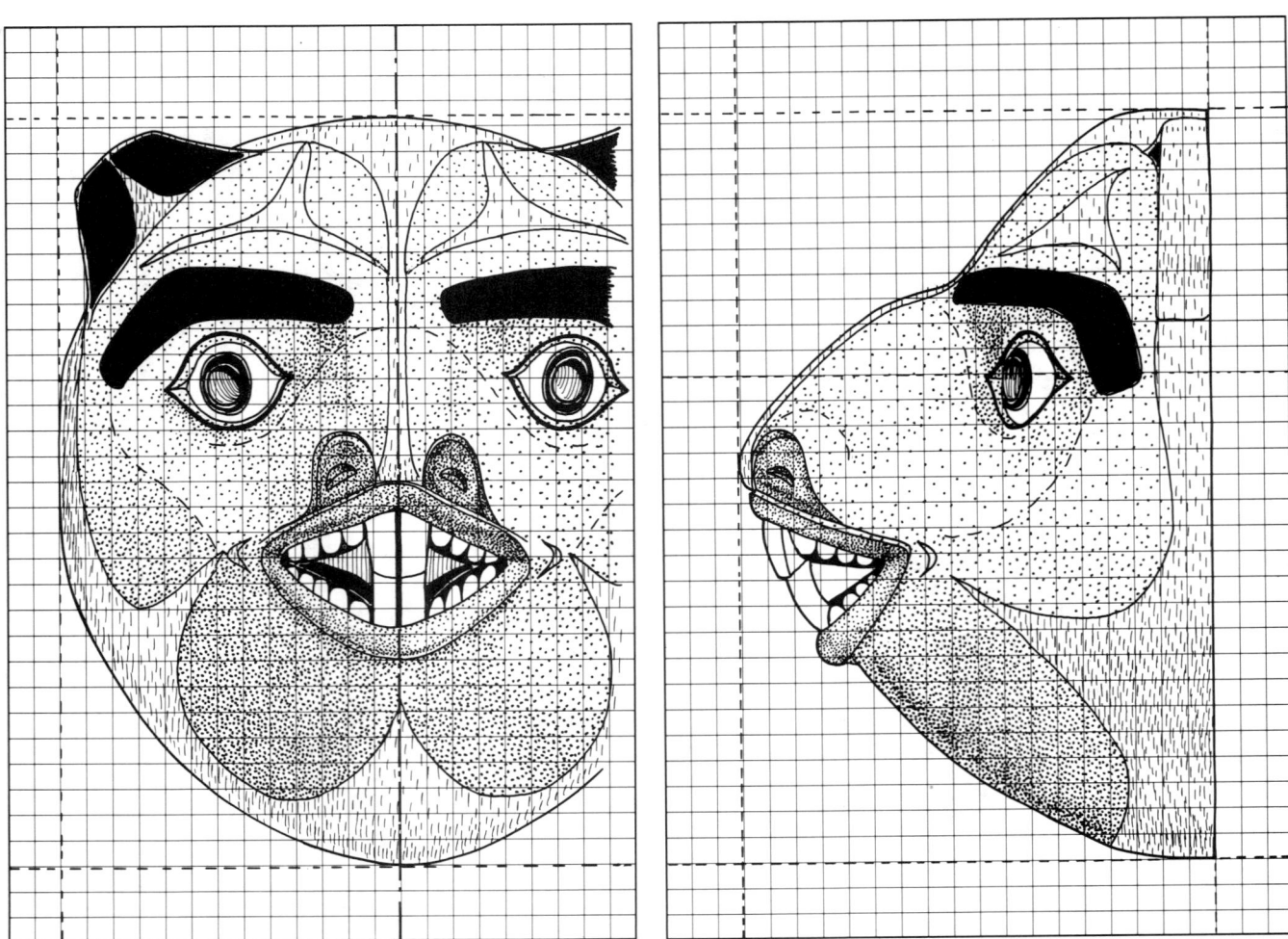

10-4   *Painting grid—front and side views—at a grid scale of three squares to one inch.*

PROJECT MAKING STAGES

Drawing Out the Design

1. Start by having a good long look at the inspirational drawings (refer to **10-1**), the working drawings (refer to **10-3**), and the painting grids (see **10-4**). If you have any doubts as to how the carving might look in the round, then make a Plasticine maquette of the whole work, or at least of the details that you think might be a problem.

2. Being mindful of the depth of this carving, and of the fact that it is symmetrical, draw out clear front and side views, and views showing the painted imagery (see **10-3** and **10-4**).

3. Make tracings, and put the master drawings to one side so that they are out of harm's way, but in clear view. Make two small detailed tracing-paper templates—one of the mouth–nose–nostrils, and one of the eyes and brows.

Making the Blank

4. As you prepare to build a laminated blank, carefully select your pieces of wood, and group them according to thickness and quality. So, for example, the total 6in (15cm) thickness might be made up from three 2in (5cm) layers, or two 2in layers and two 1in (2.5cm) layers.

5. Plane the pieces to size, and arrange the stack so that potentially difficult pieces either get to be cut away with the waste, or occur at the back of the mask where they can't be seen. For example, knots can occur at the back of the mask, or at the sides, but the central area must be made up from pieces of first-grade wood. It's best if the entire nose–mouth–nostril area is made up from a single block of wood.

6. Have a dry-run clamping—so that you know what goes where—pencil-mark the pieces, and then smear glue on mating faces and clamp up.

7. When the glue is completely dry, press-transfer the imagery to the working face of the wood, and then either cut the profile out on the band saw, or if your saw isn't big enough—ours wasn't—clear the bulk of the waste with a hand saw, and chop the profile out with a gouge and mallet (see **10-5**).

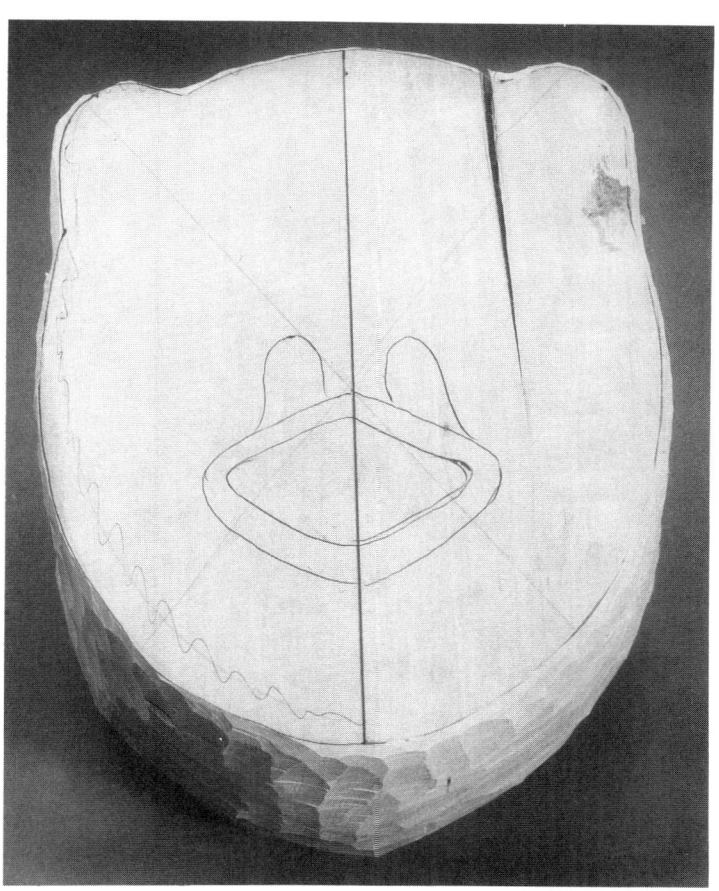

10-5 After clearing the bulk of the waste with the handsaw, use the gouge and mallet to chop out the profile.

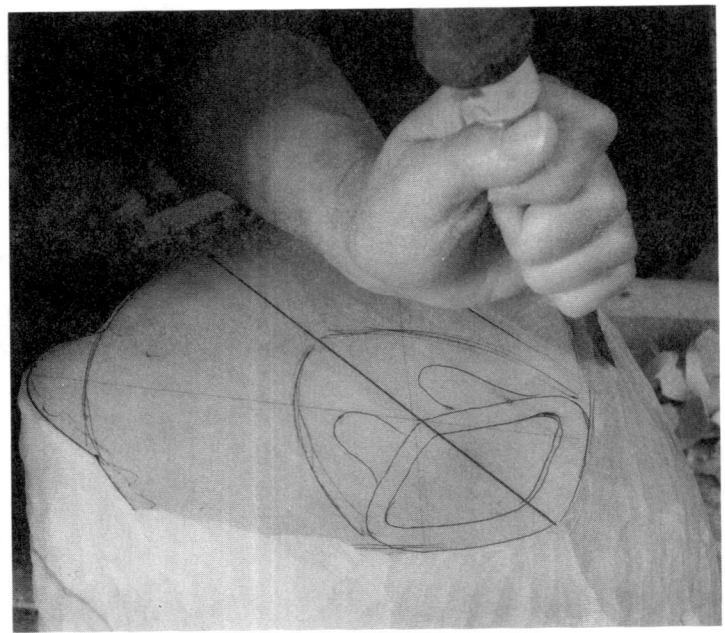

10-6 Use a large shallow-sweep gouge to clear the waste from the whole chin/neck area. Work in a full curve—from ear to ear—all the while cutting from high to low wood.

Roughing Out

8. Having achieved a good clean blank and drawn in the centerline and the overall outline of the nose and mouth details, take the largest shallow-sweep, straight gouge that you can manage, and clear the waste from the entire under-mouth area. Work in a smooth curve—from one ear, down and around the chin, and then up to the other ear. Aim for a full-curved, fat chin shape (see **10-6**).

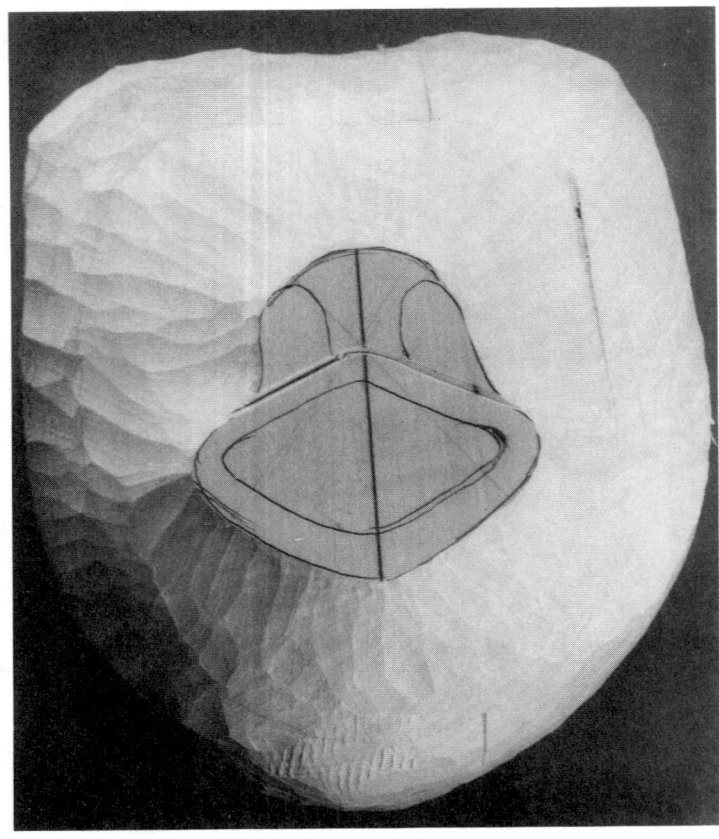

10-7 Use the large gouge to clear and shape the whole area of waste from the cheek–mouth line—leaving a bridge-like curve to mark out the top of the nose.

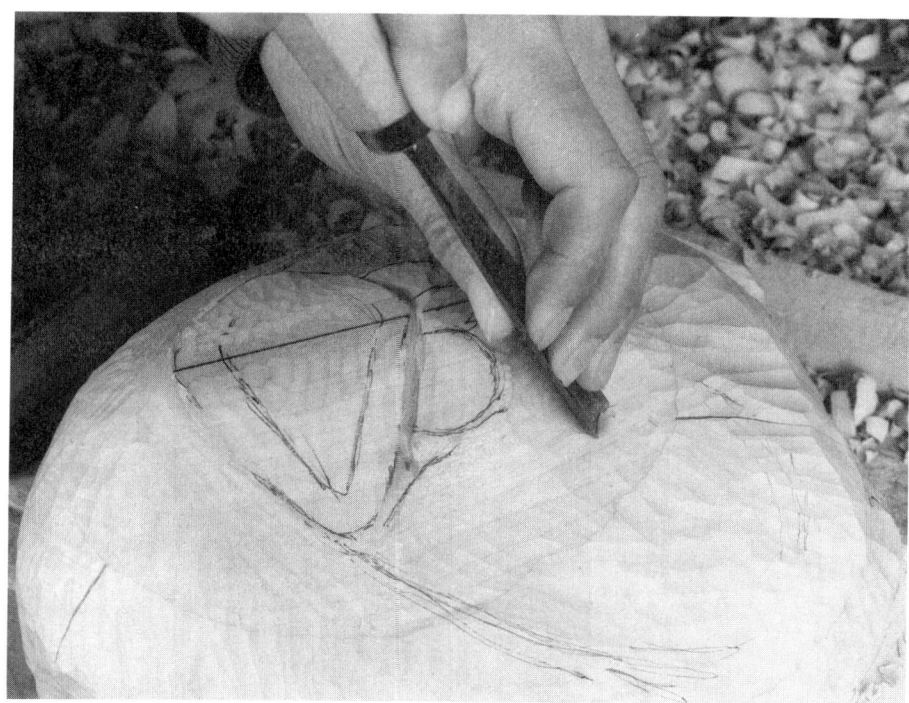

10-8 Using a small gouge to go over the roughed-out surface, refine the contours and cut away the wood from either side of the mouth and nose. Cut the eye sockets deeper and leave the middle line proud—higher than the ground.

9. Still working with the large shallow-sweep gouge, clear the waste from above the nose so that the whole upper surface of the mask slopes down from the bridge-like curve at the top of the nose (see **10-7**). Don't worry, at this stage, about the break where the ears meet the forehead; just make sure that there is a slight concavity at the cheek side of each nostril and between the ears.

10. When you have cleared the rough so that the mouth and nostrils are standing in relief like a plateau, take a smaller shallow-sweep gouge, and cut away the wood at either side of the mouth and nostrils so that the top surface of the plateau is arched (see **10-8**). While you are working around this area, start to clear some part of the waste from around the eye sockets.

Modeling

11. Draw in the shape of the mouth—and the line that runs in a sweeping curve from one corner of the mouth over the brow and down to the other corner of the mouth—to make a heart shape that encompasses the whole of the front of the face. This done, take a large shallow-sweep, bent gouge, and scoop away the dished area at either side of the nose (see **10-9**). While you are clearing the eye sockets, reduce the forehead so that it runs in a tight over-and-down curve from the brow line to the ears.

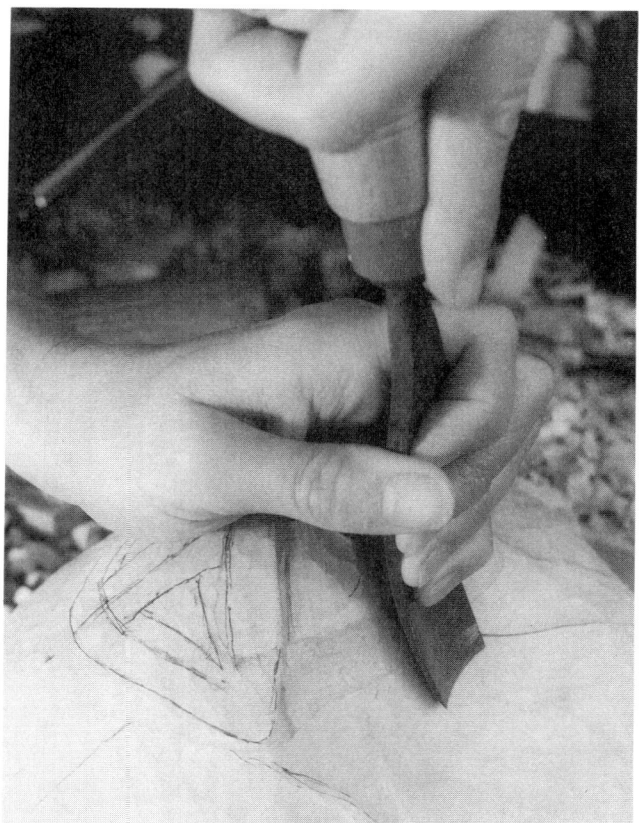

10-9 Employ the large shallow-sweep bent gouge to dish the areas at either side of the nose. Hold the tool with a firm grasping-and-guiding grip—all the while being ready to brake if you feel the edge beginning to run into the grain.

127

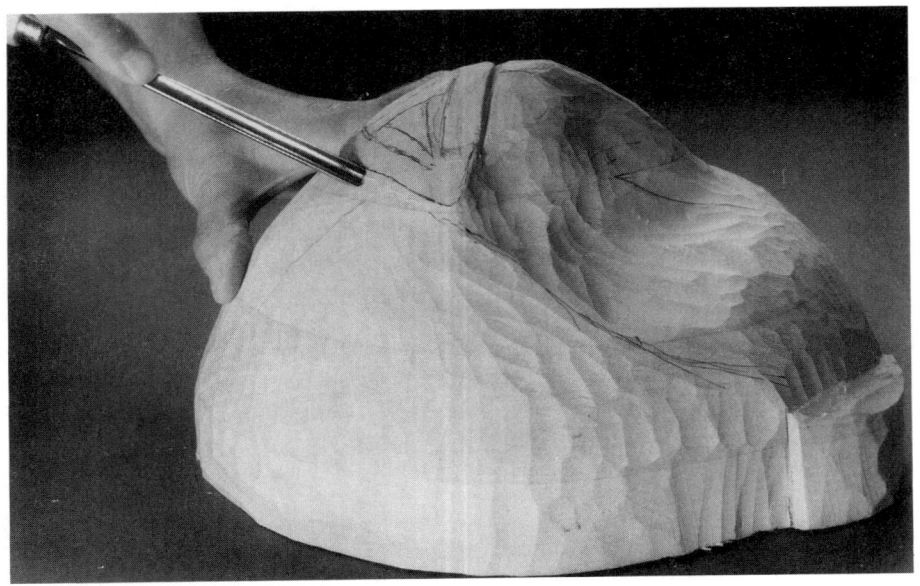

10-10 *Take a small-width, deep U-section straight gouge and model the pouting curve around the inside of the bottom lips. Avoid cutting into end grain by working from center to side.*

12. Take a small U-section straight gouge, and clear the wood from under the bottom lip so that there is a crisp "pouting" curve from the lip to the chin (see **10-10**). The mouth is one of the most important features of this carving, so spend time getting it right.

Special Tip

Northwest Coast carvings need to be crisp, clear-cut, and stylized, with the overall image coming across as cool, free-flowing, uncomplicated, and confident. Yes! they are tricky, and there is very little room for trial and error. You do have to get the modeled details right the first time around.

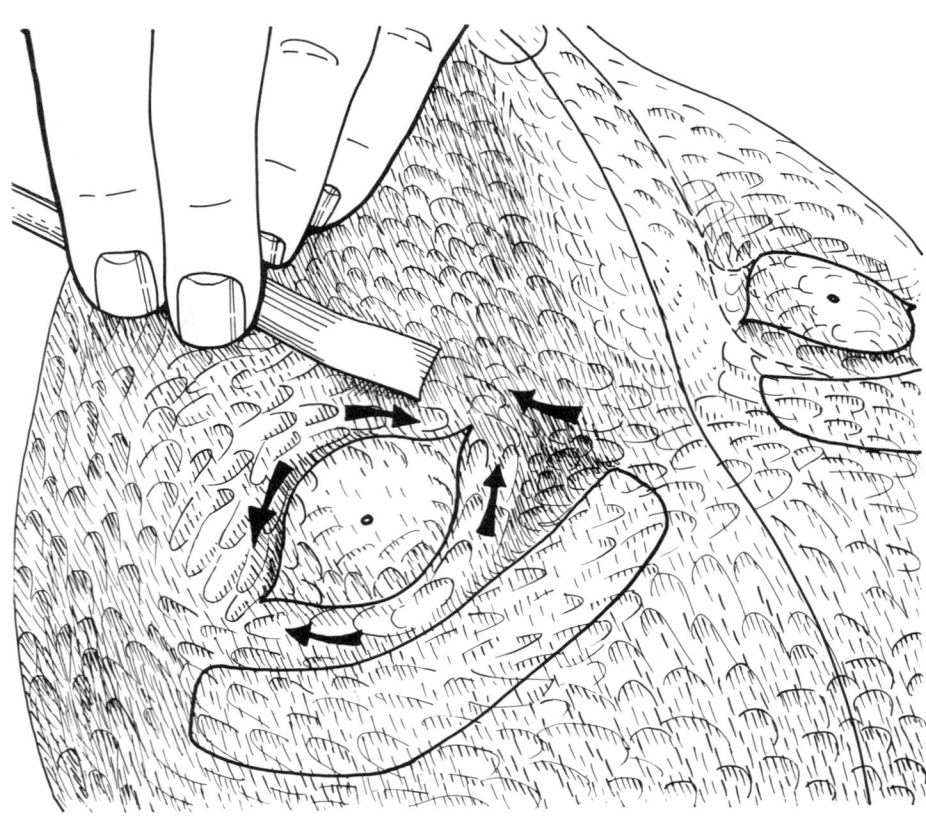

10-11 *Be aware of the changing contours when you come to carve around the eyes—work in the direction of the arrows, and be ready to change to smaller tools as you near completion.*

13. Once you have established what you consider is a good mouth shape, and after you have lowered the eye socket areas to the extent that the nose stands proud, then use the tracing-paper templates to establish the shape of the eyes and brows.

14. Being mindful that the contours around the eyes and brows will require you to be changing your angle of approach to suit the run of the grain, use the small bent and small back-bent gouges to model the moated areas around the shape of the eyes. If you are doing it right, the almond eye shape will stand proud—like a little hill-like feature (see **10-11**).

Special Tip

The deeply dished area between the nose, brow, and eye—in other words, the corner of the eye socket nearest the nose—is very tricky. No matter how we approached it, the tools seemed to catch and do damage to the grain. At the end of the day, we found that the best technique was to scoop out with a hooked knife and a small spoon gouge, and then to grind out with a scrap of fine-grade sandpaper—in a tight thumb-pressing screwing action.

15. Every now and then along the way as you remove wood and get closer and closer to the desired features, keep reestablishing and modifying the drawn lines.

16. To model the mouth: after the mouth is carefully drawn in place, take the knife and sink a stop-cut line around the inside of the lips. This done, lower the whole of the inner mouth area by about ¼in (6mm).

17. Still working with the knife, model the surface of the lips so that they run in a smooth curve down from the outer-lip line to the lip–teeth, stop-cut line. Repeat this stop-cut-and-lowering procedure several times, until you have established the full, rounded shape of the lips and fixed the level of the teeth.

18. Draw the shape of the teeth, and then use a small knife to lower the side teeth and the inside-mouth area. Aim to have the side teeth about ⅛in (3mm) lower than the two front teeth, and the inside-mouth hollowed out to a depth of about 1in (2.5cm) (see **10-12**).

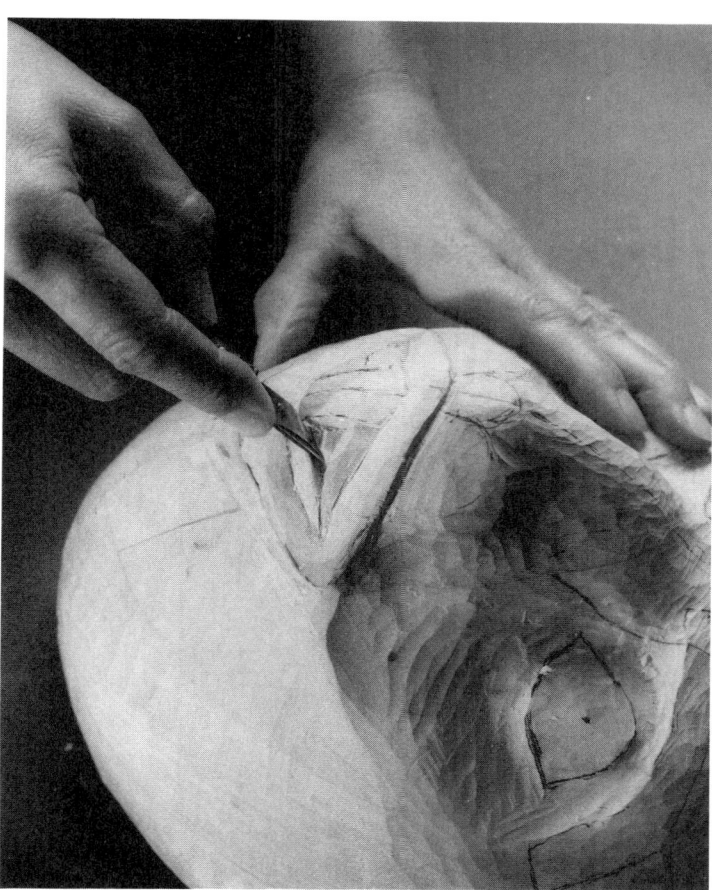

10-12 Use a skew-bladed knife to sink stop-cuts to mark out the shape of the inside mouth. Aim to lower the mouth cavity to a depth of about 1in (2.5cm).

19. With the inside-mouth cavity nicely established, pickle away with the knife and small spoon gouge at either side of the front teeth to undermine them until they bridge the underlying cavity (see **10-13**).

20. And so continue modeling the nose, underlips, and eyes, drilling the eye holes—and so on—in much the same way as already described in the other two Northwest Coast projects (see projects 8 and 9). (See *Hollowing* in the "Tools,

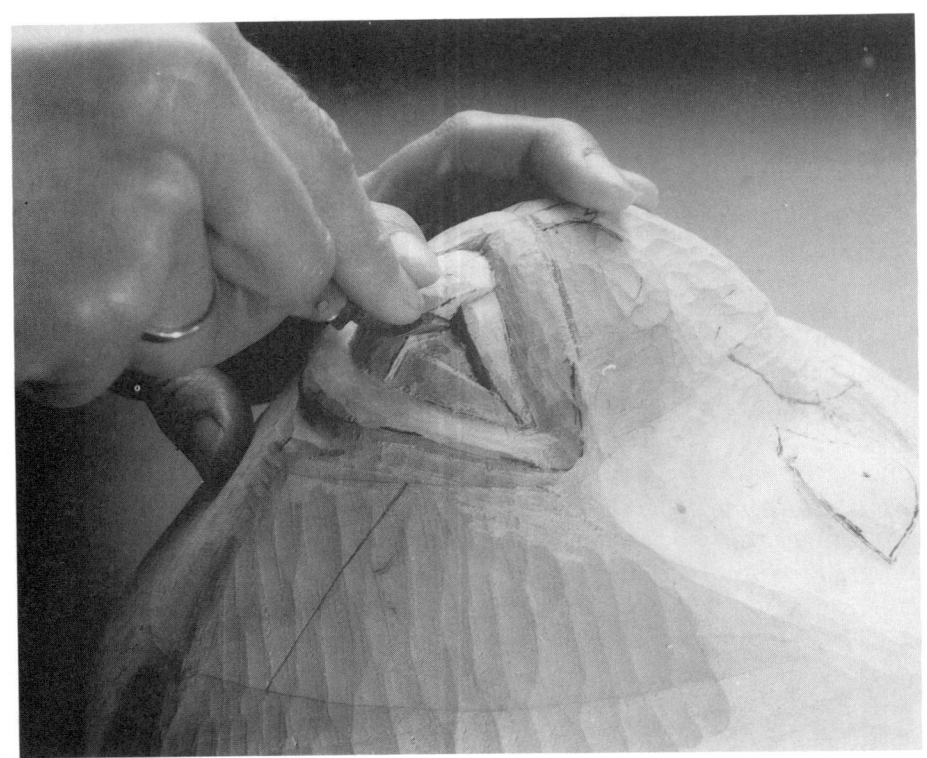

10-13   Once you have used the knife to establish the stop-cuts and have removed as much waste as possible, then use a small gouge to tidy up the cavity.

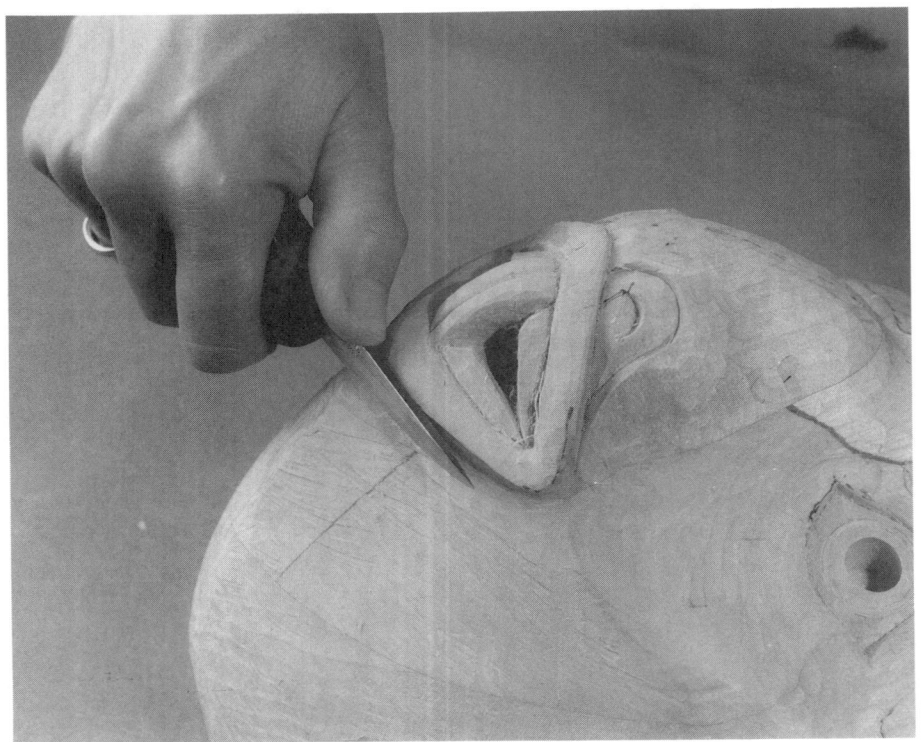

10-14   Take the knife and roll the blade in a tight, levering action down-and-around the underside of the lip to define and refine the surface.

Techniques & Materials—A–Z Guides," if you want to carve away the back of the mask.)

FINISHING

21. Once you have worked backwards and forward over the carving—all the while modeling and modifying the lines of the design—then comes the wonderfully satisfying task of using the knife to skim the details to a fine finish.

22. Keep in mind that the best approach is to move swiftly from one feature to another, all the while advancing the whole carving:

- Take the knife and roll it around and under the lips to achieve a fine, clean line around the mouth (see **10-14**).
- Use the point of the knife to refine and define the shape of the nostrils (see **10-15**).
- Use the knife to refine the lines around the eyes (see **10-16**).

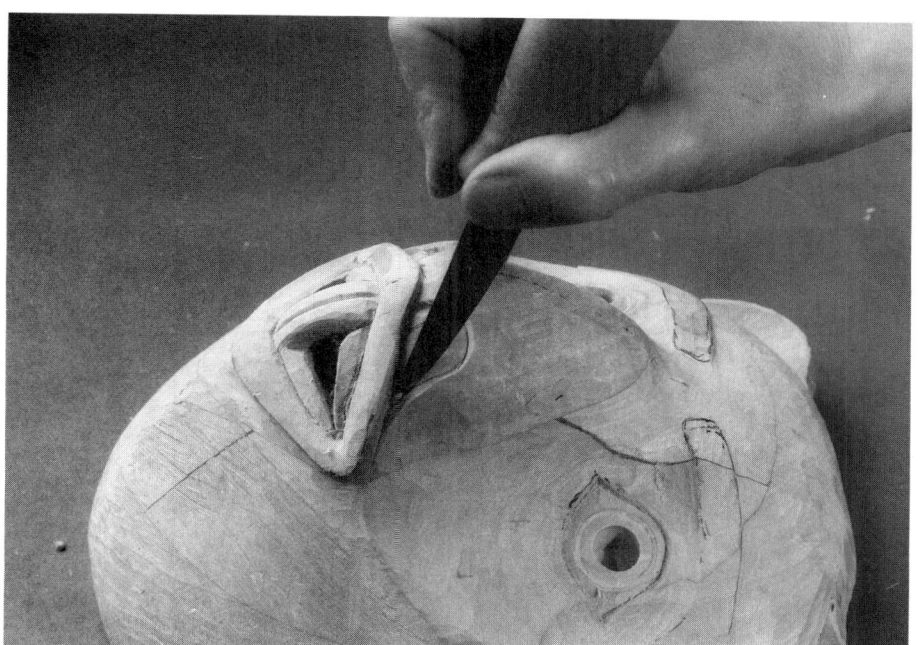

10-15 Working with the tip of the knife, use precise, carefully controlled cuts to clear the crumbs of waste from the difficult-to-reach areas.

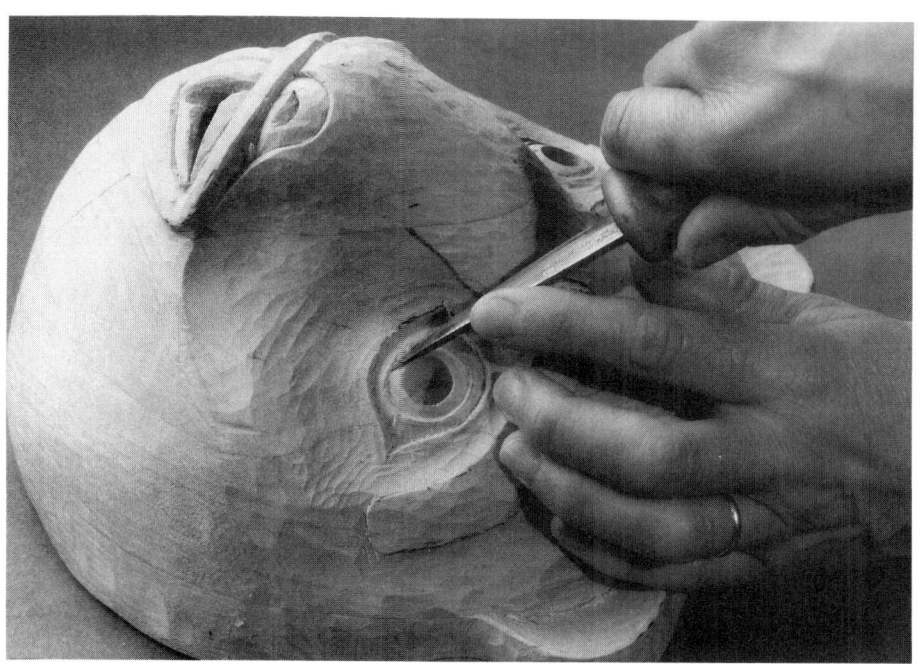

10-16 Define and refine the lines around the eyes—work with a two-handed bracing and levering cut.

10-17   Run the gouge—at a low angle—to skim the waste from inside the ears.

- Use the gouge to scoop out and hollow the inside of the ears (see **10-17**) and generally spend a lot of time very carefully shaving, trimming, and skimming the details.

23. Once you are happy with the carving—and this might take anywhere from hours to weeks, depending on your skill level and motivation—take a scrap of fine-grade sandpaper, and swiftly rub down all of the surfaces to a smooth finish.

24. Wipe away the dust, mix the water paints to a thin wash, and paint:

- the lips and nostrils red,
- the brows black,
- the areas around the eyes and mouth blue-green,
- the eyeballs and teeth white,
- the inside-mouth cavity, the tooth lines, and the lines around the eyes black.

25. Wait for the paints to completely dry, then take a sheet of fine-grade sandpaper and rub down the whole carving to break through the painted surfaces and produce areas of "wear."

Special Tip

When the Native American carvers painted their masks, they, of course, put down areas of flat color and left it at that—and you might well choose to do the same. Nevertheless, we think that the aging procedure as described—meaning rubbing through the paint—gives the finished mask a special dynamic quality, with the scuffed areas helping to enhance and give emphasis to the shapes and forms within the carving.

26. Finally, wipe over the whole carving with the beeswax polish, and burnish it to a rich, dull-sheen finish.

PROBLEM-SOLVING

- Since this is a fairly hefty mask, there is good reason why you have to make sure that the wood is well seasoned and dry. Be warned—if

your wood is straight from the tree, then be ready for the warping and splits!
- The success of this project hinges on your tools—especially the knives—being razor sharp. There is no excuse for working with a cheap or dull-edged knife. Maybe you feel you can't afford a new carving knife, but we know that it is easily possible to buy old high-quality knives at secondhand shops and flea market stalls for almost nothing. If you are looking for such a knife, then it's best go for one made sometime around the 1930s—the sort of rusty-bladed, bone-handled kitchen knife that your great-grandmother and mine used for chopping vegetables. Grind and hone it to shape to suit your carving needs.

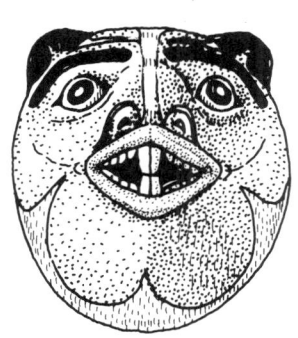

·11·
Barong Mask

Bali, Indonesia

The uniquely rich Indonesian masking tradition has its roots in the wave upon wave of immigrants who came to the islands from the Asian continent.

The Balinese Barong type mask—as featured in this project (see **11-2**)—is particularly interesting in that there is a link between this mask and the

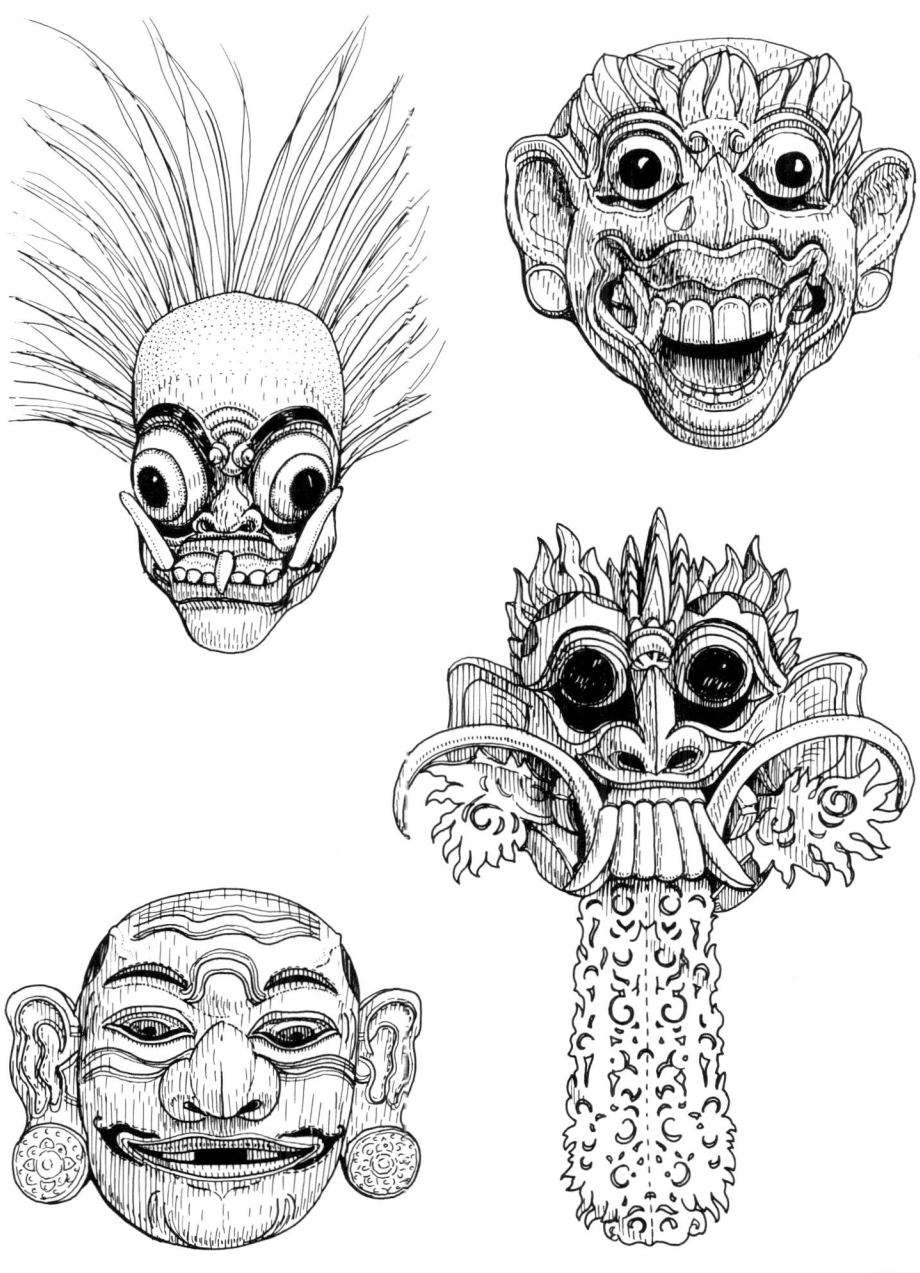

11-1 Inspirational drawings. (Top left) Mata Gde mask—Bali. This mask represents the demon servant of the evil witch Rangda. Rangda is the angry window, queen of the witches. Note the addition of tusks and horsehair. (Top right) Leyak Barak mask—Bali. This mask represents an apprentice witch associated with violent storms and troubles—the character receives power directly from the god Brahma. (Bottom left) Merdah mask—Bali, outside the Barong tradition. Servant to Rama. (Bottom right) Rangda mask—Bali—with added tusks and a cut and pierced leather tongue.

Sivaistic deity masks, as found in the Hindu tradition that is connected with the Indian goddess Duraga.

The Balinese Barong plays, or dramas, tell the story of the magical contest between the Barong—meaning the spirit of the Balinese village—and the evil witch Rangda. Although the masks of the Barong type are many and varied, they all conform to the same shape and form. That is to say, all the masks are characterized by having bulging eyes, big nostrils, prominent teeth and tusks, a large hanging tongue, and an aura of flames—and all are brilliantly painted and gilded.

As to which particular character our mask portrays, it's not so easy to say—it might be an evil witch, a mythical bird, or any one of the demonic creatures that feature in the Barong plays. The Barong plot or story line goes something like this: The evil, repulsive, child-eating witch Rangda is challenged to a fight by the not-so-evil but still-pretty-grisly demon Keket, with all manner of apprentice witches and demons putting in their two cents' worth. The story wraps up with a horrible battle, at which time the evil Rangda comes to a noisy and bloody end! Great fun and wonderful masks!

11-2 Project picture—the finished mask.

THOUGHTS ON SHAPE, FORM & TECHNIQUE

Have a look at the working drawings (see **11-3**) and see how, at a grid scale of four squares to one inch, the mask is a miniature that measures about 6½in (16.5cm) from the top down to the tip of the tongue, and is about 4½in (11.5cm) wide and 3in (7.5cm) thick from back to front. Study the painting grids (see **11-4**), and note how the mask is stylistically painted in brilliant colors. Note the characteristic bulging eyes, the prominent upper teeth, the tusks, and the way the tongue laps down from the open and pierced mouth.

Although most of the Barong-type Balinese masks that are currently being imported into North America and Europe are no more than quietly executed carvings for tourists, it's fair to say that they, nonetheless, are carved to a pretty high standard, most of the imagery being true to the original. If you want to get a close-up look at one of these masks, then you could visit a large city museum, and/or you could search out a shop that carries such ethnic items and buy the same type of miniature mask that inspired this project.

CHOOSING YOUR WOOD

Although it looks to us as if most of the Balinese masks—as seen in shops and galleries—are now being carved from soft, lightweight, easy-to-work wood types like jelutong, we have opted to use lime/linden and to build up the blank from several layers. Although the color characteristics of your chosen wood are not important—because after all the mask is heavily painted to the extent that all the underlying wood is blocked off from view—

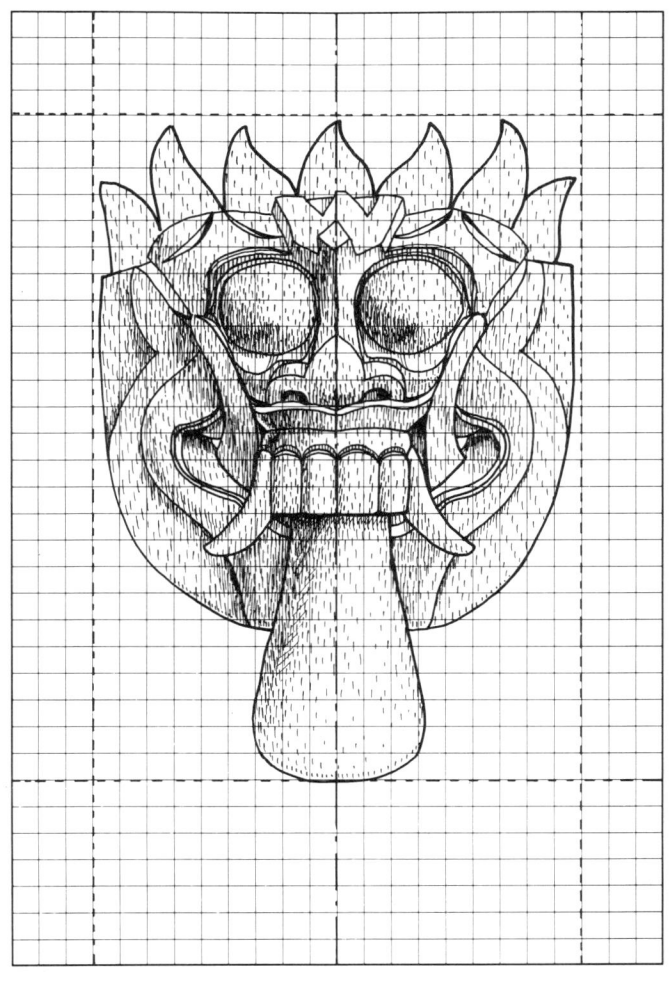
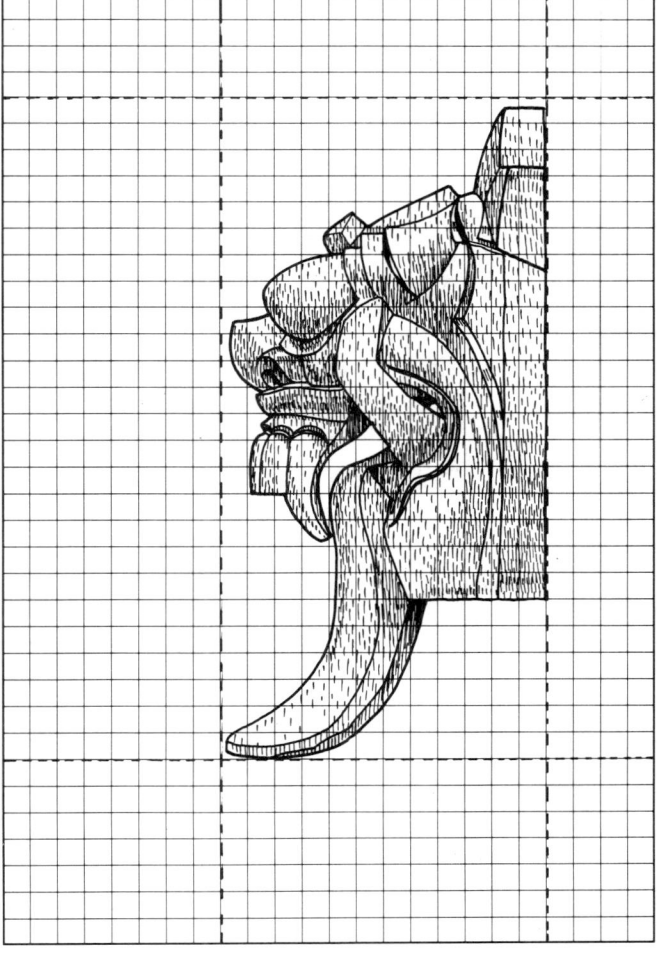

11-3   Working drawings—front and side views. The grid scale is four squares to one inch. Note the complex side-profile view.

you do need to make sure that your chosen wood is smooth and tight grained with a minimum of knots.

Special Tip

Many who are new to woodcarving have in mind a link between masks and exotic woods—the line of thinking being that their carvings are going to be that much better if they go for "quality" woods. And, of course, they usually choose the first fancy wood that springs to mind—namely, mahogany.

These beginners are misguided on many counts. A good many so-called mahoganies are raggedy and generally difficult to carve, so that they are not suitable for masks; they are overly expensive; and they have, in many instances, been plundered from endangered forests.

And finally, of course, why use an expensive, raggedy not-so-great wood, when there are many other inexpensive types that will do the job so much better?

Suggested Tools

- workbench with a vise and holdfast
- medium-weight mallet of a size and shape to suit your needs
- good selection of medium-sized carving gouges and chisels
- a good sharp, long-bladed knife—we use a Swedish sloyd knife with a laminated steel blade
- use of a small band saw
- pencil, ruler, and pair of dividers
- one sheet each of workout and tracing paper
- acrylic paints in the colors bright red, bright red-orange, yellow, black, and gold
- two soft-haired brushes—a broad- and a fine-point—as used by watercolorists
- small quantity of umber oil paint—as used by artists

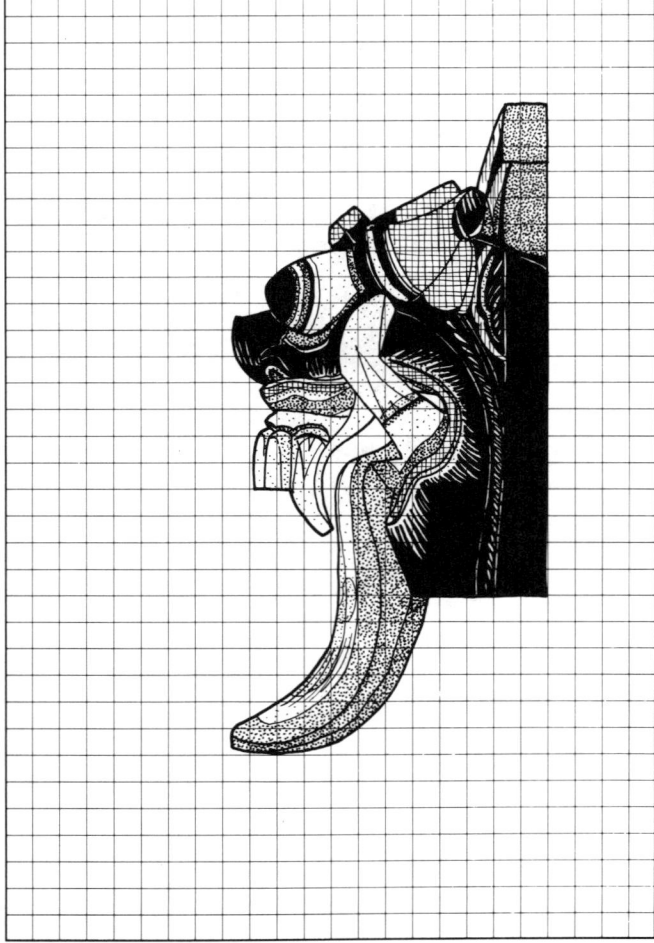

11-4 Painting grids—front and side views at a grid scale of four squares to one inch.

- small can of spar varnish
- typical workshop tools and materials such as sandpaper, oilstone, oil, sharpening slips, Plasticine, dust mask, and PVA (polyvinyl acetate) adhesive.

PROJECT MAKING STAGES

Drawing Out the Design

1. Start by having a good long look at the project pictures (refer to **11-2**), the working drawings (refer to **11-3**), and the painting grids (refer to **11-4**).

2. When you have studied and are familiar with the shapes of the various views and the overall size and character of the carving, make sure that you have a clear idea of just what tools and techniques are necessary for carving a project of this complex character. In our opinion this is one of the most difficult masks to carve. When you are ready to proceed, draw or photocopy the images up to full size, and make a clear tracing of both the front and side views.

3. Pin up the master drawings so that they are within view, and generally get ready for the task ahead. We recommend that nervous beginners make a full-sized Plasticine maquette of the carving.

Making the Blank

4. When you have carefully selected your wood—and either laminated up a block from a collection of prepared pieces or simply cut a solid block to size—use a handsaw to slice down the wood so that all faces are square and true.

5. Set down the "front" view tracings on the front face so that the grain runs from crown to chin, and press-transfer the imagery to the wood. This done, repeat the transferring procedure, only this time around, press-transfer the "side" view to the side face. Make sure that the two views are aligned with each other.

6. Having double-checked that all is correct and as described, move to the band saw, and very carefully fret out the "side" view image. Try for the minimum number of cuts and don't discard the offcuts of waste.

7. Set the offcuts back onto the partially sawn block—as needed, stick them in place with double-sided sticky tape—then turn the wood over and saw out the "front" view image. At the end of this finger-twisting procedure, you should be left with a whole heap of waste, and a mask that is sawn out in two views (see **11-5**).

11-5 The blank sawn out in both views—with a piece of the cut-away wood to the side.

Roughing Out

8. Having achieved a blank that is well sawn out in both views, draw the mask image in on the wood, plus as many guidelines as you think fit. Then butt the workpiece hard up against a bench stop, and set out your tools so that they are close at hand.

9. Use the small range of straight tools—the chisels and gouges—to swiftly round over the sawn form. Angle the top of the forehead so that it runs down from the brow line, cut away the sides, and start to clear the rough from under the steps that run down from the top jaw to the tongue and the lower jaw (see **11-6**).

10. Use the small gouge and the knife to establish all the levels that mark out the various peaks that make up the relatively complex form of the face.

Modeling

11. Having cleared the bulk of the rough and generally established the various blocks and levels, set the workpiece alongside the tracing. Use the pencil and dividers to mark on the wood all of the salient high points, step-offs, and valleys that make up the design (see **11-7**).

12. With the tongue roughed out so that there is a crisp step-down from the teeth to the tongue and the tongue to the chin, and with the position and size of the teeth clearly drawn in, take a knife—or you might prefer to use a V-tool—and set-in the bottom edge of the row of teeth with a stop-cut.

13. Take one of the bent gouges, and slide down the length of the tongue and into the stop-cut (see **11-8**). Repeat this procedure several times, all the while shaping the "ski slope" curve of the tongue and undercutting the teeth.

11-6 Use the gouge to establish the various stepped levels that run down from the front teeth and to the chin at the underside of the tongue.

11-7 Work with the pencil and dividers to mark on the wood all the high points, step-offs, and valleys that make up the design. If you have made a maquette, then so much the better—you will have a clearer understanding of how the imagery looks in the round.

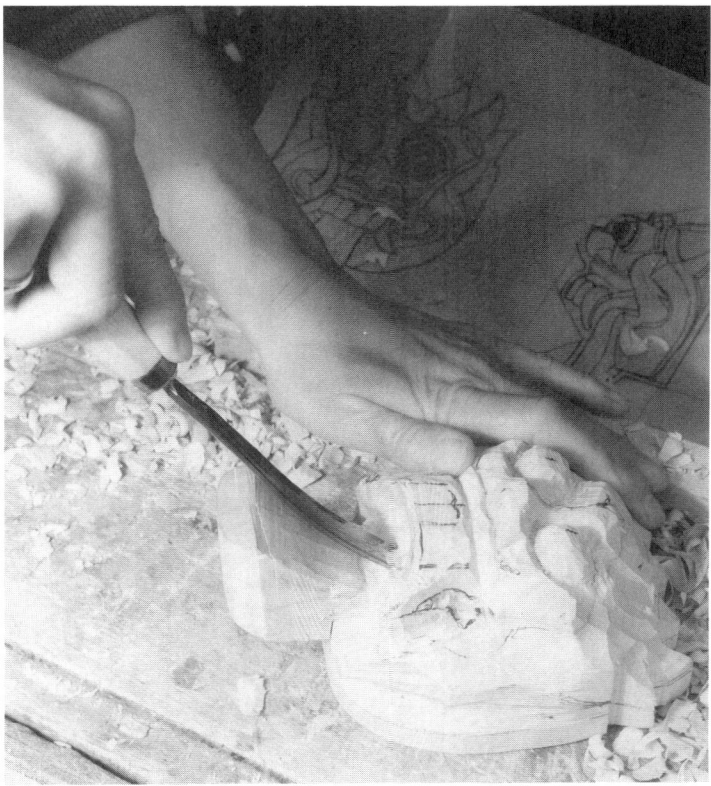

11-8 Use a bent gouge to scoop out the waste from the back of the tongue and mouth cavity.

11-9 Reduce the wood at the sides—where the cheeks step down towards the back edge of the mask. Be watchful that you don't split off the short grain areas at the side-back rim.

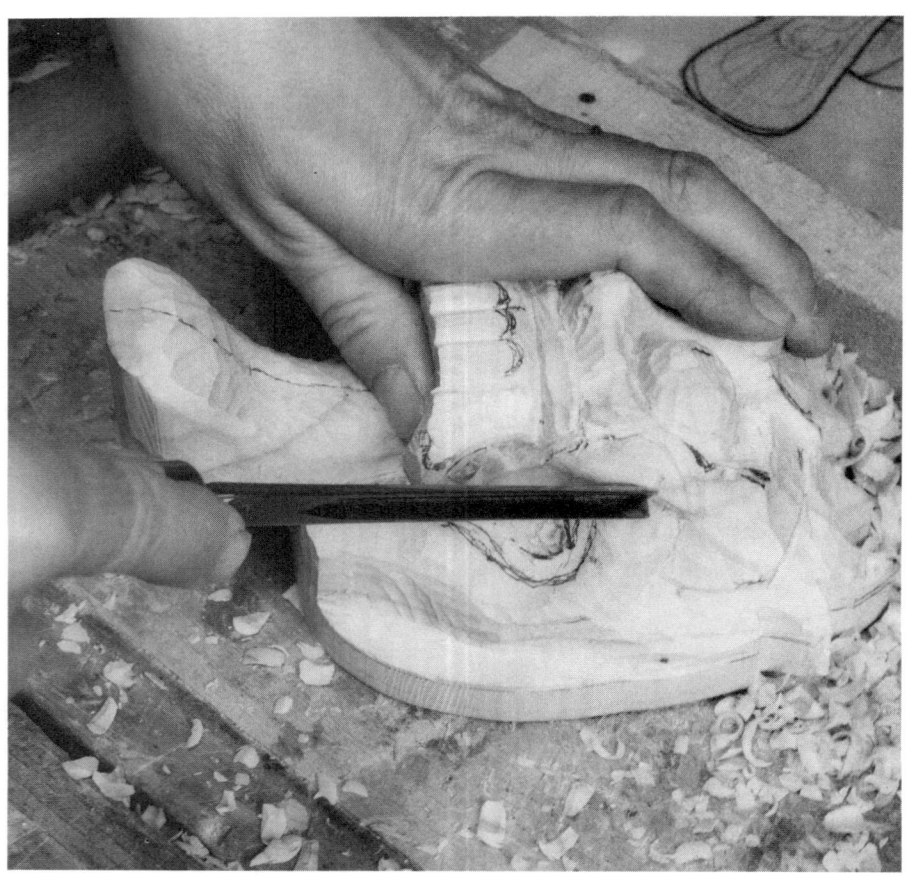

11-10 When you have first very carefully established a good grid of guidelines, then set the secondary stop-cuts in with the V-tool.

14. When you have achieved a step-down from the teeth to the root of the tongue of about ¾in (2cm), turn the bent gouge over so that the back of the tool is hard up against the teeth, and then slide the tool down-around-and-in to shape the roof of the mouth and deepen the mouth cavity.

15. Have a close-up look at the working drawings and the project picture, and see how there is a rolled-edge step-down from the side cheeks to the side edges of the mask. After this, take a small shallow-sweep gouge, and shave and round over the cheeks so that they curve down from the edge of the mouth. Aim for a rim thickness at the side of the mask of about ⅜in (1cm) (see **11-9**).

16. Take the V-tool and go over the carving setting in the secondary stop-cuts. For example, there is a stop-cut on either side of the tusks that spring up from the bottom jaw (see **11-10**); there is a stop-cut between the top lip and the teeth.

17. Be mindful when you are modeling the inside curve of the tongue that you must work with or down the run of the grain—that is, from the tip of the tongue down into the mouth. Use a shallow-sweep gouge to lower and model the sides of the tongue so that it is a full convex curve in cross section. Keep redrawing and referring to a centerline (see **11-11**).

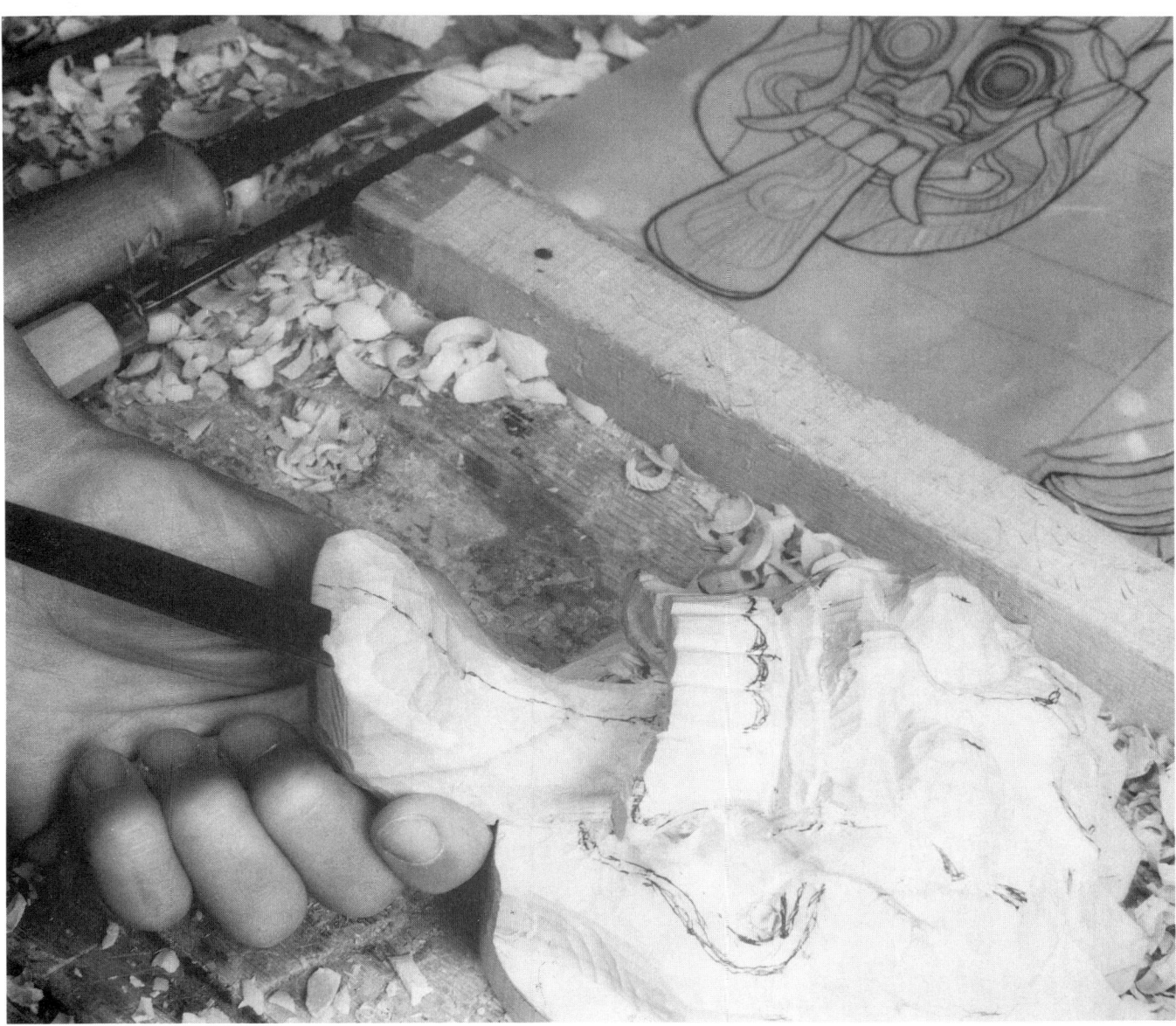

11-11   Keep redrawing the centerline and using it as a reference to lower and model the sides of the tongue.

18. Use a selection of small straight chisels and gouges to deepen and model the hole that occurs at the side of the mouth—the hole between the tusk and the curve at the corner of the mouth. Sink the hole in to a depth of about ¼in (6mm) (see **11-12**).

19. Select a gouge with a sweep section to match the curve at the top of the teeth, and then very carefully set-in a stop-cut to mark out the teeth–gum line (see **11-13**). If you have done it right, the initial V-section stop-cut line that you set-in several stages back will result in the crumbling away of the small area of waste wood at the top of the teeth. After this procedure use the point of a knife to tidy up the surface at the top of the gums.

20. Continue working with the knife by modeling around the snout and the eyes (see **11-14**), cutting the divisions between the teeth (see **11-15**), and generally bringing the carving nearer to the envisaged shape.

Note: If you want to carve the back of the mask, see *Hollowing* in the "Tools, Techniques & Materials—A–Z Guides."

11-12 Remove the waste from between the lower tusks and the curved corners of the mouth. Be careful not to do damage by levering the tool against the upper tusks.

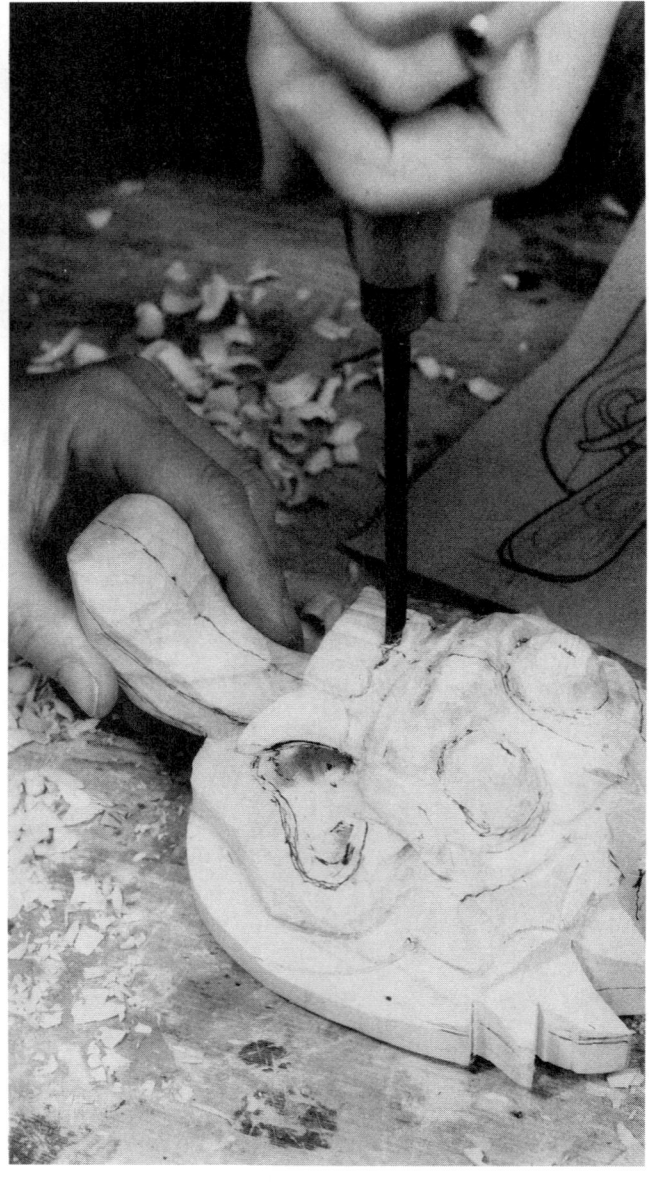

11-13 Match up a gouge with the top of the teeth—that is, match the curved sweep of the gouge to the curve of the teeth—and then set-in the teeth–gum line.

11-14   Modeling with the knife: gradually model and refine the overall shape by removing smaller and smaller slivers of waste. Limit yourself at this stage to working with a small tight, controlled cut.

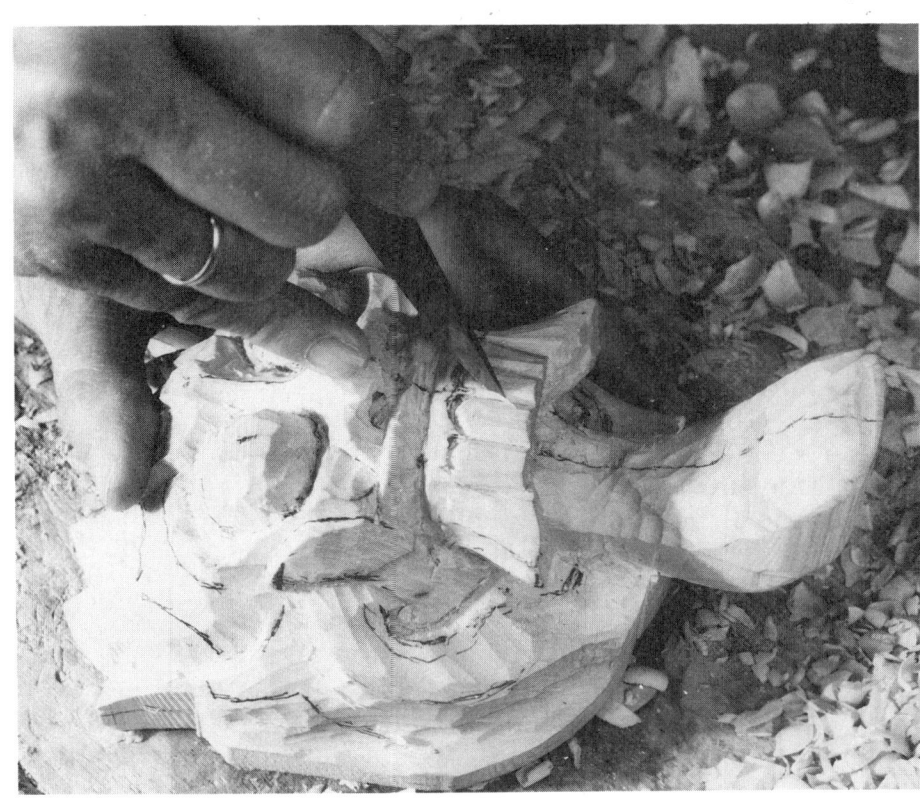

11-15   Round over each tooth—by first deepening the initial between-tooth stop-cuts and then rounding down the sides. The line of teeth needs to follow the curve of the upper jaw.

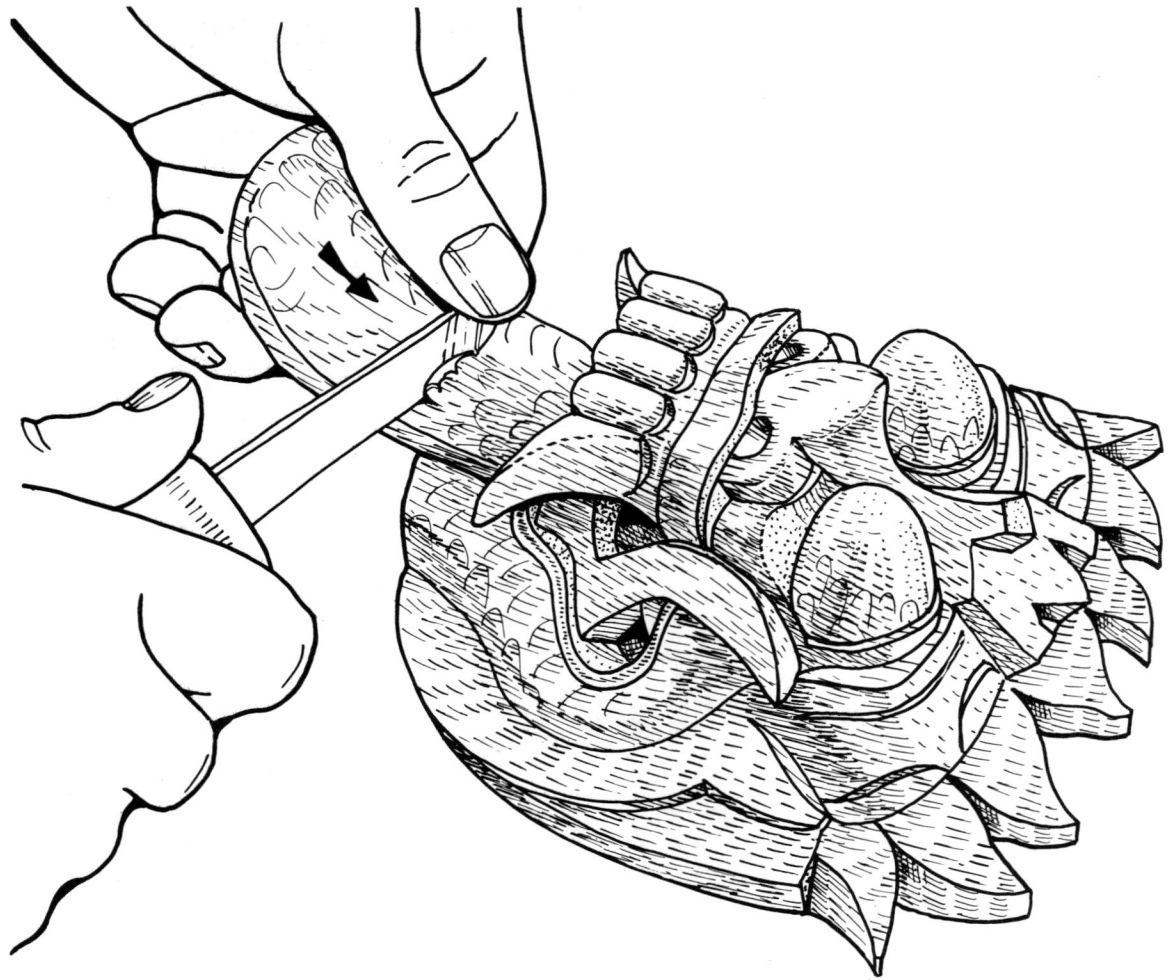

11-16 Use the knife to refine and define the modeling—by clearing the waste from crevices, and by skimming and scraping the raised curved surfaces.

FINISHING

21. When you have modeled all of the features—the teeth, lips, tusks, snout, eyes, cheeks, brows, flames, tongue, and the rest—then take the knife to skim and scrape down all the surfaces to a smooth finish (see **11-16**).

Scraping is a wonderfully efficient method of bringing the surfaces to order, but only if you work with the run of the grain—or, we might say, from high to low wood. Don't forget that this is an unusually multifaceted form, with lots of small peaks of wood breaking through the grain; so be doubly aware of the run of the grain, and try to direct the scraping accordingly. For example, scrape down the tongue to the teeth (see **11-16**), down-and-around the bulges that go to make the eyes, and up the teeth, tusks, and flaming hair.

22. Having finished the scraping and tidied up with the sandpaper, wipe away the dust and move to the area set aside for painting. Mix the acrylic paints to a nonrunny consistency. Then paint the whole background of the mask black, the gums, tongue and nostril holes red, the teeth, tusks, and eyes yellow, and so forth. Wait for the ground colors to dry completely, then take a small fine-point brush and paint in the secondary detailing: black on the peaks of the eyes, black and red rings around the eye bulges, black lines between the teeth, and so on. Last, use the fine-point brush to pick out the areas of gold—the line around the mouth and the brow and hair flames.

23. Finally, once the paint is completely dry, decant a little of the varnish, and mix it with the smallest dab of umber oil paint so that you have a thin golden varnish glaze. Give the whole carving a single all-over coat.

PROBLEM-SOLVING

- As with all the projects, if you want to truly get a handle on the mask—meaning when, where, and why the original mask was made—then you will really want to visit a museum and get to see Bali masks. Treat this trip as a day out for research—lots of sketching, buying a few photographs, and maybe, although not likely, getting to hold and touch the masks.

- Although in many ways, the small size of this mask—if you are working on the tight scale as described—makes it exciting, it does mean that it is a bit tricky. If this worries you, then you could double the scale to go for a larger mask.

- If you find that the mask is difficult to hold and secure when you are carving, you might consider using a bench screw (see *Woodcarving Basics,* also published by STERLING).

·12·
Lombok Mask

Timor, Indonesia

Indonesian masks were traditionally considered to have an active and powerful function. The idea was that the wearer could positively influence everyday problems such as illness or bad luck by taking on another identity and physical shape. So, for example, with the mask wearer perceiving a particular illness as being such and such a demon, he would attack the demonic character by taking on the more powerful personality contained within the appropriate mask (see **12-1**).

12-1 Inspirational drawings. (Top left) Topeng mask—Central Java—7in (18cm) high. (Top right) Solo mask—Java—7in (18cm) high. (Bottom left and right) Two Wayang Topeng face masks—early masks were held by the dancer gripping a peg or strap with his teeth. Note the characteristic upturned nose and the way the eye slits are under the painted eyes.

149

Masks were used by Timor Lombok tribes at their feasts to personify evil spirits that threatened the rice crop. By working through set-piece mask dramas, the priests made sacrifices and exorcized evil.

Of all the wood-carved masks made in the Timor group of islands, the masks of the Lombok tribes are considered by many collectors to be the most impressive (see **12-2**). Although they were traditionally made from extremely hard, dense, difficult-to-carve woods, most of the trade masks that currently reach Europe and America are made from easy-to-carve imported woods like jelutong.

12-2   Project picture—the finished mask.

THOUGHTS ON SHAPE, FORM & TECHNIQUE

Have a look at the working drawings (see **12-3**) and see how, at a grid scale of four squares to one inch, the mask measures about 8in (20cm) high, 4¾in (12cm) wide, and 2in (5cm) from back to front. Although this mask is clearly too small to wear, and there are no eye slots—suggesting that it is no more than a trade item—we know that some small masks were also used traditionally as a convenient, portable, second line of defense—a bit like a Christian wearing a small crucifix. It may not be as powerful as a full-sized mask, but it's the next best thing.

Although we decided to block this mask up from two 4in (10cm) by 4in (10cm) square sections, you can use a single slab.

If you study the mask in front and side views, you will see that although the overall form is rather straightforward, the details are extremely subtle. For example, if you look closely at the mouth, you will see that the serene expression is achieved by having the lips closed tight, while at the same time the edge of the lips is cleanly and clearly defined. And then again, if you study the lines above the eyes, you will note that the eyelid fold line is characterized by having a little flick or upturn at the end.

All in all, we think that many beginners will find this project to be something of a challenge. This is not so much because the individual details are in any way extra difficult, but rather because the sum total of bringing all the details together is a trying business. To put it another way, the nose, the mouth, and the eyes are all relatively easy to carve—but how to carve them so that they all fit?—that's the trick!

CHOOSING YOUR WOOD

Although nineteenth century Indonesian masks were traditionally made from such hardwoods as box, Burmese ebony, Lauan mahogany, padauk, satinwood, teak, and the like, we have noticed that currently many Lombok masks are made from softwoods that have been variously stained, painted, and waxed. When we look closely at our modern Lombok mask—the mask that inspired this project—of course, we can't know for sure the species of wood, but our experienced guess is that it is jelutong. We say this because not only is there a great similarity in weight and grain pattern, but, perhaps more to the point, we know that jelutong, or "jungle rubber wood," is grown in Java, Borneo, and the surrounding area.

Our advice, if you are a beginner, is to start by using a softwood like jelutong, lime/linden, or basswood, and then, when you have finished making mistakes, go for a more substantial wood. That said, why use a precious endangered wood like mahogany, when a piece of carefully stained, quick-growing, low-cost softwood fills the bill?

Suggested Tools

- workbench with a vise and holdfast
- medium-weight mallet of a size and shape to suit your needs
- good selection of carving gouges and chisels—including a small-sized straight gouge, a straight chisel, a spade or fishtail gouge, and a small V-section tool
- a good sharp long-bladed knife—we use a Swedish sloyd knife with a laminated steel blade
- use of a small band saw
- pencil, ruler, and pair of dividers
- small open-toothed rasp
- one sheet each of workout and tracing paper
- small quantity of wood sealer
- quantity of brown wax boot polish
- selection of artists soft-hair watercolor brushes
- fine-point, spirit/alcohol-based, felt-tip pens in the colors black, gray, and red-brown
- beeswax polish
- typical workshop tools and materials such as sandpaper, oilstone, white spirit, oil, sharpening slips, a quantity of Plasticine, dust mask, and white PVA (polyvinyl acetate) adhesive

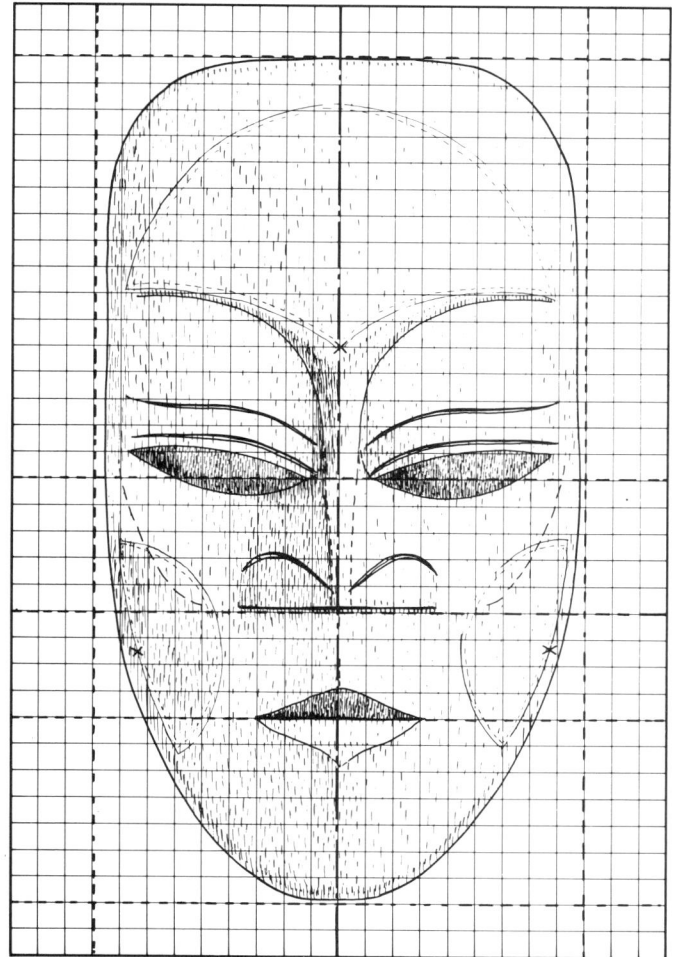

12-3 Working drawings—front and side views. The grid scale is four squares to one inch. Note the position of the part-circle areas of pattern on the front view—with the compass center points being marked with an

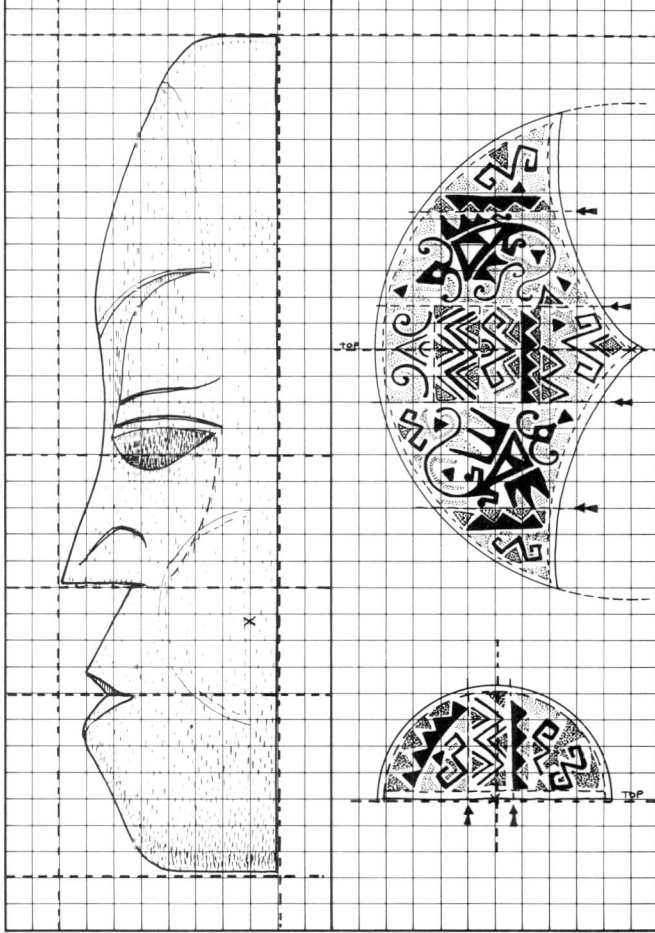

X. Note the part-circle areas of pattern on the side view—with the dotted guidelines and the center points.

PROJECT MAKING STAGES

Drawing Out the Design

1. When you have gathered your tools, selected your wood, and generally organized the working area, then take your sheet of workout paper, and draw the front and side views of the mask to full size. Have a centerline running from top to bottom, and registration lines that link the two views (see **12-3**).

Special Tip

We find that a good deal of the pleasure of carving masks has to do with hunting down originals in museums, galleries, and tourist-type shops. It's always a good idea, prior to carving, to find out as much as you can about the country of origin and the culture that produced the masks.

2. Once you are happy with all the precarving research and preparations, as well as the resultant drawn elevations, then take a pencil tracing of both the front and side views. Rework the back of the tracing with a soft pencil, and establish clear center- and guidelines.

Special Tip

If your drawing skills are not strong, then it's best to use our designs. In that case, either directly transfer the imagery using gridded paper or use a photocopy machine.

3. Pin the master drawings up so that they are within view of the working area, have a last good long look at any inspiration photographs or books, and then to work!

Making the Blank

4. Align the front elevation tracing with the various center- and guidelines, fix with tabs of masking tape, and then use a hard pencil to press-transfer the drawn lines to the wood. If you are working with two blocks of wood, then repeat the procedure, and press-transfer the side views to the sides of the blocks.

5. Having reworked the transferred profile outline and shaded in the waste areas so that there is no doubting what wood needs to be cut away, run the wood through the band saw to cut out the drawn profile—as seen in front and side views (see **12-4**).

Note: As the side profile of this mask is made up from quite subtle forms, we decided not to saw out the fine details as seen in side view at this early stage.

6. After you have checked that all is correct and as described, smear a generous amount of PVA (polyvinyl acetate) glue on mating faces, set the two cutouts together so that the various drawn features are carefully aligned, and then clamp.

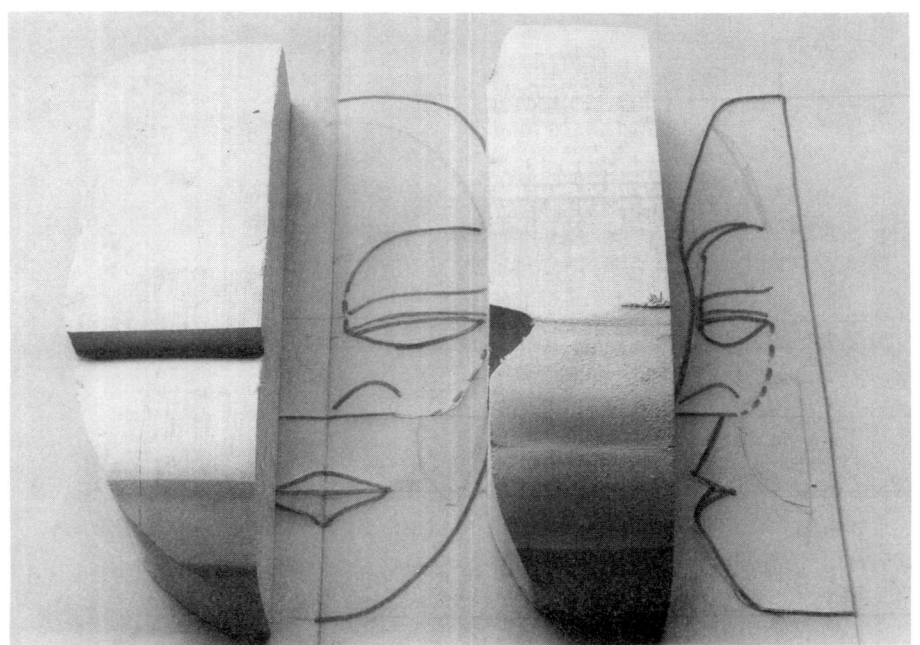

12-4 Run the wood through the band saw, and cut out the drawn profile. Repeat this procedure for both views.

Roughing Out

7. Wait for the glue to dry, then remove the clamps, and spend time making sure that all the drawn imagery is clearly and correctly established. If needed—meaning that you have made a bit of a mess-up with the alignment—sand off the drawn lines and adjust them accordingly.

8. Establish the position and width of the nose, and then use the saw to set in the bottom-of-nose line with a stop-cut. Run the saw down to within ¼in (6mm) of the full depth of the nose. This done, use a good size gouge to swiftly round over the edges of the profile.

9. Clear the bulk of the rough from the area around the mouth and the under-nose stop-cut. Aim for a side-view profile that runs in a smooth full curve up from the bottom of the mask to the nose stop-cut (see **12-5**).

Modeling

10. When you have achieved the overall shape of the mask, then take the ruler and dividers, and very carefully plot out all of the step-offs that make up the design. Being mindful that the success of the carving hinges on the proportions and symmetry being carefully rendered, spend a lot of time at this stage making certain that all the details are well placed.

11. With all the primary step-off points and guidelines established, take the knife, and lower the area between the eyes and the brow. The best procedure is to first set in the brow line with a deep stop-cut, and then to shave the wood by making low strokes that run from the top of the eye to the stop-cut (see **12-6**). If you work in this way, you will always be making the most efficient cuts.

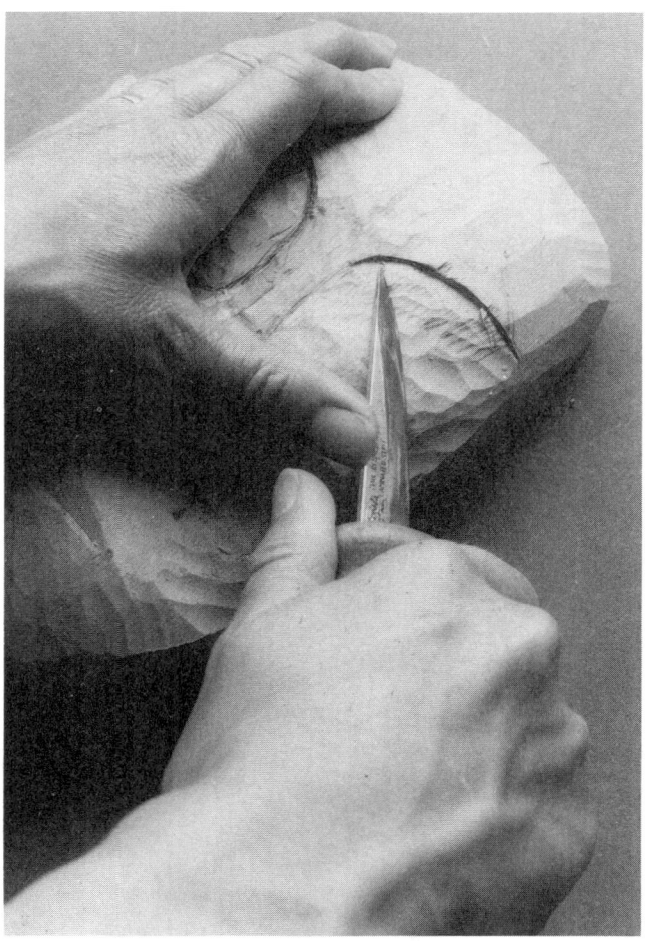

12-5   Clear the bulk of the rough from around the mouth, and use the dividers to plot out all the step-offs that make up the design.

12-6   First set-in the brow line with a deep stop-cut, and them make low knife cuts towards the stop-cut to remove slivers and shavings of waste.

12. After you have roughed out the eyelids, then very carefully set to work lowering the wood between the underside of the eyes to the mouth. Remembering to allow for the almond shape of the actual eyes—this will require a deal of careful measuring and setting out with the dividers—aim for a smoothly curved surface that runs in a clean scoop from the eye down into the hollow of the outer eye socket, and then up through to the top lip (see **12-7** and the project picture **12-2**).

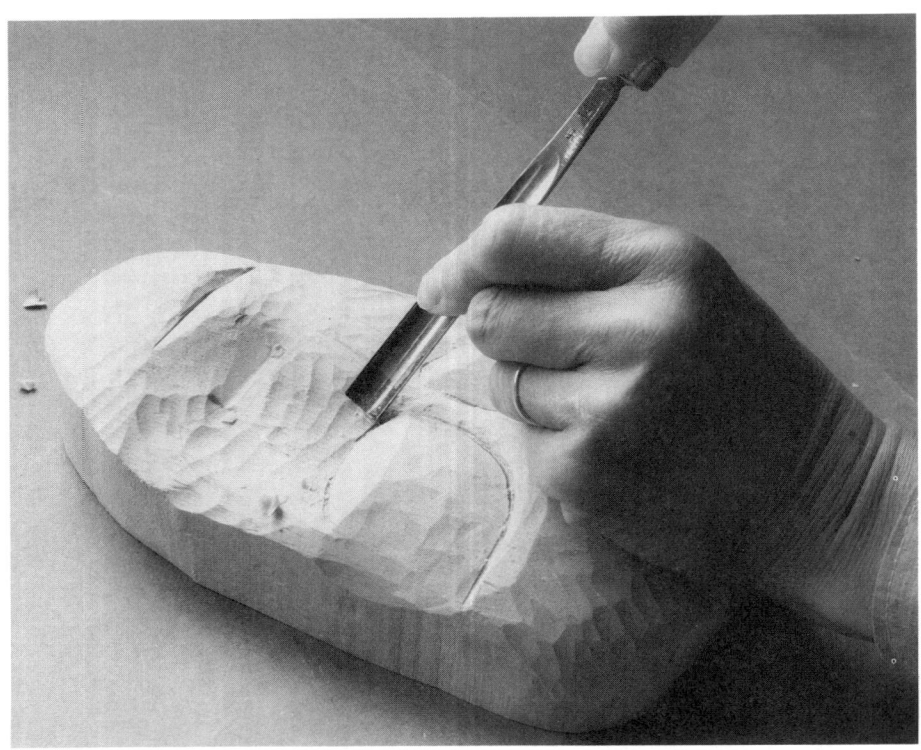

12-7   Lower the wood from the underside of the eyes, through to the mouth.

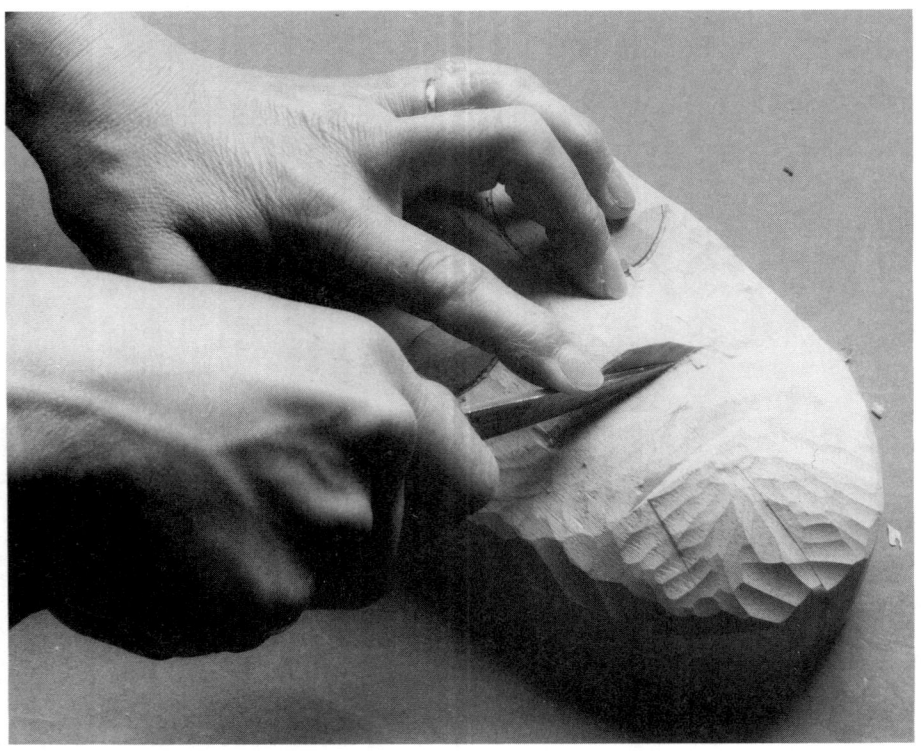

12-8   Use the knife to model the nose and the area around the mouth.

13. When you get to the stage where the procedure of lowering the waste leaves the nose, mouth, and lip areas standing in relief, then take the knife and set to work modeling these features (see **12-8** and **12-9**).

Special Tip

When you are working on a collection of details, the best procedure is to flit about, like a bee going from flower to flower. That is to say, you carve a little bit here, then a little bit there, and so on, all the while adjusting details one to another. This way of working allows you to stand back and assess the sum total of the carving. On no account should you attempt to take one isolated feature to completion, and then try to carve everything else to fit. It just doesn't work!

14. Keeping in mind that the success of this mask has to do with your being able to bring together many subtle details so that they seem to be part of a single organic form, you must be prepared for a slow, little-by-little approach. Skim down the features to shape, stand back, pencil in areas that need to be lowered (see **12-10**), shave away the marked areas, stand back for another reassessment, and so on.

12-9   To create the very subtle curves of the mouth, very gradually deepen the divide between the lips.

12-10   Shade in the areas that need to be reduced. Go at it slowly, all the while taking time to check your carving off against the designs, and being mindful that you can't put the wood back once it has been cut away.

12-11 Remove thin slivers of wood. Work with a two-handed slicing-and-levering stroke.

FINISHING

15. Once you have finished the primary modeling—when you are within a hair's breadth of finding the personality of the mask that was "hidden" within the wood—rehone your knife to a razor-sharp edge. Then rework the whole carving by skimming the details back to a good finish. Pay particular attention to the shape of the eyes and the curve of the lips (see **12-11**). Continue shaving finer and finer skims from the surface of the mask, until the carving is finished. This done, take the knife, and cut the delicate, incised V-section lines that decorate the eyes and the nostrils.

16. Rub down the surface of the wood to a good finish, clear away the dust and debris, and give the mask a coat of sealer. When it is dry, use the pencil and dividers to draw out the part-circle shapes that go to make the decorative patterns (see **12-12**).

17. Having first studied the patterns (refer to **12-3** side view, right), take the felt-tip pens and set to work drawing in the little zigzags and stylized forms that go to make the design.

18. Mix a small amount of the brown wax polish with the white spirit—until you have a wash or glaze—and then lay on repeated coats. Continue until the wood is a rich red-brown mahogany color. Leave the part-circle areas the natural pale color of the wood.

19. Finally, when you consider the mask finished, burnish it to a dull sheen—and the job is done.

12-12 Use the dividers to draw out the part-circle shapes that mark out the areas of pattern.

PROBLEM-SOLVING

- If you really do want to work this project in an exotic hardwood, then it's best to have a trial run with an easy-to-carve wood.
- If you are thinking of using an exotic hardwood, then keep in mind that you might have to adjust the procedures. For example, you might not be able to skim the wood with the knife, your chosen wood might be so oily that it doesn't need to be sealed, or you might need to use files to achieve a fine finish.
- If you do decide to use an exotic hardwood, then make sure that it's nontoxic. We say this because we personally find that the dust from some hardwoods makes the eyes itch and nose run!
- If you are a nervous beginner, then we would always recommend that you start by making a Plasticine maquette—so that you have a three-dimensional prototype from which to work.
- When we say "Choose a mallet to suit your needs," we mean just that. For example, you might enjoy using a heavy brass mallet; then again, you might prefer an inexpensive lightweight mallet; or then yet again, you might want to sculpt a mallet from a piece of hedgerow wood or whatever. The choice is influenced by any number of factors: your body strength and height, the character of the wood that you are carving, and how much money you are prepared to spend.

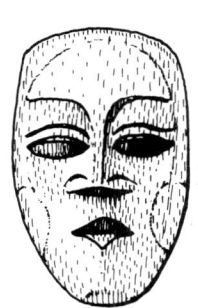

Metric Conversion

Metric Conversions

1 mm = 0.039 inch
1 m = 3.28 feet

Feet and Inch Conversions

1 inch = 25.4mm
1 foot = 304.8mm

Inches to Millimeters and Centimeters
mm—millimeters   cm—centimeters

inches	mm	cm	inches	cm	inches	cm
⅛	3	0.3	9	22.9	30	76.2
¼	6	0.6	10	25.4	31	78.7
⅜	10	1.0	11	27.9	32	81.3
½	13	1.3	12	30.5	33	83.8
⅝	16	1.6	13	33.0	34	86.4
¾	19	1.9	14	35.6	35	88.9
⅞	22	2.2	15	38.1	36	91.4
1	25	2.5	16	40.6	37	94.0
1¼	32	3.2	17	43.2	38	96.6
1½	38	3.8	18	45.7	39	99.1
1¾	44	4.4	19	48.3	40	101.6
2	51	5.1	20	50.8	41	104.1
2½	64	6.4	21	53.3	42	106.7
3	76	7.6	22	55.9	43	109.2
3½	89	8.9	23	58.4	44	111.8
4	102	10.2	24	61.0	45	114.3
4½	114	11.4	25	63.5	46	116.8
5	127	12.7	26	66.0	47	119.4
6	152	15.2	27	68.6	48	121.9
7	178	17.8	28	71.1	49	124.5
8	203	20.3	29	73.7	50	127.0

Index

A

Animals
    Combined powers, 8
    Part human, 87–88
Apple wood, 23

B

Balinese spirit mask characteristics, 136
Band saw, 13
Bapende mask, 87, *color section C*
Barong mask, 135, *color section H*
Basswood, 23
Baule mask, 67, *color section H*
Beeswax, 36
Bench, 13
Blank, 13
Blemishes, 24
Bow saw, 14
Braque, Georges, 57, 78
Brushes, 14

C

Calipers, 14
Canary (American whitewood), 23
Cedar, 23
Centerline, 30, 41, 50, 72, 80, 115, 152
Checks, 24
Cheeks, 63, 127, 143
Chisels, 16
Clamps, 14
Color section *follows page* 96
Compass, 14
Coping saw, 14
Cubist art, 57
Curls, 45
Cushion or bag, 14

D

Decay, 24–25
Deep-carved, 15
Derain, Andre, 78
Designing, 15
Dividers, 15
Drawing the design, 30, 40, 50, 60, 70–71, 72, 80, 82, 90, 101, 113, 125, 139, 152
Drawknife, 15

E

End grain, 25
Epstein, Jacob, 57
Eye details, 35, 45, 50, 51, 53, 55, 72, 74, 84, 94, 96, 99, 104, 106–107, 117, 119, 127, 129, 150, 154
Eye hole, 84, 88, 119, 130

F

Fang mask, 77, *color section E*
Finish, 15
Finishing, 36, 45–46, 55, 64–66, 76, 85, 96, 108–109, 120, 131–132, 146, 156
Flour spout mask, 37, *color section G*
Fool, dancing, 121
Fool mask, 47, *color section B*
Forstner drill bits, 15, 75, 93

G

Glues and adhesives, 16, 40–41
Gouges, 16, 36
Grain, 25
Green Man mask, 27, *color section G*
Green wood, 26, 66
Grinding, 17
Grounding or wasting, 17

H

Haida mask, 111, *color section A*
Hair, 83, 85, 146
Hardwoods, exotic, 26
Hold-down, 17–18
Hole cutting, 75
Hollowing (back), 18–19, 38, 46, 65, 76, 86, 96, 120, 144

I

Incised cut, 19
Indians, Pacific Northwest, 9, 97–98, 111, 121–122
    Cedar masks, 24
    Characteristics of carvings, 109, 122
Inspiration designs, 17
Ivory Coast, 67–68

J

Jelutong wood, 24, 78–79, 150

K

Knives, 14
    To suit your needs, 133
Knots, 26
Kwakiutl mask, 97, *color section C*

L

Laminated or built-up, 19, 38, 40, 46, 48, 49, 58, 61, 68, 78, 88, 100, 102, 112, 123, 125, 139, 152
Linden/lime wood, 24
Lombok mask, 149, *color section E*

M

Making the blank, 30, 40, 50, 60–61, 71, 80, 90–91, 101–102, 113, 125, 139–145, 152
Mallet, 19–20, 157
Maquette, Plasticine, 40, 50, 71, 80, 90, 125, 139, 157
Masked fool, 47–48
Masks
    Ancient world, 12
    Bapende, 87, *color section C*
    Barong, 135, *color section H*
    Baule, 67, *color section H*
    Characteristics, 9
    Dancers, 8, 122
    Deity, Indonesian, Hindu, 135–136
    Definition, 7
    European traditions, 37
    Fang, 77, *color section E*
    Flour spout, 37, *color section G*
    Fool, 47, *color section B*
    Green Man, 27, *color section G*
    Haida, 111, *color section A*
    Indonesian, 149–150
    Kwakiutl, 97, *color section C*
    Lombok, 149, *color section E*
    As magic, 7
    New identity, 12
    Origin, 8–9
    Part human, part animal, 87–88, 122
    Powers conferred, 9, 88, 150
    Shaman's drama, 111–112
    Transformation type, 97
    Tribal cultures, 37
    Tsimshian, 121, *color section F*

Ugandan, 57, *color section D*
Worn as helmet, 58, 98
Matisse, Henri, 78
Measure, 20
Modeling, 32–35, 43–45, 52–55, 62–63, 72–76, 82–85, 93–95, 105–108, 117–119, 127–131, 139–145, 153–155
Modifying, 20
Motifs
  Animal, 121
  Beaver, 122
  Bird, 136
  Clan, 108
  Corn, 37
  Devil/demon, 37, 136
  Fertility, 37
  Foliage, 27, 28
  Human body parts, 38
  Spirit, 121
  Teeth, 137
  Tongue, 137
  Tusks, 137
  Witch, 136
Mouth-nose details, 35, 43, 44, 52–53, 55, 62, 72, 74, 83–84, 96, 115, 117–118, 127, 129, 153

N

Nostrils/holes, 55, 74, 119

P

Painting, 20, 100, 108, 114, 120, 124, 132, 138, 146
Pencil-press transferring, 20, 41, 60, 70, 71, 80, 91, 101, 124, 125, 139, 152
Picasso, Pablo, 57, 78
Pine, 24
Plateau wood, 20
"Primitive" African art, 57
"Primitive" art movement, 77–78

R

Roughing out, 20, 32, 41–42, 50–51, 61–62, 71–72, 81, 92–93, 103–104, 113–117, 126–127, 139, 153

S

Sanding, rubbing down, 21
Setting-in, 21
Setting-out, 21
Shakes and splits, 26
Shaman's masked drama, 111–112
Shape, form, technique, 28, 38, 48, 58, 68, 78, 88, 98–99, 112, 122–123, 137, 150
Sharpening, 21–22
Slips, 22
Softwood, 26
Stepping, 58
Stop-cut, 22
Sycamore, 24
Symmetry, asymmetry, 28, 60, 63, 70, 76, 99

T

Teeth, carving, 64, 129, 140
Template, 23, 125
Texture, 96
Tips, 19, 28, 36, 40–41, 43, 50, 59, 60, 66, 68–69, 71, 78–79, 80, 82, 85, 90, 94, 101, 109, 112, 115, 119, 120, 123, 124, 128, 129, 132, 138, 152, 155
Tongue, 50, 140
Tools for project, 29, 39, 49, 59, 69, 79, 89, 100–101, 112, 124, 138–139, 151
Totem poles, 98, 101
Tracing paper, 23
Tree worship, 28
Tsimshian mask, 121, *color section F*

U

Ugandan mask, 57, *color section D*
Undercutting, 23

V

V-cuts, 23
Vise, 23
Vlaminck, Maurice de, 78

W

Wood, choosing your, 28, 38–39, 49, 58, 68, 78, 89, 99–100, 112, 123, 137–138, 150–151
Wood
  Faults, 24
  Nonallergenic, 59
  Nontoxic, 39, 58
Working drawing, 17, 29, 39, 49, 59, 69, 79, 89, 99, 113, 123, 137, 151
  Tracing, 40, 90, 101, 114
Workout paper, 23, 152
Workshop, 23